AF581193

THE IN-BETWEEN

Intimate and Candid Moments of Broadway Stars

JENNY ANDERSON

Foreword by Ariana DeBose

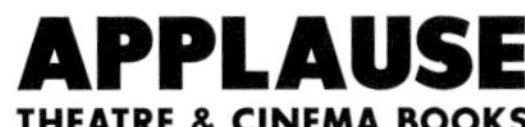

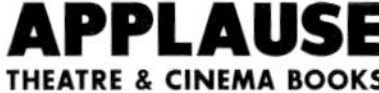

Applause Theatre & Cinema Books
Bloomsbury Publishing Inc, 1385 Broadway, New York, NY 10018, USA
Bloomsbury Publishing Plc, 50 Bedford Square, London, WC1B 3DP, UK
Bloomsbury Publishing Ireland, 29 Earlsfort Terrace, Dublin 2, D02 AY28, Ireland
www.ApplauseBooks.com

British Library Cataloguing in Publication Information available

Library of Congress Cataloging-in-Publication Data

Names: Anderson, Jenny, 1984- author. | DeBose, Ariana, 1991- author of foreword.
Title: The in-between : intimate and candid moments of Broadway stars / Jenny Anderson ; foreword by Ariana DeBose.
Description: Lanham : Applause, 2025. | Includes index.
Identifiers: LCCN 2024048443 (print) | LCCN 2024048444 (ebook) | ISBN 9781493088119 (cloth) | ISBN 9781493088126 (epub)
Subjects: LCSH: Theater—New York (State)—New York—History—Pictorial works. | Broadway (New York, N.Y.)—Pictorial works. | LCGFT: Photographs.
Classification: LCC PN2277.N5 A36 2025 (print) | LCC PN2277.N5 (ebook) | DDC 792.09747/10904—dc23/eng/20241021
LC record available at https://lccn.loc.gov/2024048443
LC ebook record available at https://lccn.loc.gov/2024048444

For product safety related questions contact productsafety@bloomsbury.com.

∞™ The paper used in this publication meets the minimum requirements of American National Standard for Information Sciences—Permanence of Paper for Printed Library Materials, ANSI/NISO Z39.48-1992.

to my momma for my love of theatre
to my daddy for my love of photography
to both for never saying “you can’t”

CONTENTS

FOREWORD

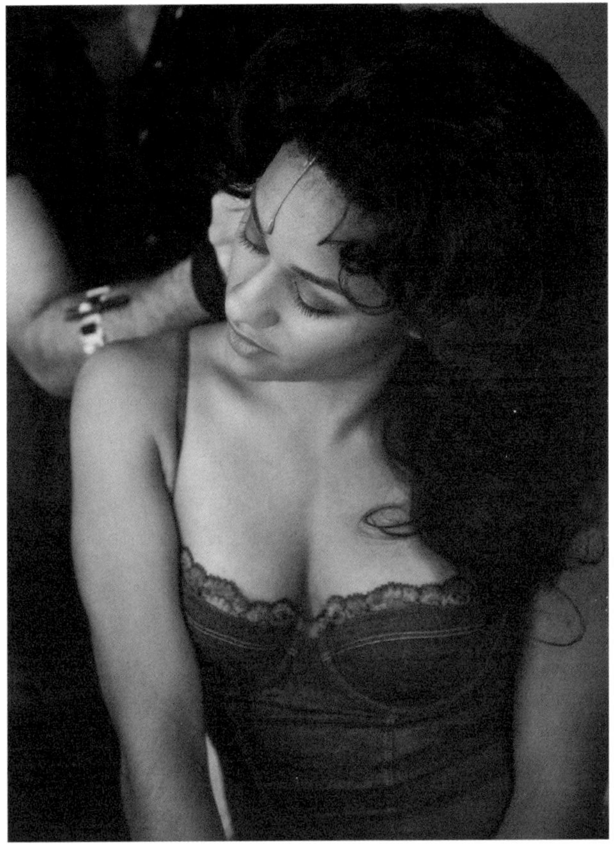

Ariana DeBose
Summer: The Donna Summer Musical
Lunt-Fontanne Theatre
2018

Here's the thing about Broadway: most people only see what happens onstage eight times a week. That magic—and it *is* magic—is shiny. It sparkles in a way that, while people wonder what happens behind the curtain, they rarely get the chance to actually move it.

Those who do are rare and special, none more so than my talented comrade in art and life, Jenny. To be honest, we as a community are not always welcoming to outsiders. I mean, what if they taint the magic? But it's never been that way with Jenny.

From the very beginning, she's pulled back that proverbial curtain with such care, compassion, and curiosity. But moreover, it is her unwavering commitment to simply being there to witness this art form that she loves so dearly and capture a moment in time amongst the people who are the beating heart of Broadway that sets Jenny apart.

Speaking of beating hearts, the same words could be used to describe her, as I don't think there's a single member of this community who can imagine a Broadway event without Jenny's presence. A New York City resident of nearly two decades, Jenny is the definition of a bona fide lady-boss hustler. I have seen her turn in immaculate work on the most insane timelines. Sure, some would say, "Hey, that's the life of a professional photographer," and yet Jenny has done it with one of the most inspiring attitudes I've ever encountered. And she has done so in the face of her fair share of adversity. Our corner of the entertainment industry may be smaller than Hollywood, but the components that have made it tick for most of the years of Jenny's residency have been male-dominant.

Perhaps it's her southern charm (she's a Mississippi gal whose parents—also theatre people—raised her right) in conjunction with her incredible vision and talent that has left a unique mark? But from where I sit, I have watched her work her way into the upper echelons by simply *doing* the work and putting her heart into the art—with a dash of standing up to the boy's club and for herself when necessary.

But more importantly, Jenny has always understood that, as magical as Broadway can be, there is a potent vulnerability in every moment. But I'd say the feeling is probably at it's peak backstage before the show for many actors. Now, let's be real. Acting is not the same as curing cancer. But it does take courage to go onstage every night and risk making an absolute ass of oneself in the pursuit of making art and connecting with the audience. Jenny understands and respects that, and you can feel it in every capture. There is no judgment and always a sense of reverence in a Jenny Anderson photograph.

Whether it be backstage just before a half-hour call or in the moments just after winning a Tony (or, in my case, when Jenny was there in the life-changing moments after I won my Oscar), there is simply no other person's face or lens you would rather see.

I have had the privilege of knowing and being photographed by Jenny Anderson for more than 10 years now, and it's true: there's absolutely no one like her. Jenny will tell you that it has been *her* privilege to capture these moments on Broadway, but in truth, it has been *our* privilege to be truly seen through the gaze of the great Jenny Anderson.

Now, enough from me. The work in these pages will speak for itself!

—Ariana DeBose

PREFACE

I've loved theatre and theatre performers since my memories began, but mine was always a different kind of obsession. Yes, I loved sitting in the rows of seats waiting for the curtain to rise and being moved to tears by a perfect performance, but I loved the world backstage more. When I was seven, my mom played Grace in the Brookhaven, Mississippi, production of *Annie*. I had auditioned to be an orphan but didn't make the cut. Oddly, I wasn't that devastated when I found out I could still spend my time running the back halls of the theatre with the other kids or sneaking into the wings to watch my mom rehearse. To me, that's where the real magic happened. That was how this unbelievable thing I got to see—a live theatrical performance—really came to life.

Still, through high school and college I auditioned and took singing lessons, trying to mirror the talents of my mother in order to find a role in the world I loved. Around that same time, my dad introduced me to photography. Women like Dorothea Lange, Margaret Bourke White, and Eudora Welty quickly became my new obsession. Their ability to capture the quiet, human moments of real life while telling a complete, mesmerizing story was exactly the same feeling I got when I ran around backstage of a show gathering glimpses of my mom in costume, ensemble members playing cards in the wings, or ladies chatting through laughter in the wig room. Magic.

In college, I leaned more into my love of photography, joining the daily newspaper, becoming photo editor, and forcing my friends to dress up and do editorial shoots in the woods. But the first time I realized I wanted to make it my career was when I was shooting backstage at the theatre department's production of *Streetcar Named Desire*—a job that I assigned myself. I was friends with several of the actors and asked if I could come backstage and capture a few moments before the show. That night, I took an image of one of the leads sitting in her vintage, satin and lace slip and putting the finishing touches on her pin curls. She was beaming with laughter—probably due to something one of the other 10 girls shoved in a small college dressing room had said. It still gives me such a visceral feeling when I think of it. That was the moment I knew I'd found my way into my favorite place in the world.

After graduating, my only goal was to get to New York City—Broadway, specifically. I sold everything I owned, bought a one-way ticket, and never looked back. I even took a job taking portraits of tourists on the Circle Line Cruise to survive those first few months. Then I landed a photo internship at Broadway.com—the place I spent hours scrolling as a theatre-obsessed teen and young adult. That internship officially started it all, getting me and my camera backstage of every theatre on Broadway. My first backstage shoot was with Laura Benanti in *Gypsy* just weeks after she won the Tony. I couldn't have been greener or more nervous, but all that washed away the second I walked into her dressing room. I've spent the last 17 years reliving that moment with dozens of icons in dozens of shows. But over all those years—which included shoots as far from dressing rooms as The White House and The Academy Awards Red Carpet—I have always come back to my love of what happens inside the halls and wings of a theatre.

These moments before a show begins, when the actors are preparing, costumes are being adorned, quiet retrospective breaths in the shadows are everything that makes theatre special. Not many get to witness these in-between moments. Even less get to capture them.

It's been my greatest honor to be that documentarian, that conduit from audience member to beyond the footlights. Sharing these images in this book opens the door and allows you into a sacred space where family is made between singing, dancing, and dialogue. This is where the endless work that leads to what you see onstage is celebrated and revered.

COLLECTION

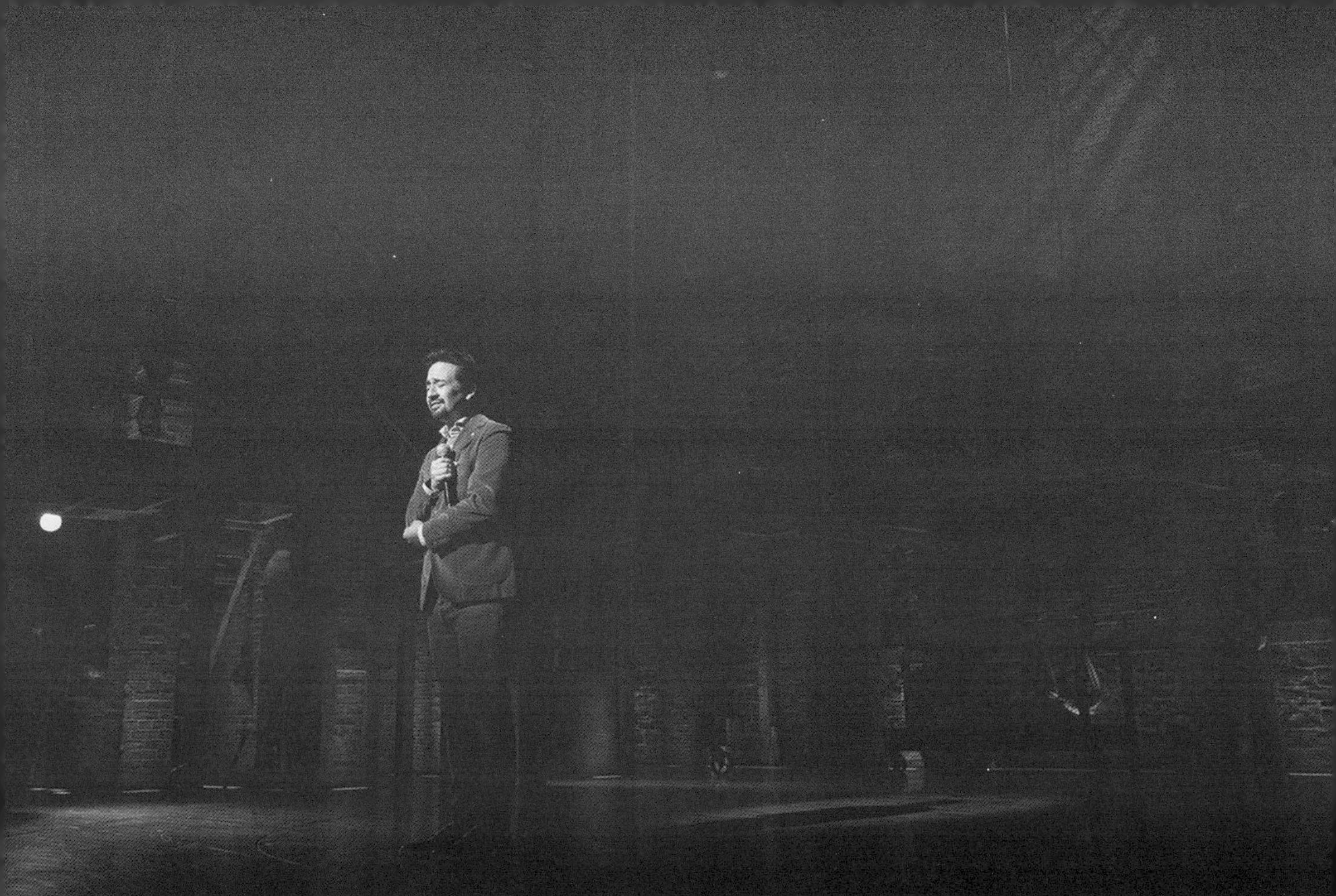

Lin-Manuel Miranda
The reopening of *Hamilton*
Richard Rodgers Theatre
2022

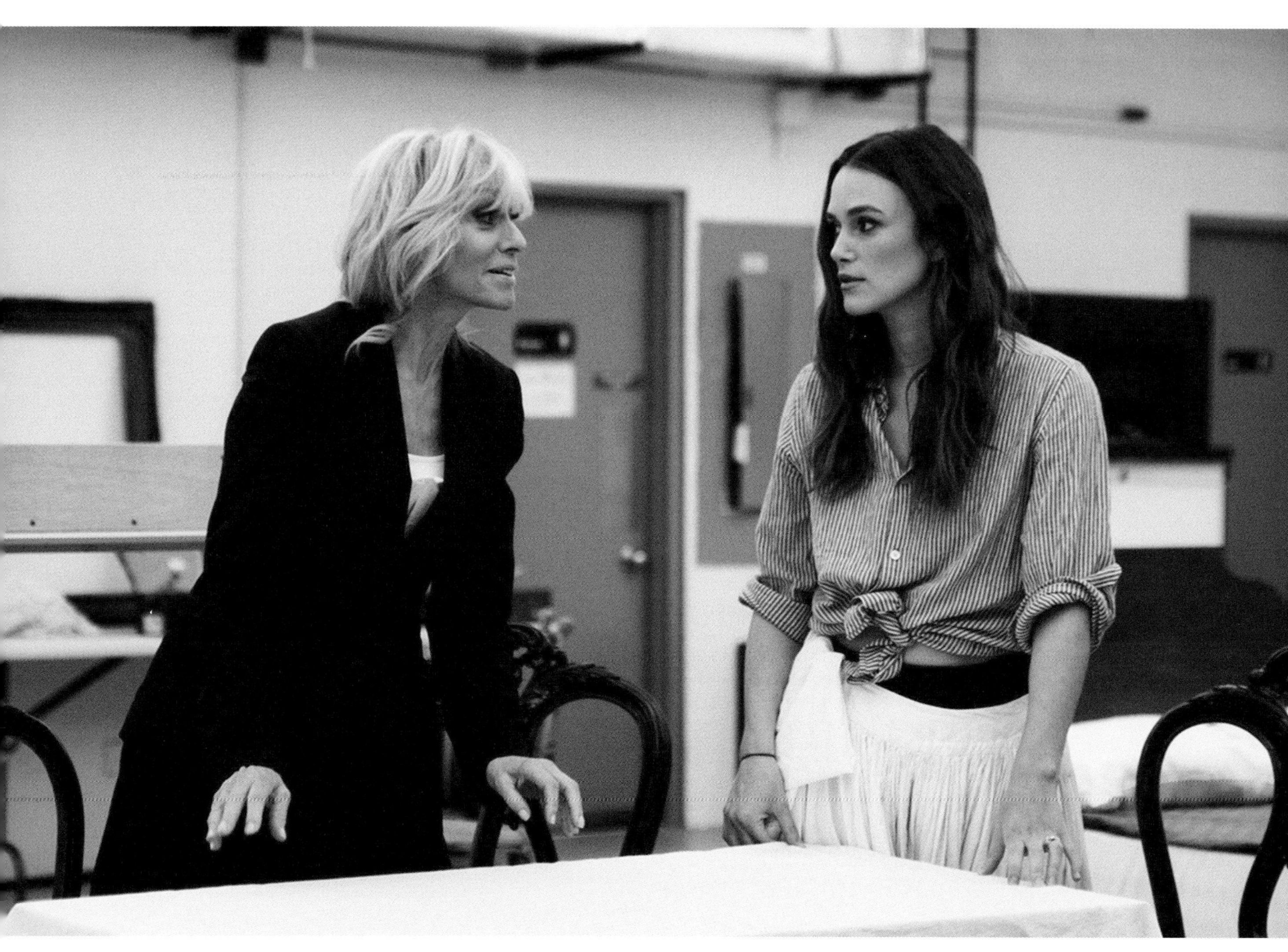

Judith Light and Keira Knightley
Rehearsal for *Thérèse Raquin*
2015

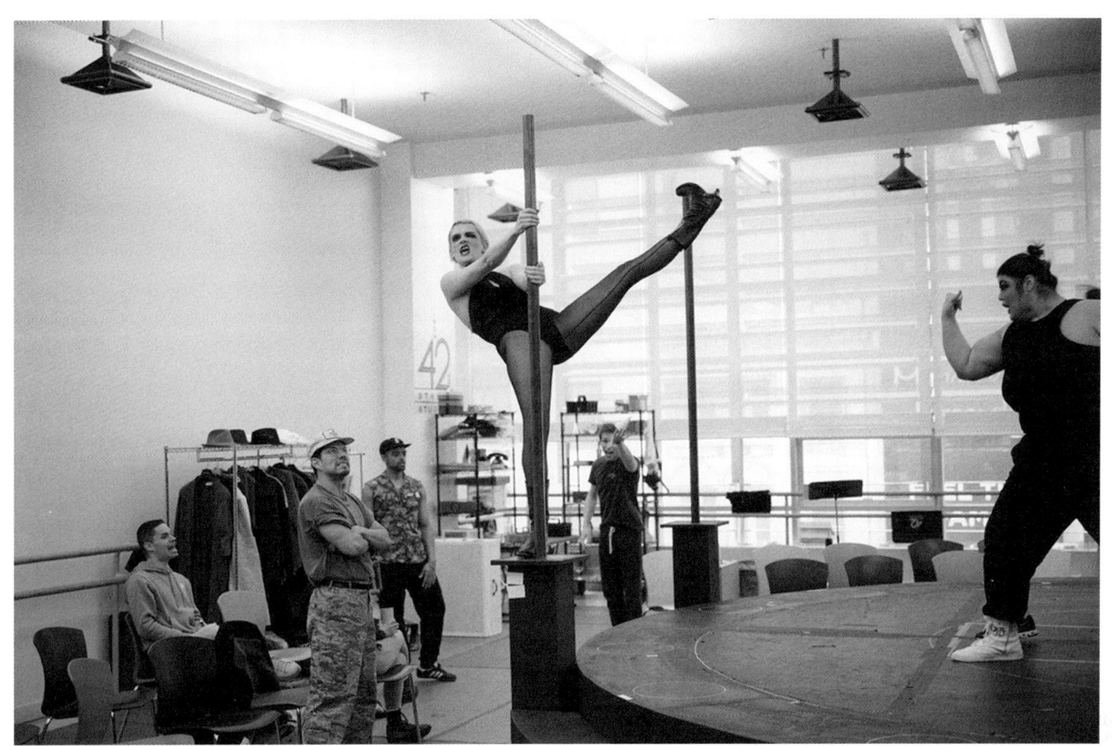

Gayle Rankin
Rehearsal for *Cabaret*
2024

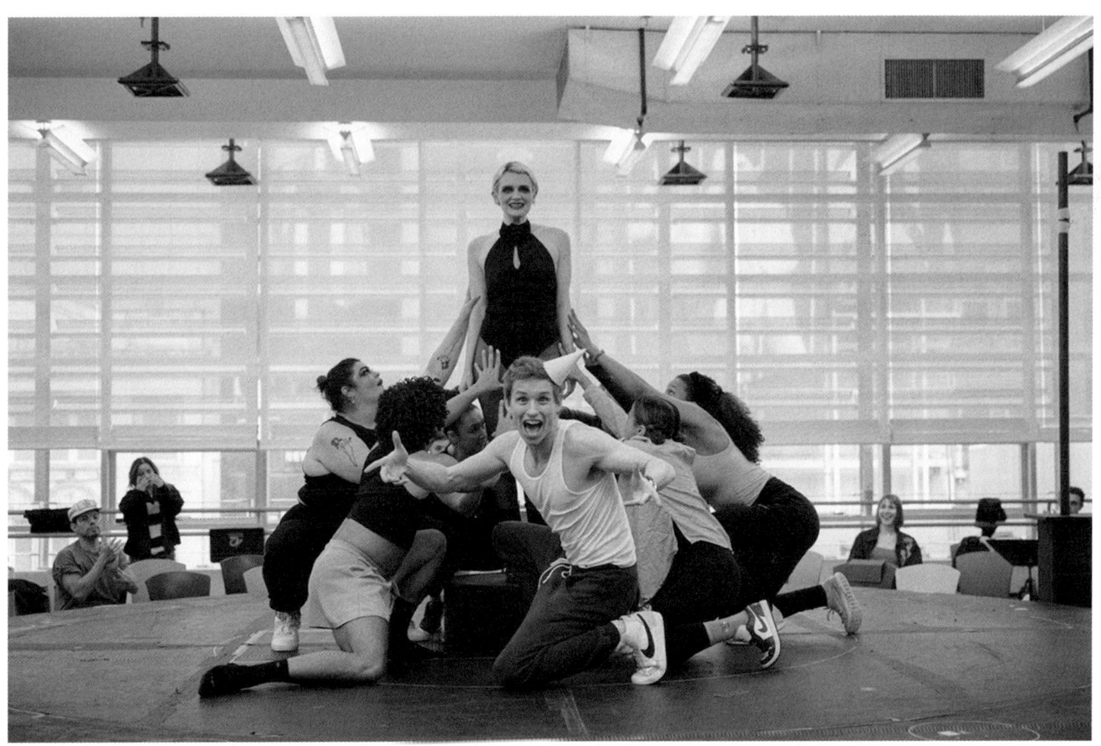

Gayle Rankin, Eddie Redmayne, and cast
Rehearsal for *Cabaret*
2024

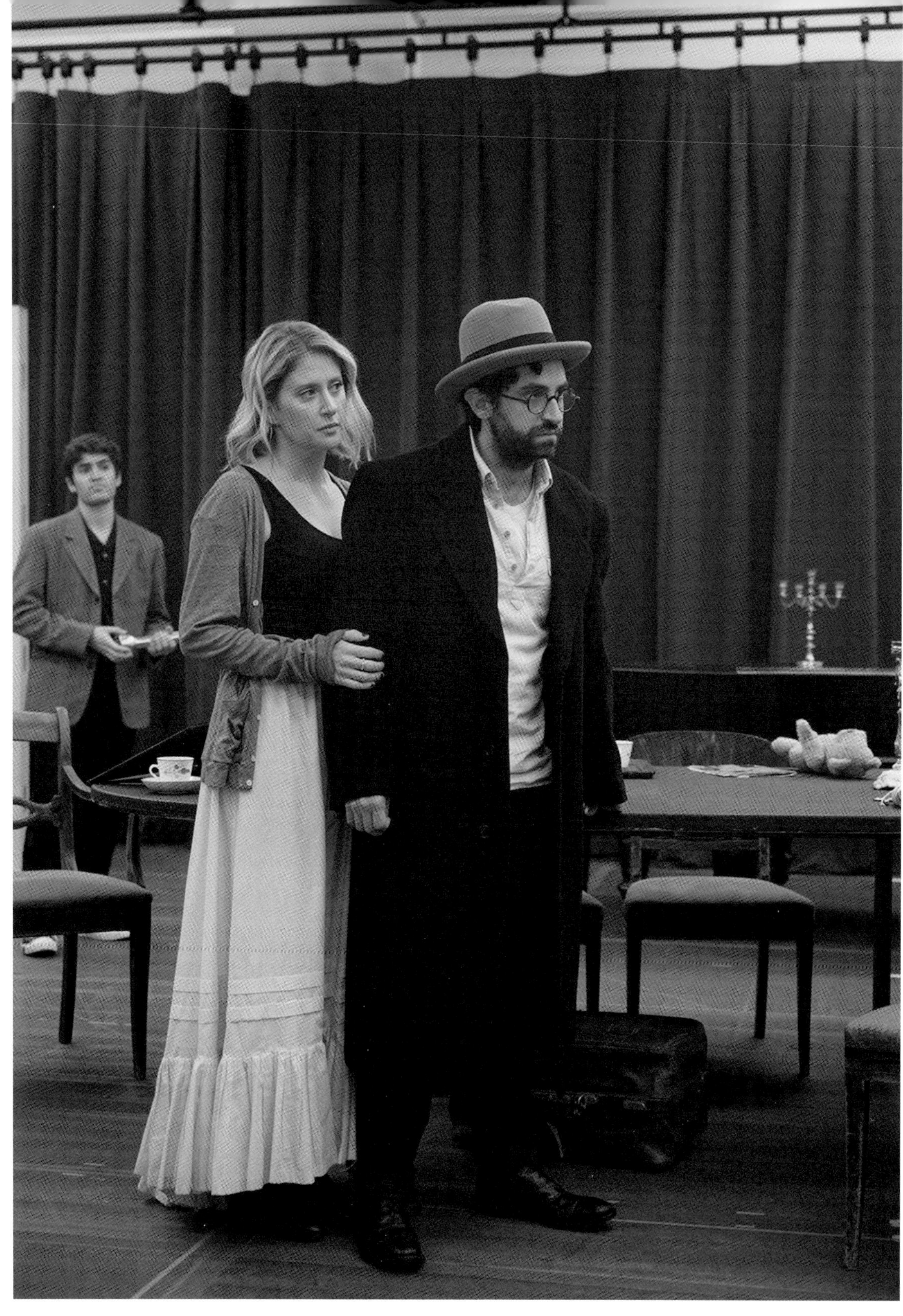

Caissie Levy and Brandon Uranowitz
Rehearsal for *Leopoldstadt*
2023

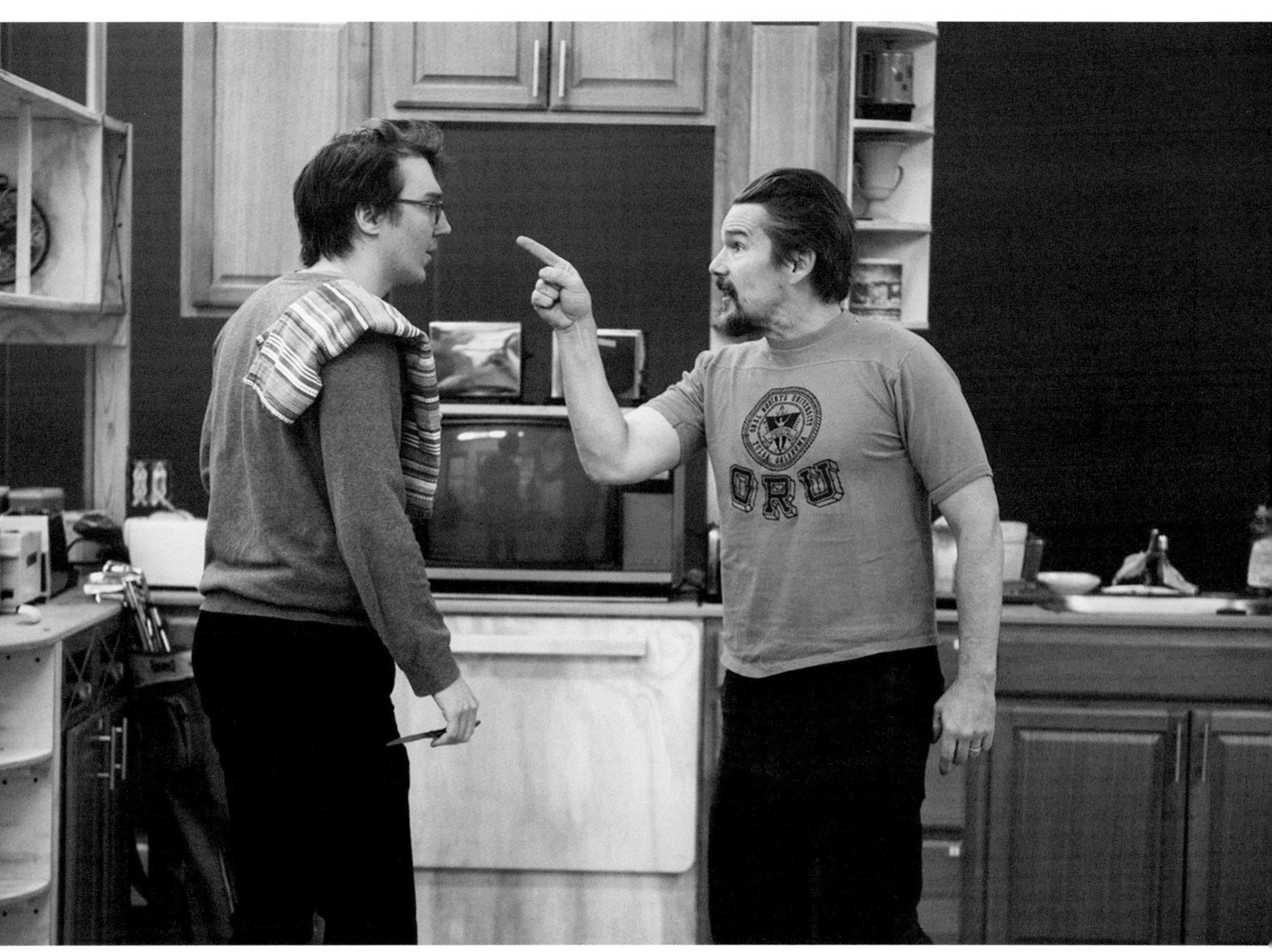

Paul Dano and Ethan Hawke
Rehearsal for *True West*
2018

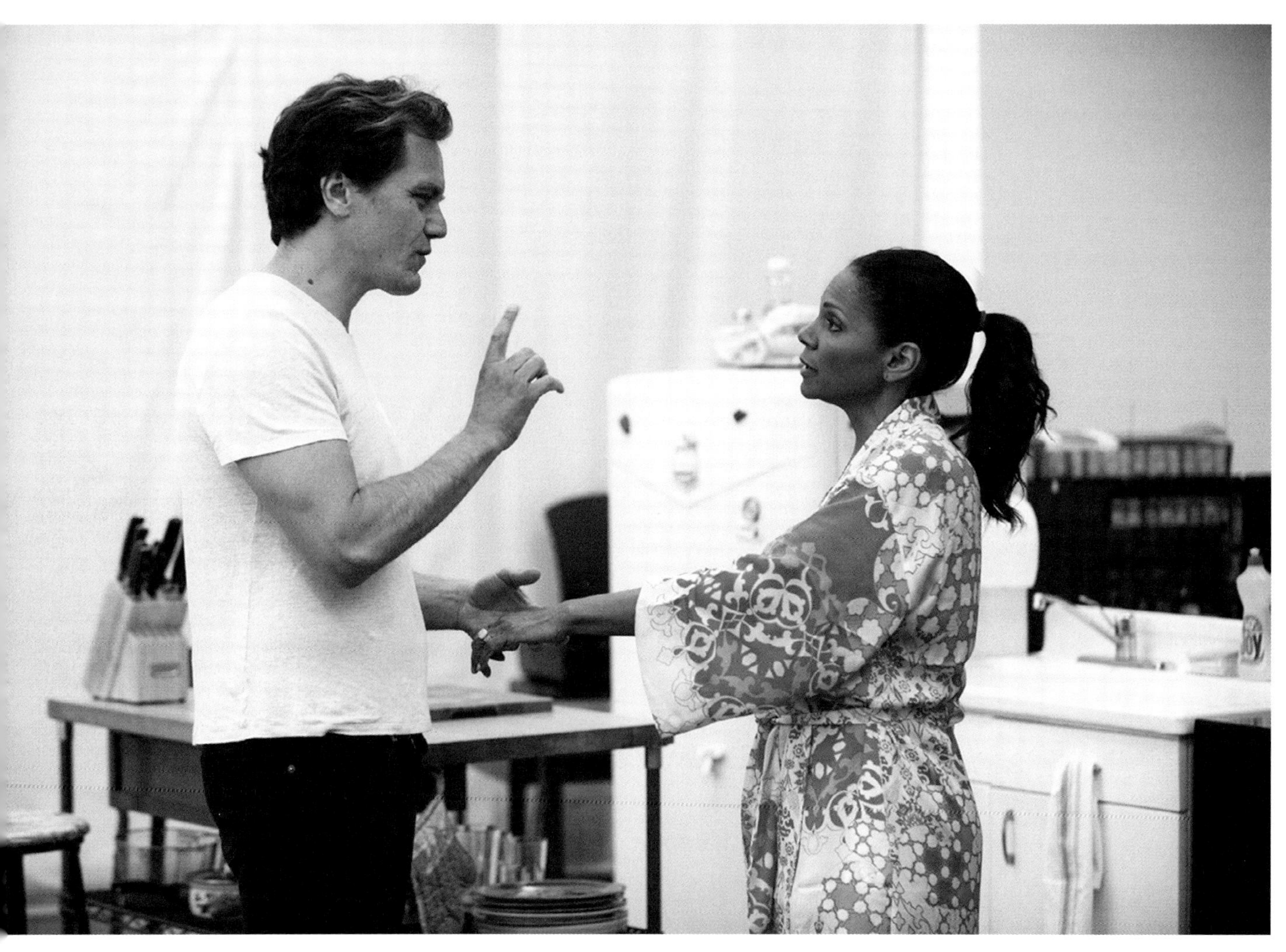

Michael Shannon and Audra McDonald
Rehearsal for *Frankie and Johnny in the Clair de Lune*
2019

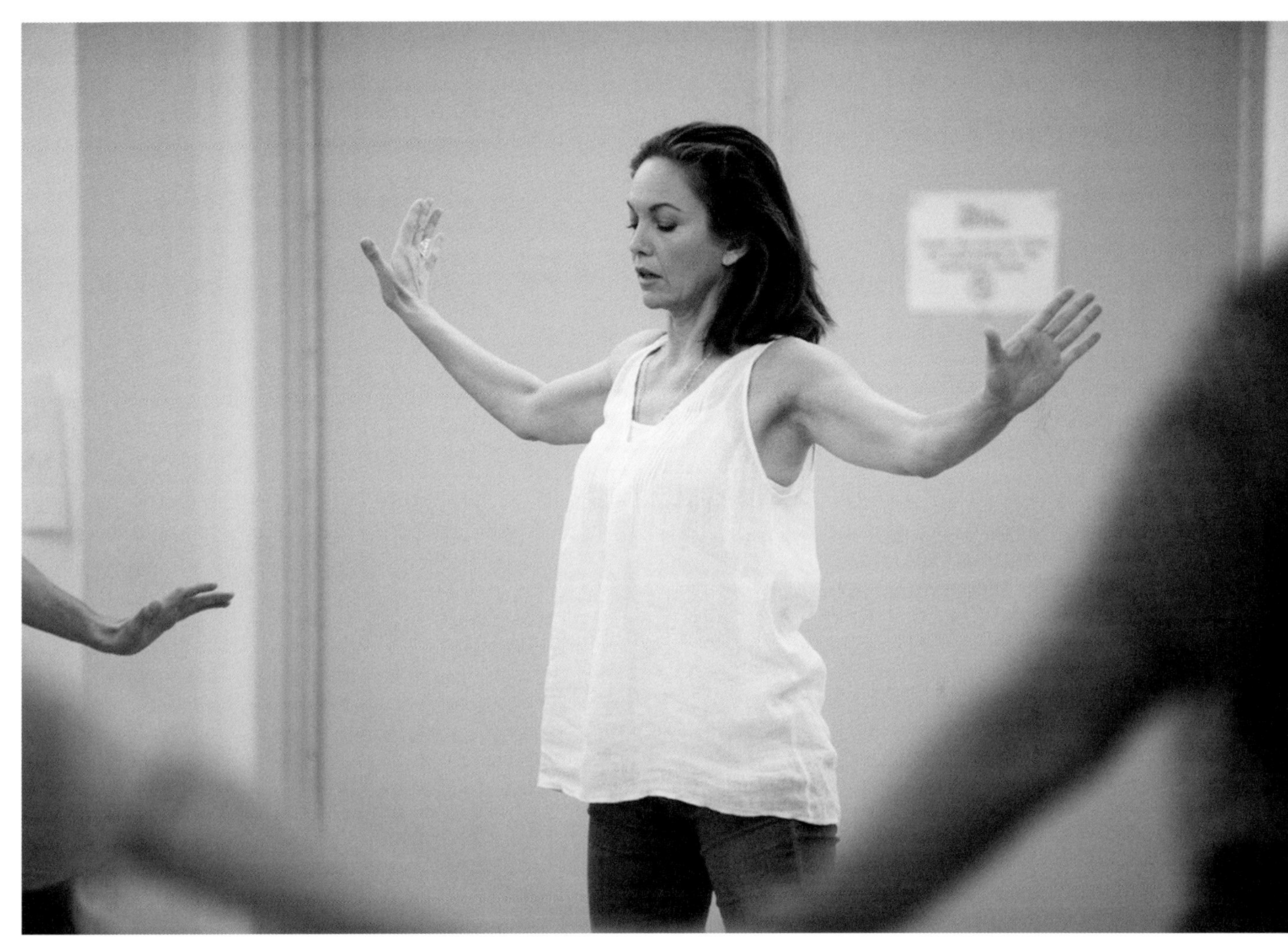

Diane Lane
Rehearsal for *The Cherry Orchard*
2016

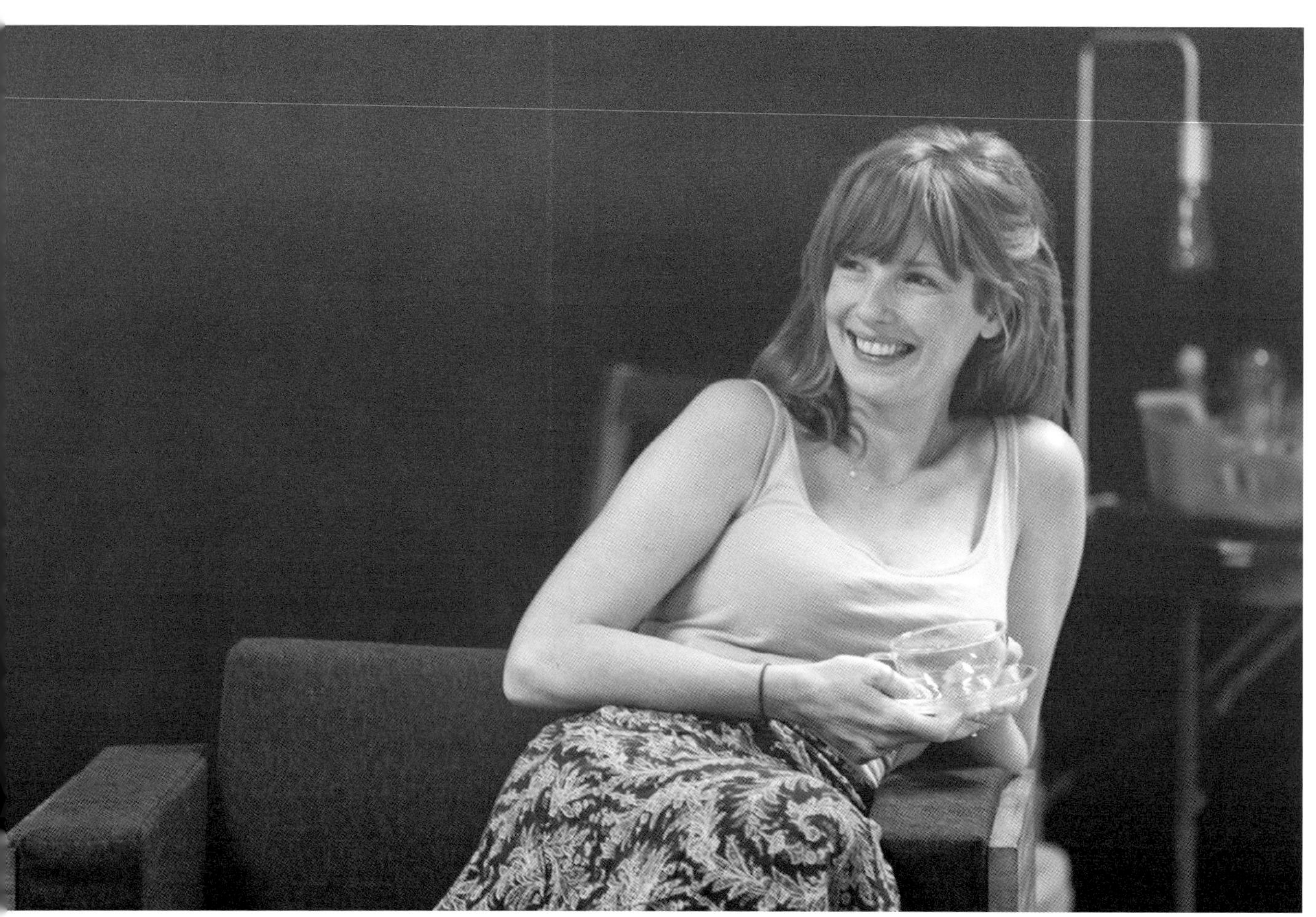

Kelly Reilly
Rehearsal for *Old Times*
2015

Lea Michele
Tech for *Funny Girl*
August Wilson Theatre
2023

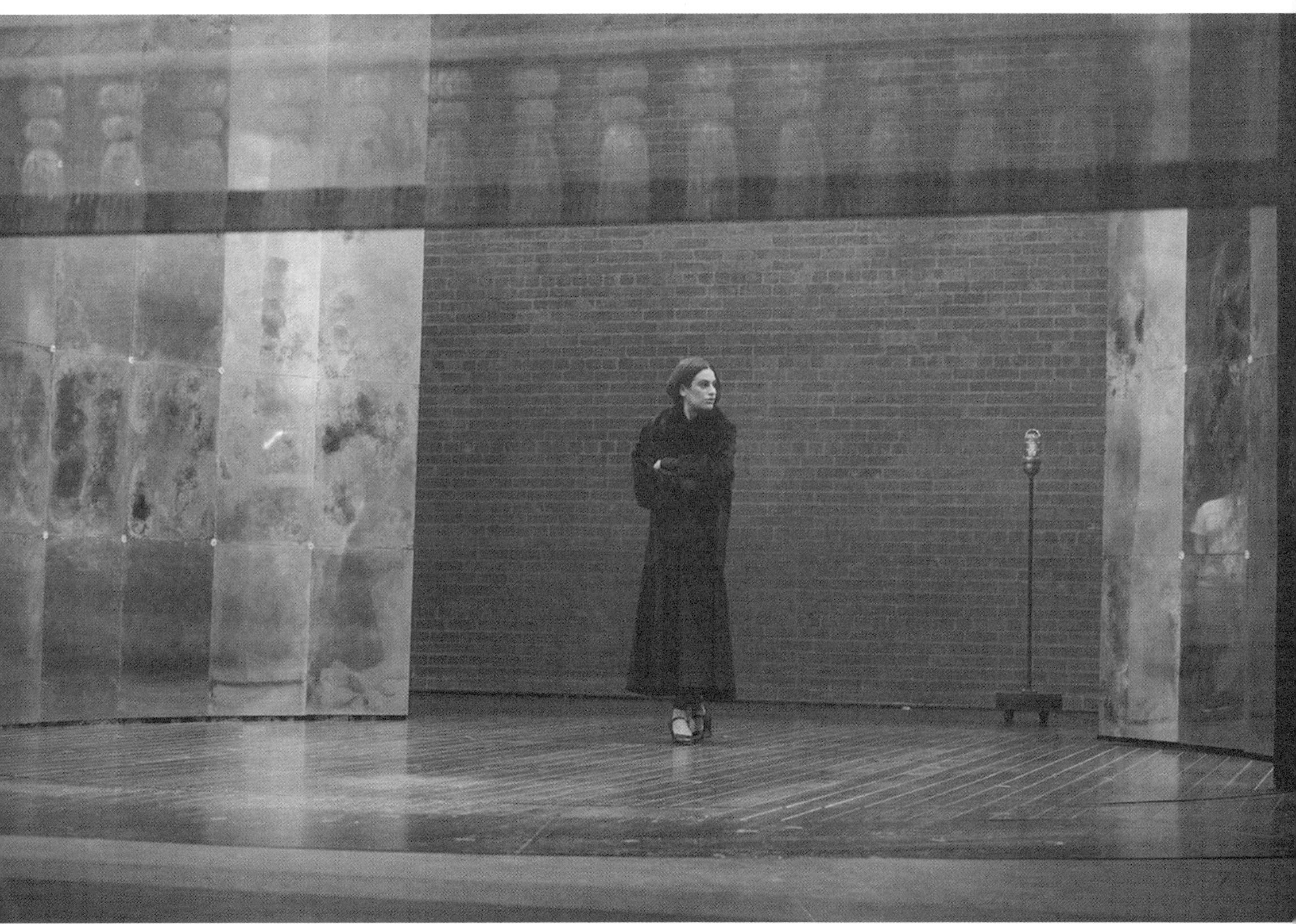

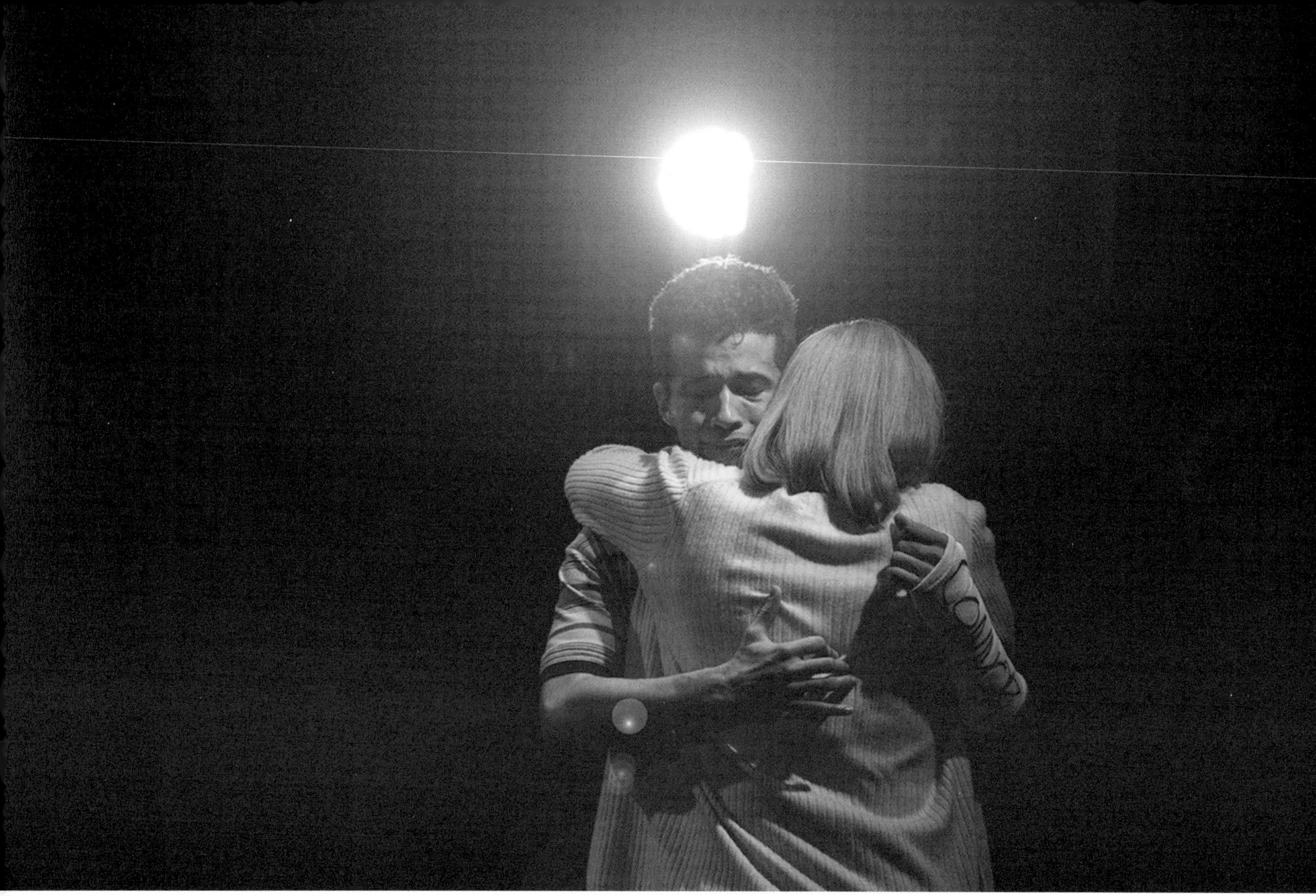

Jordan Fisher and Christiane Noll
Tech for *Dear Evan Hansen*
Music Box Theatre
2023

Caissie Levy, Gavin Creel, and Will Swenson
Rehearsal for *Hair*
2010

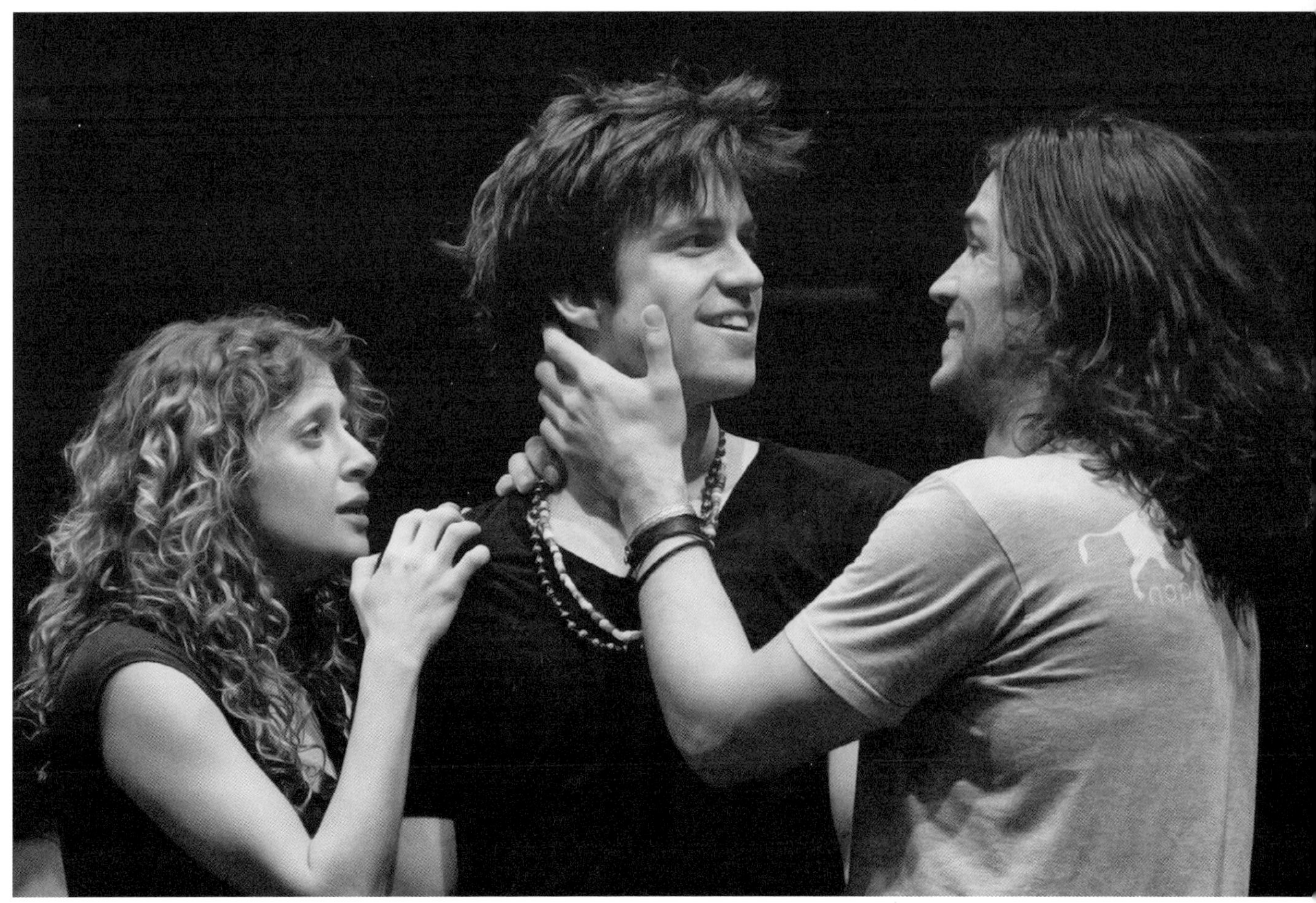

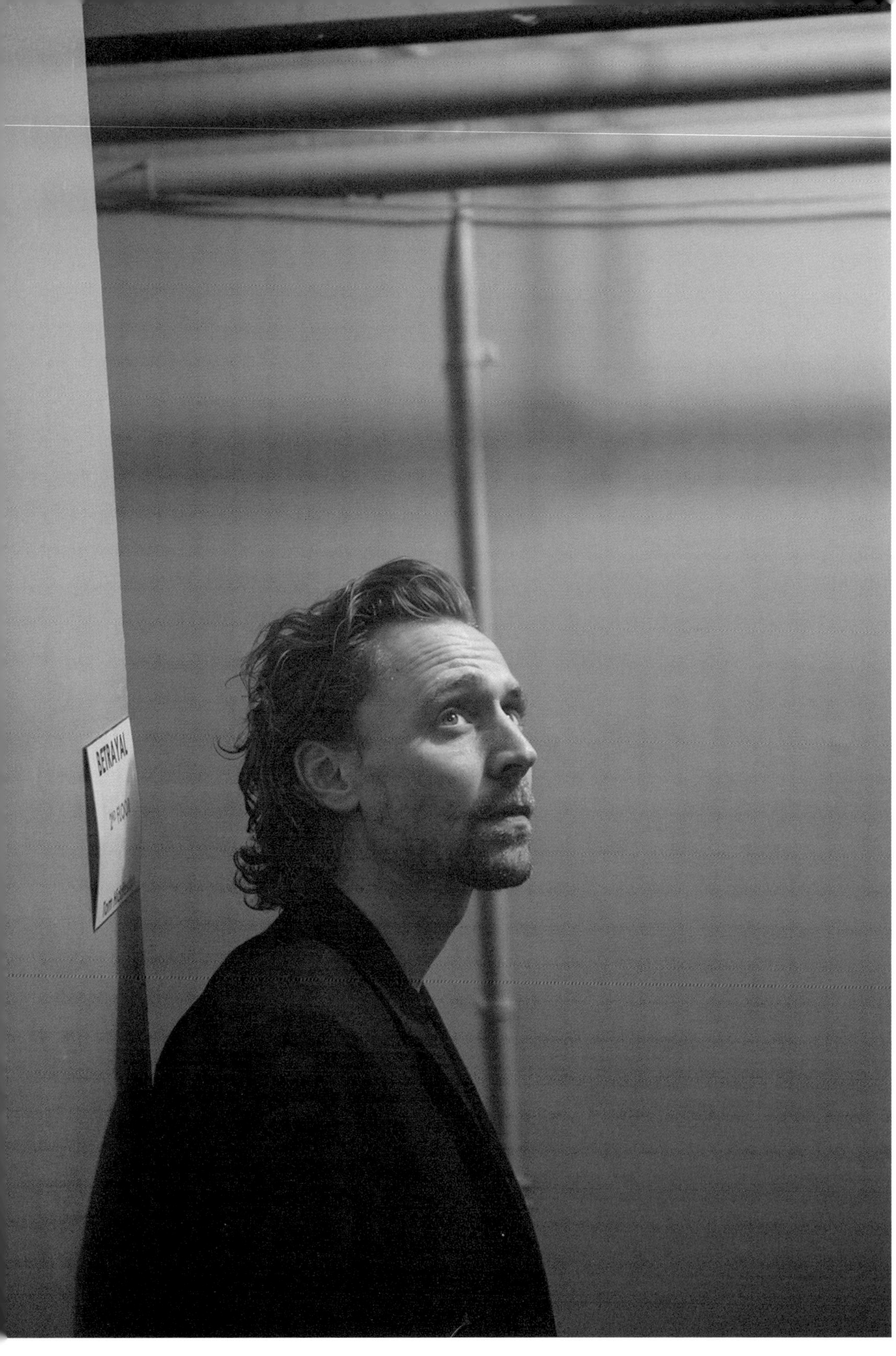

Tom Hiddleston
Betrayal
Bernard B. Jacobs Theatre
2019

John Kander and Joel Grey
The 76th Annual Tony Awards
United Palace Theatre
2023

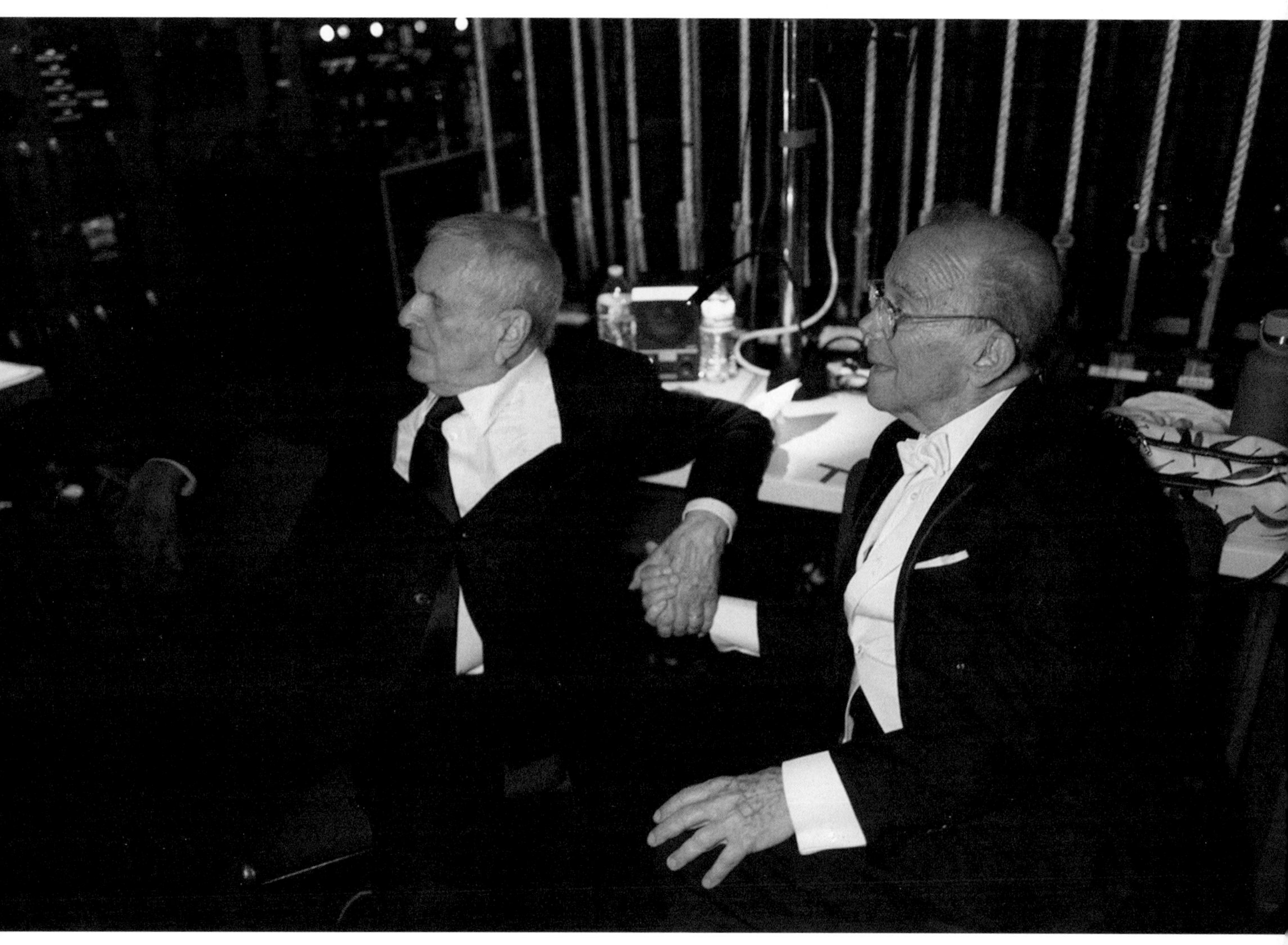

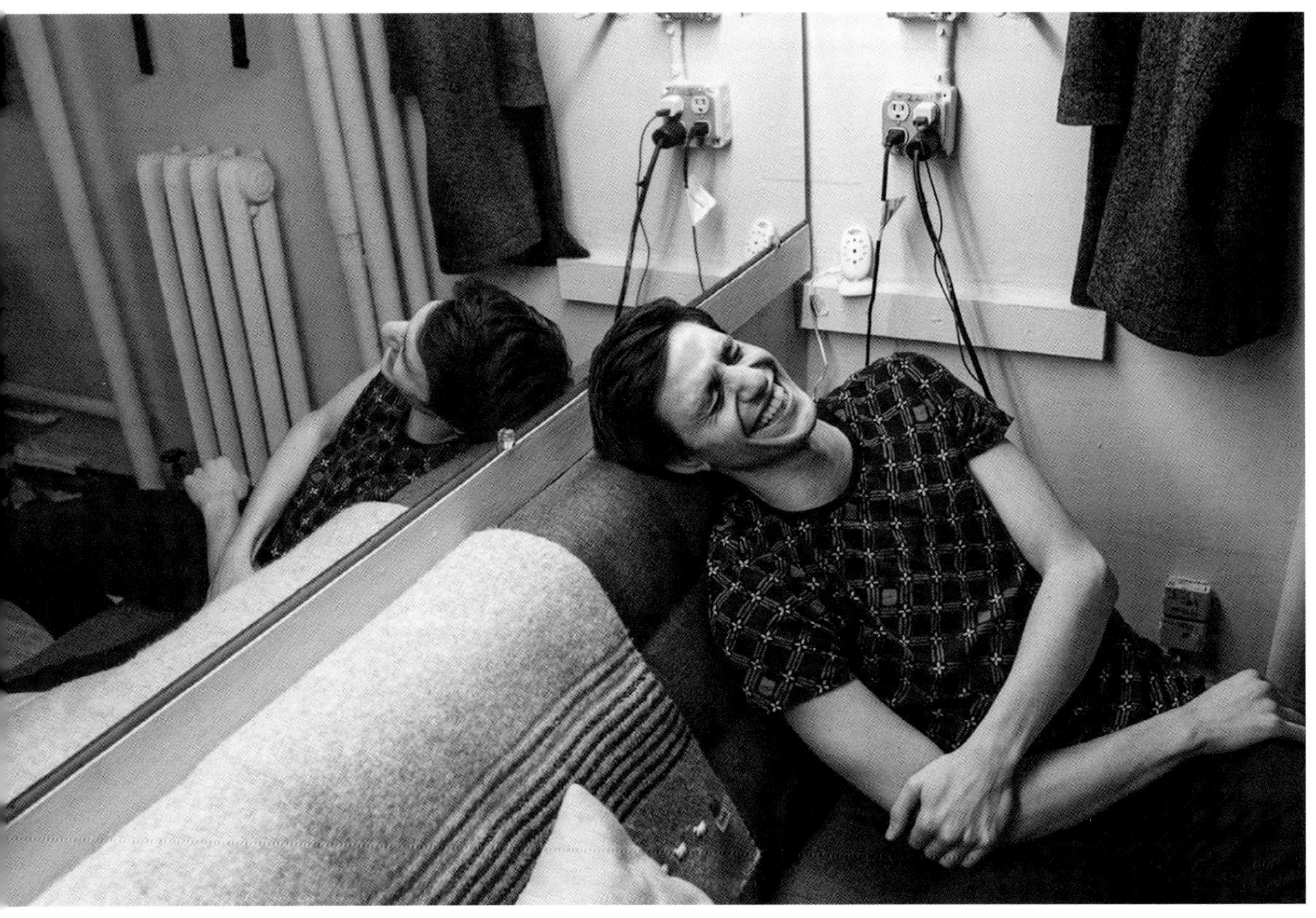

Gideon Glick
Significant Other
Booth Theatre
2017

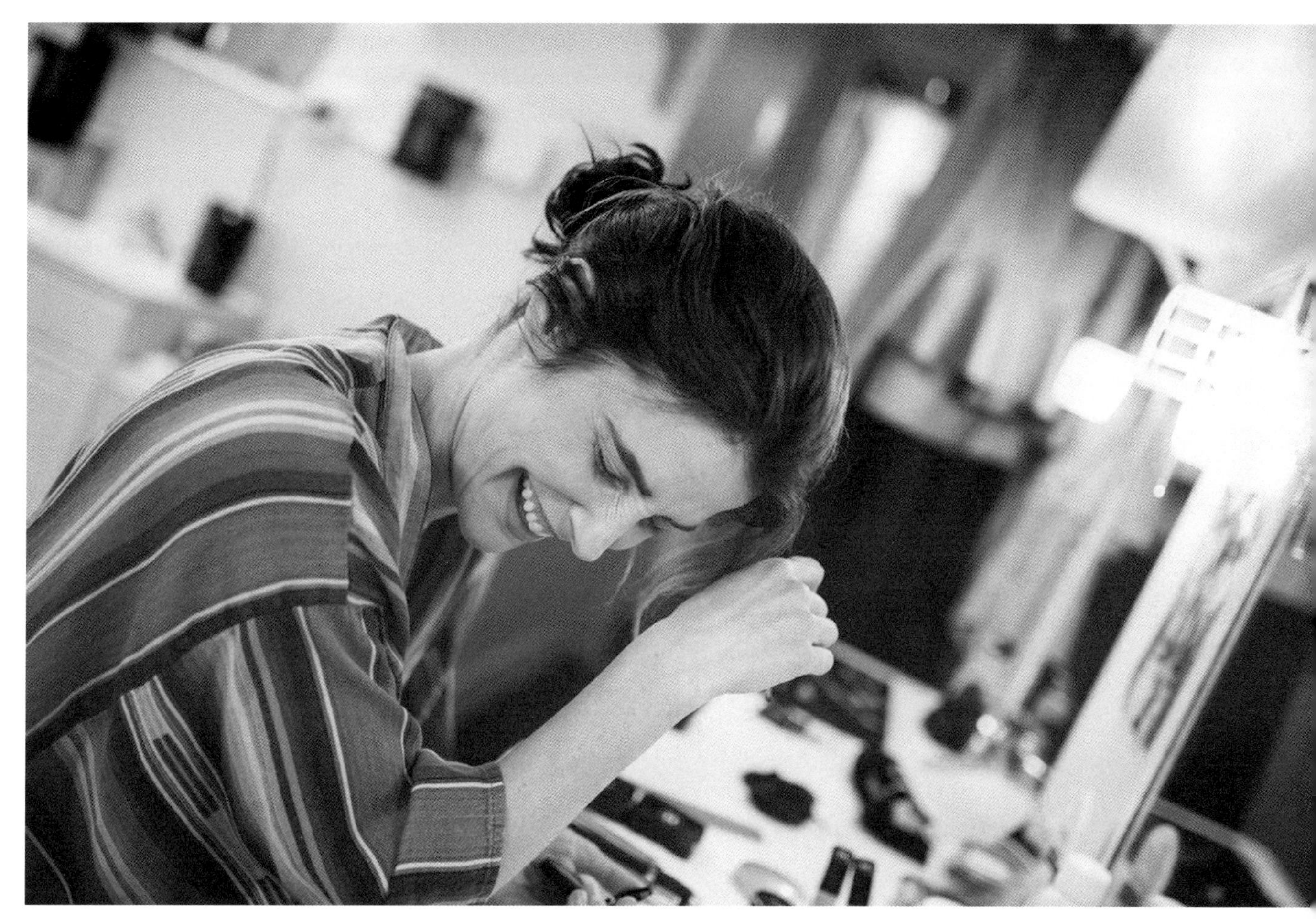

Cobie Smulders
Present Laughter
St. James Theatre
2017

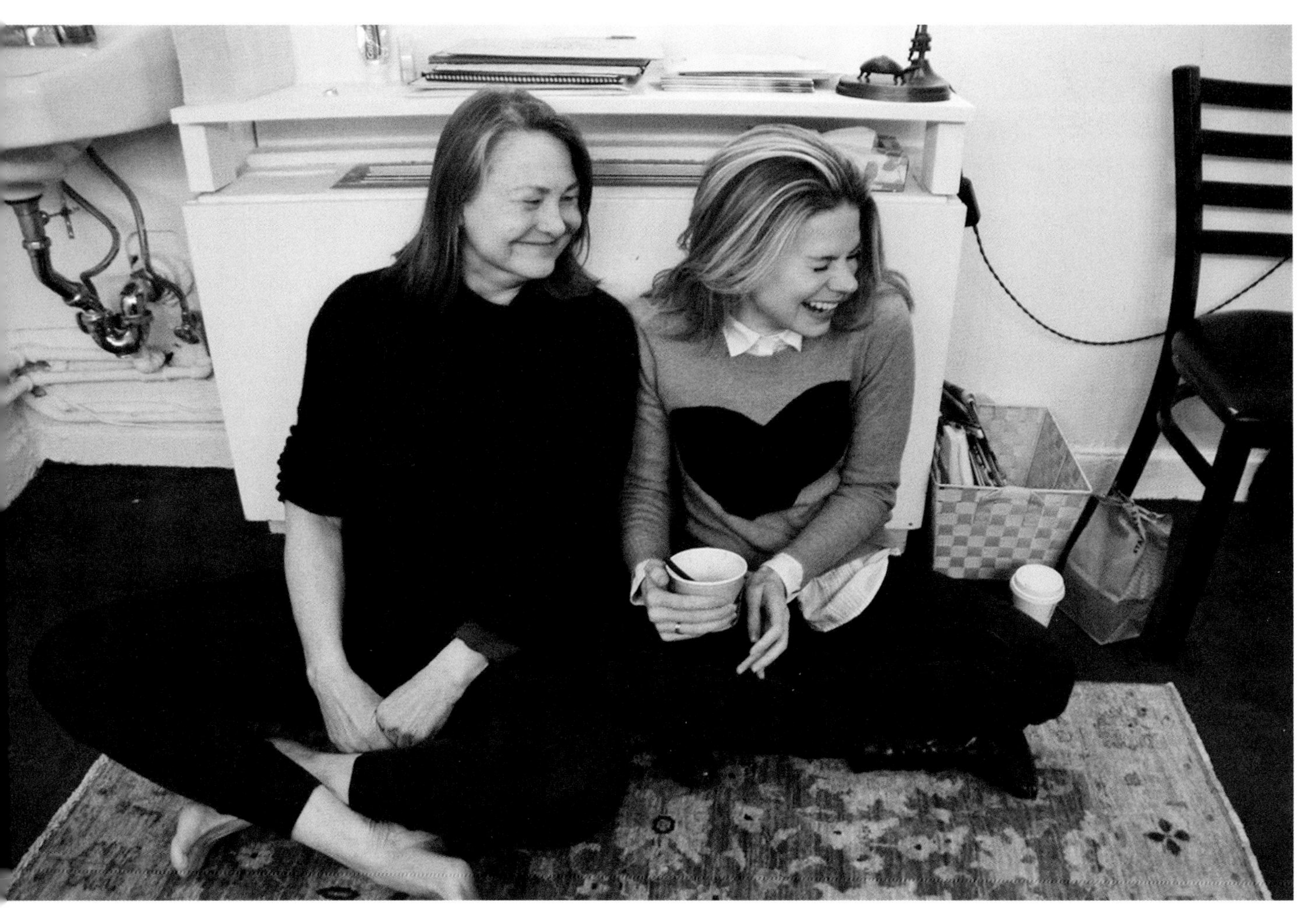

Cherry Jones and Celia Keenan-Bolger
The Glass Menagerie
Booth Theatre
2013

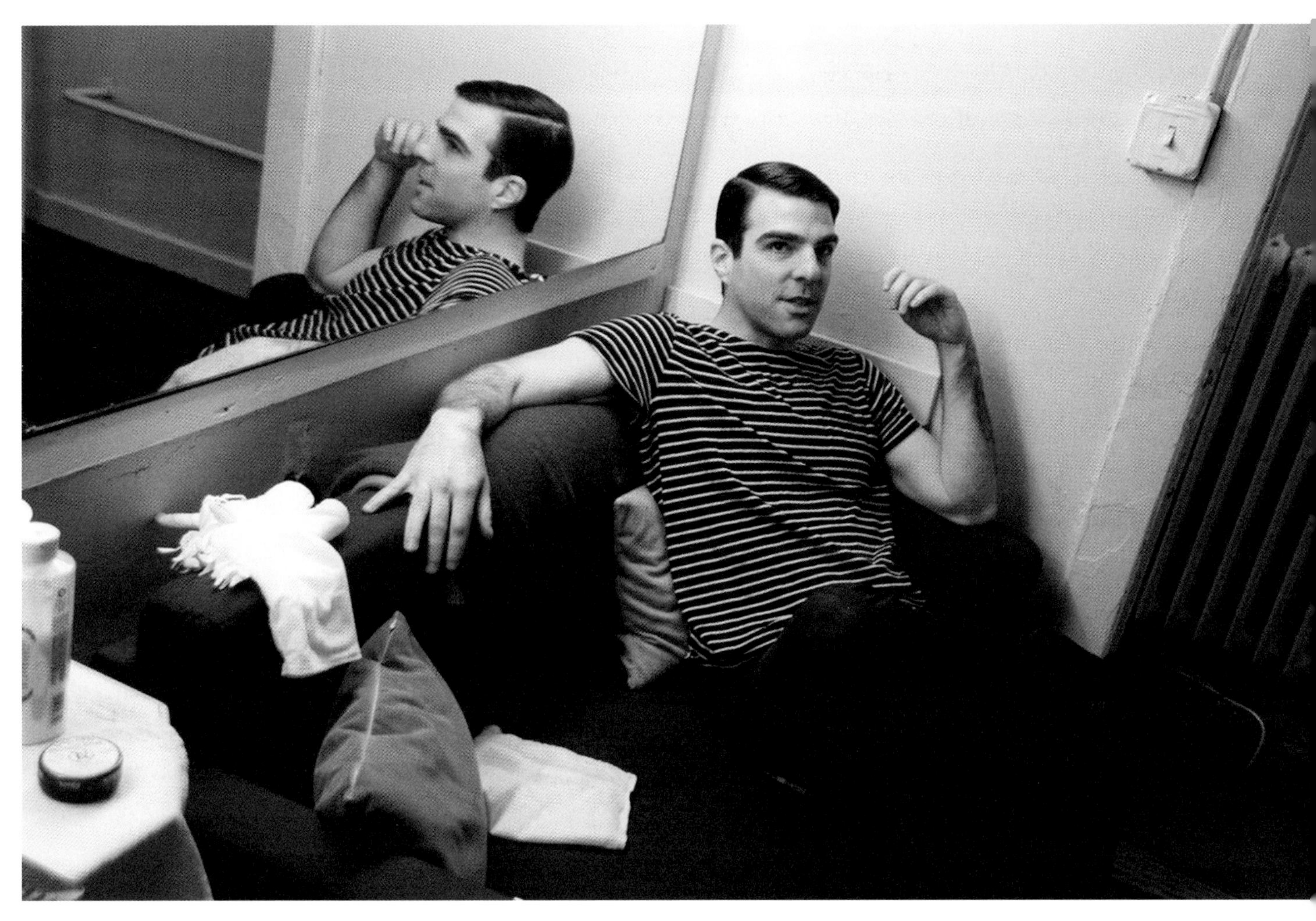

Zachary Quinto
The Glass Menagerie
Booth Theatre
2013

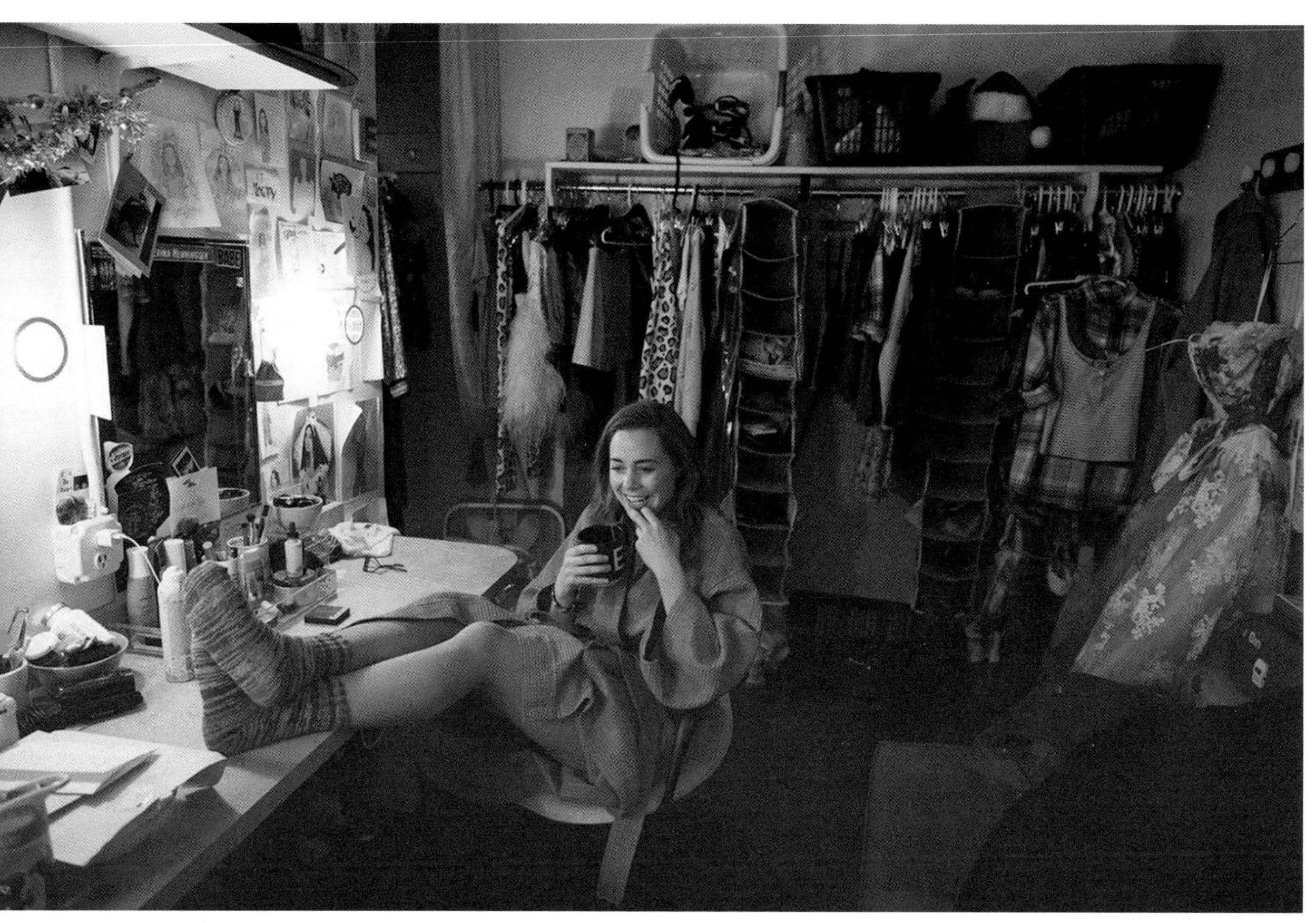

Erika Henningsen
Mean Girls
August Wilson Theatre
2018

Myles Frost
MJ
Neil Simon Theatre
2022

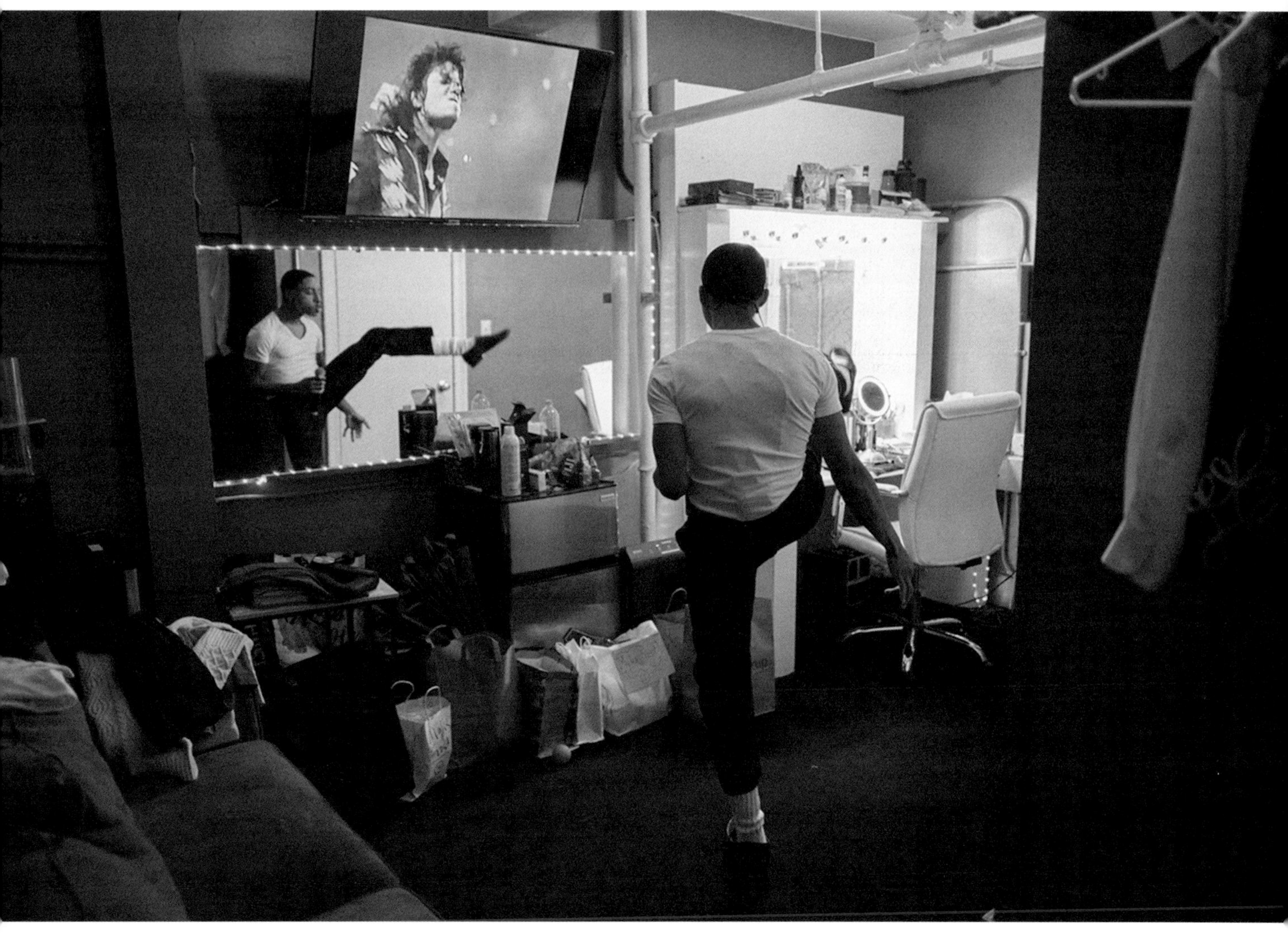

Vanessa Williams
Sondheim on Sondheim
Studio 54
2010

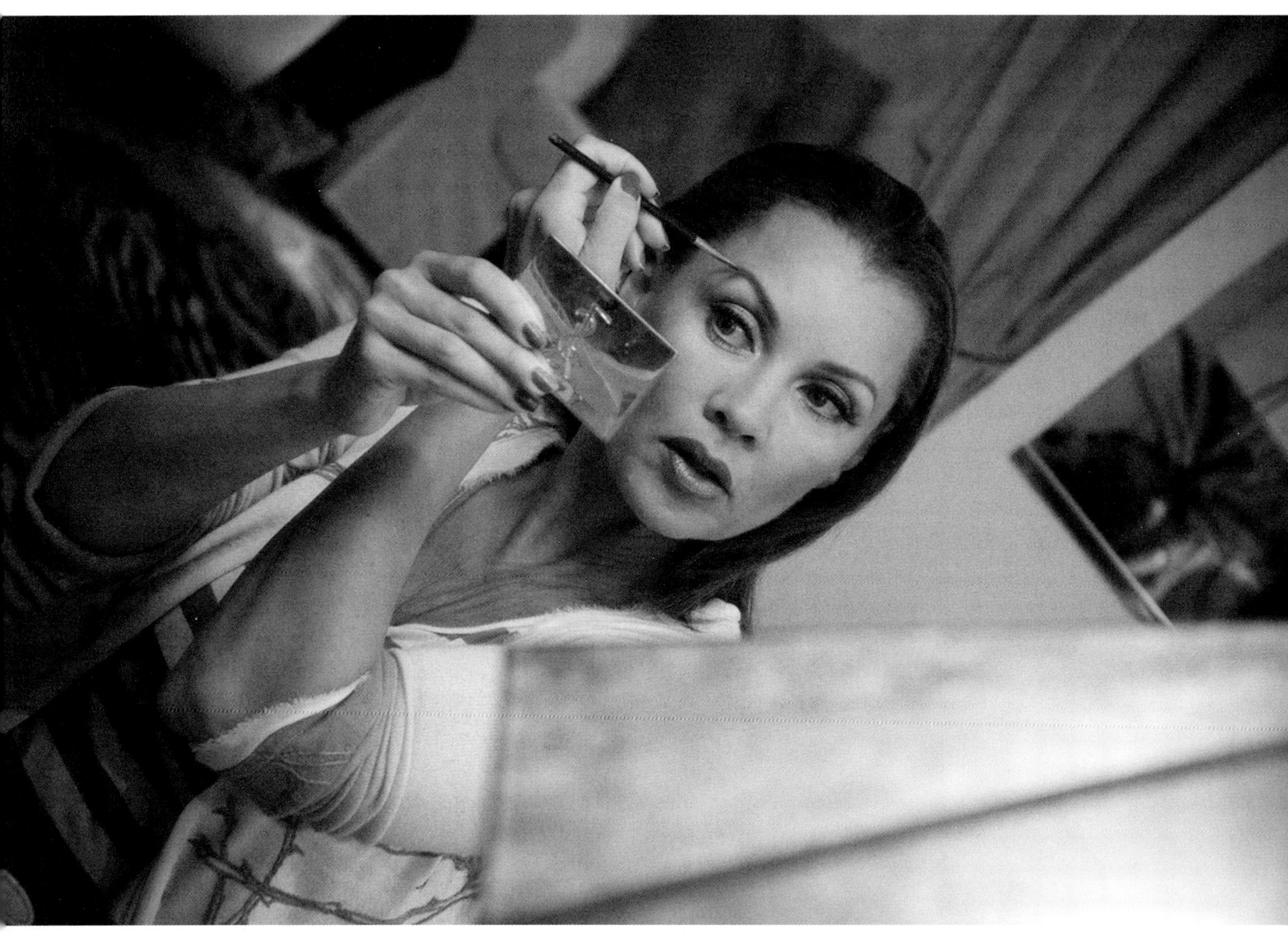

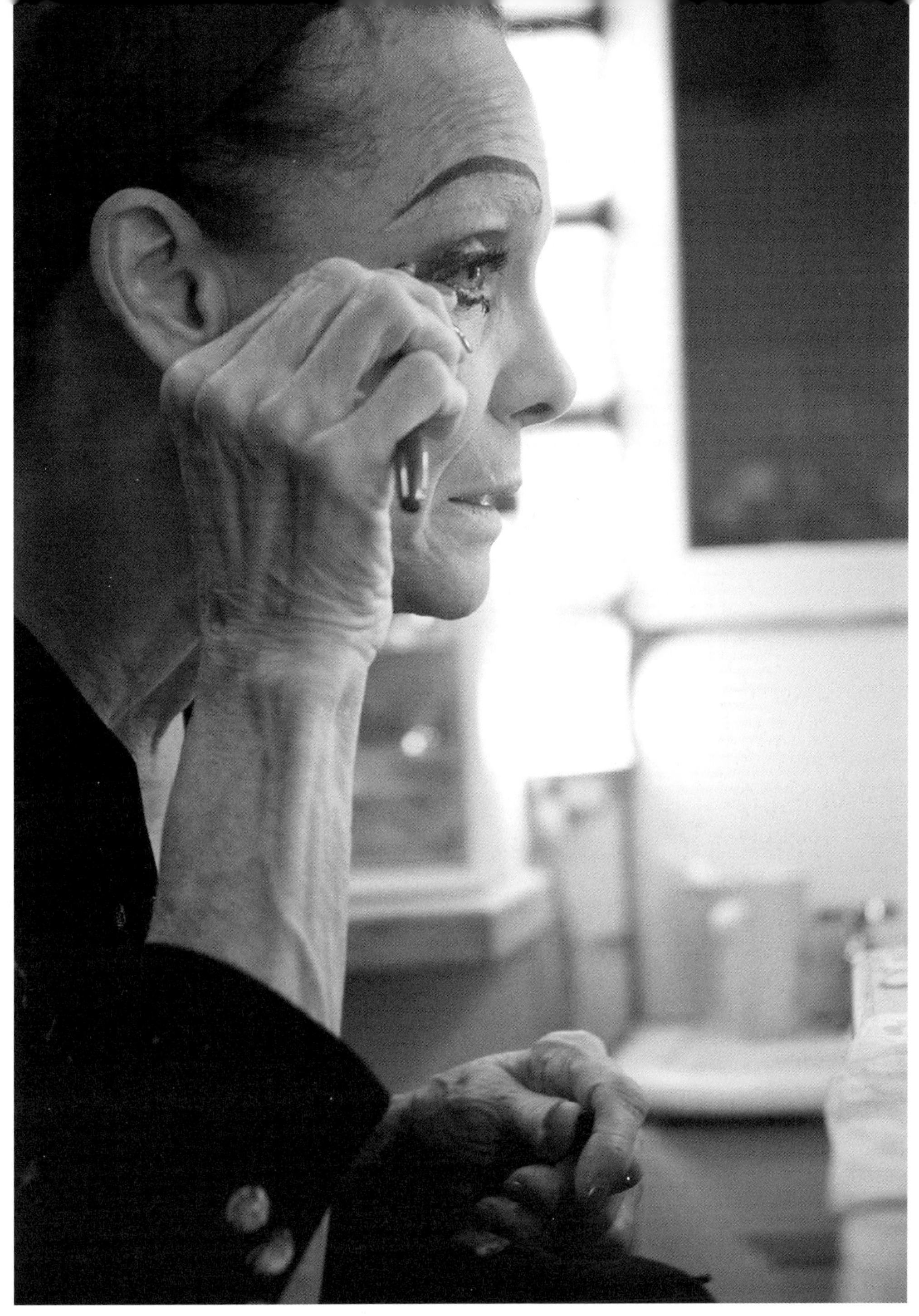

Valerie Harper
Looped
Lyceum Theatre
2010

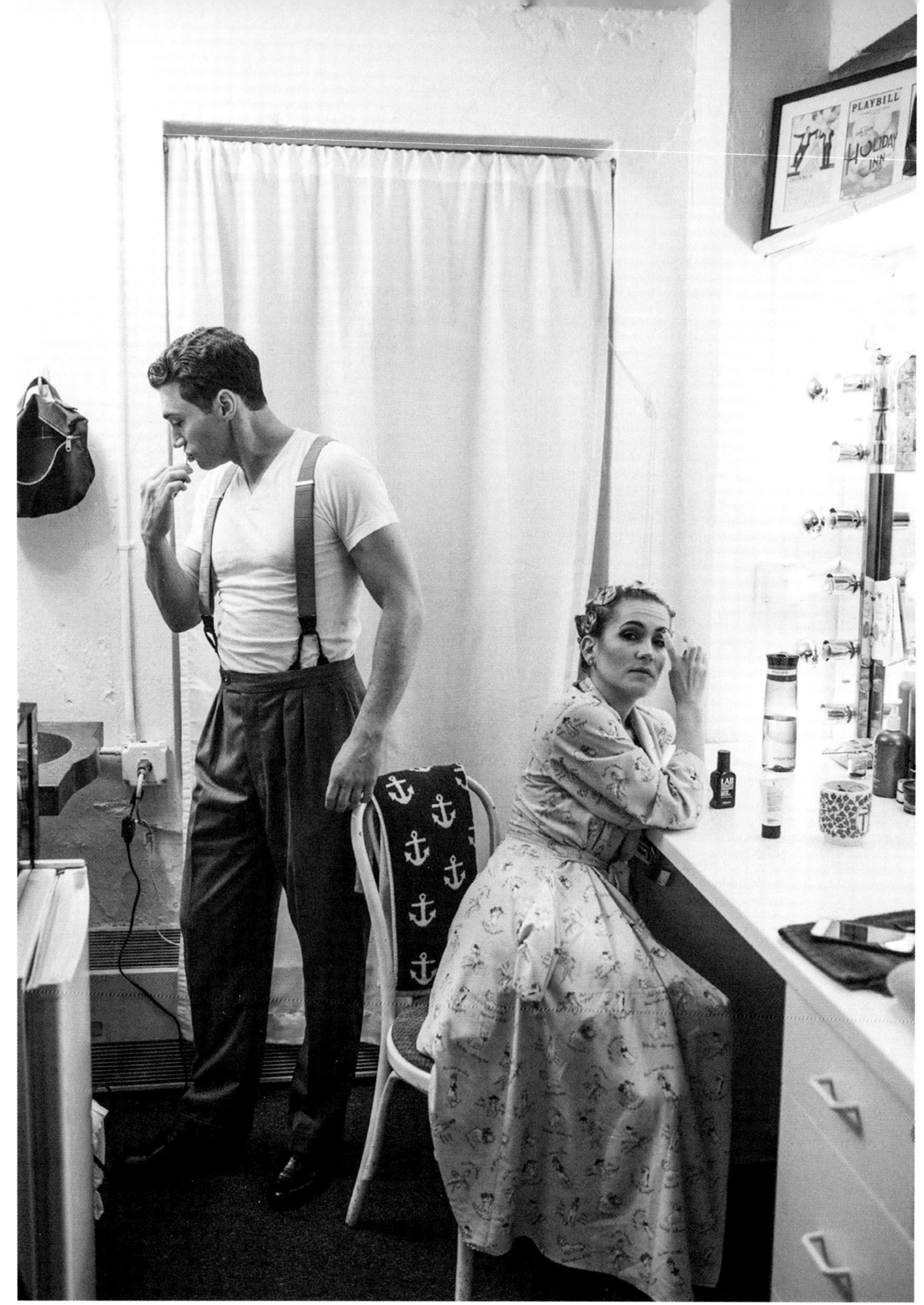

Bryce Pinkham and Lora Lee Gayer
Holiday Inn: The New Irving Berlin Musical
Studio 54
2017

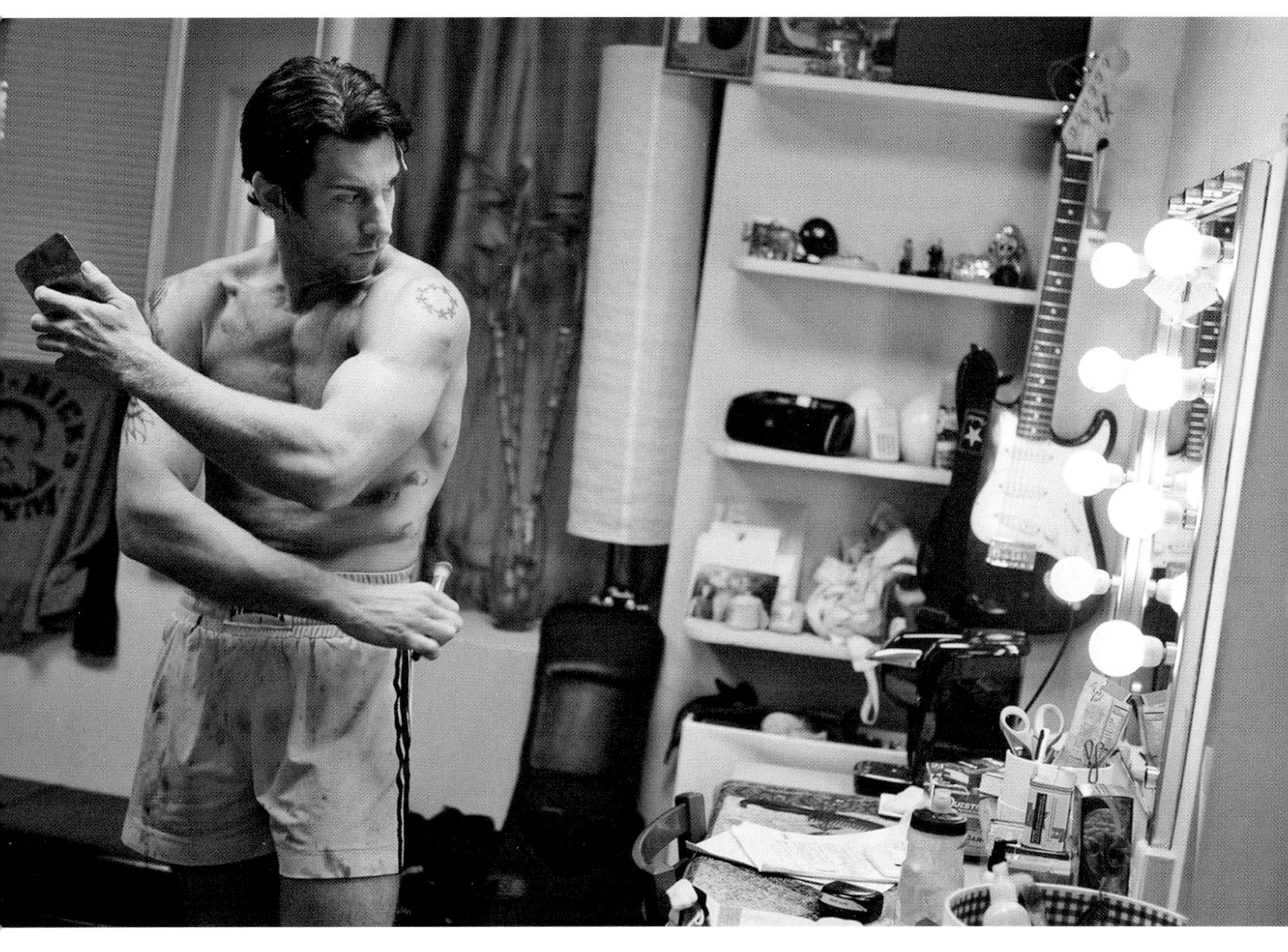

Andy Karl
Rocky
Winter Garden Theatre
2014

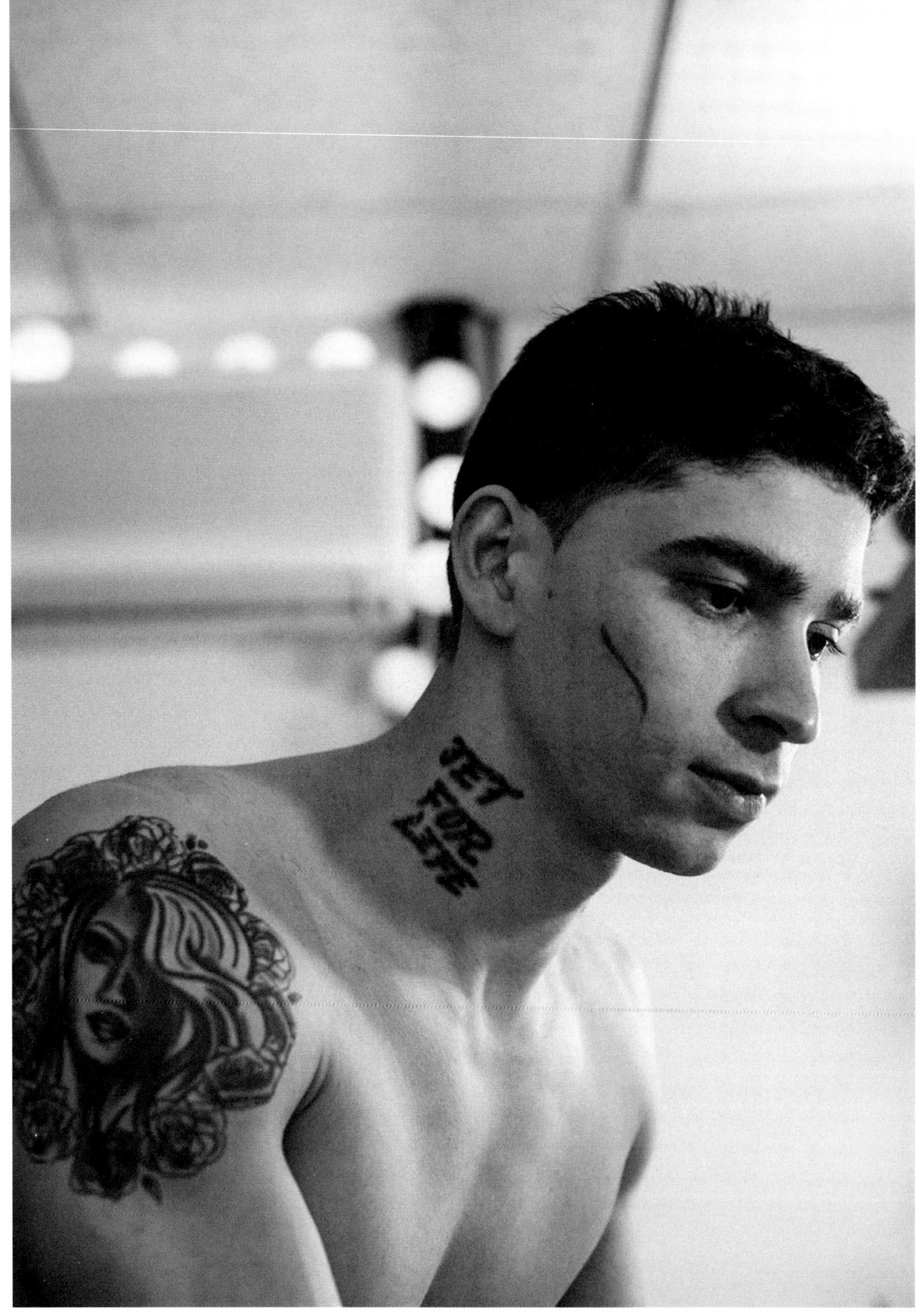

Isaac Powell
West Side Story
Broadway Theatre
2020

Gareth Saxe
The Lion King
Minskoff Theatre
2010

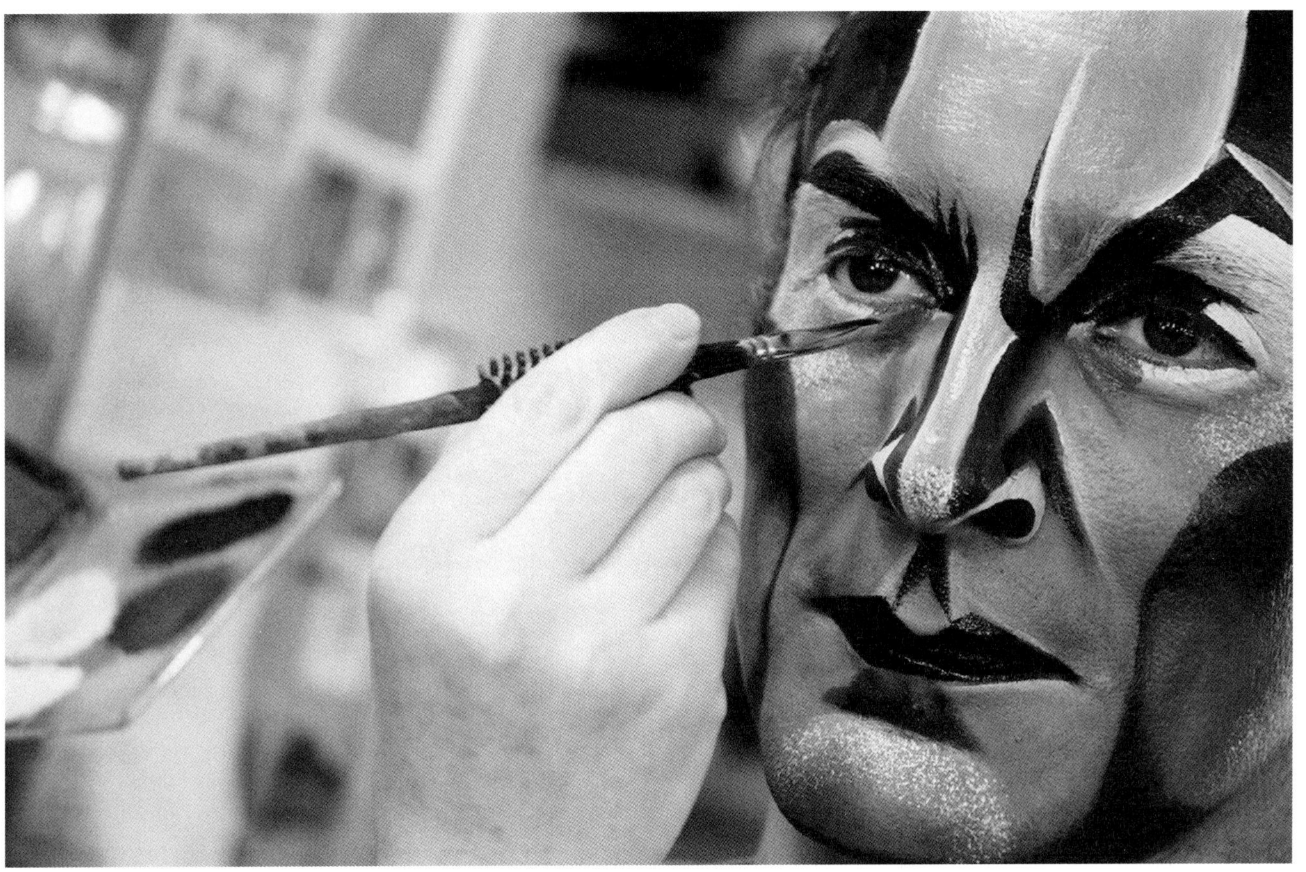

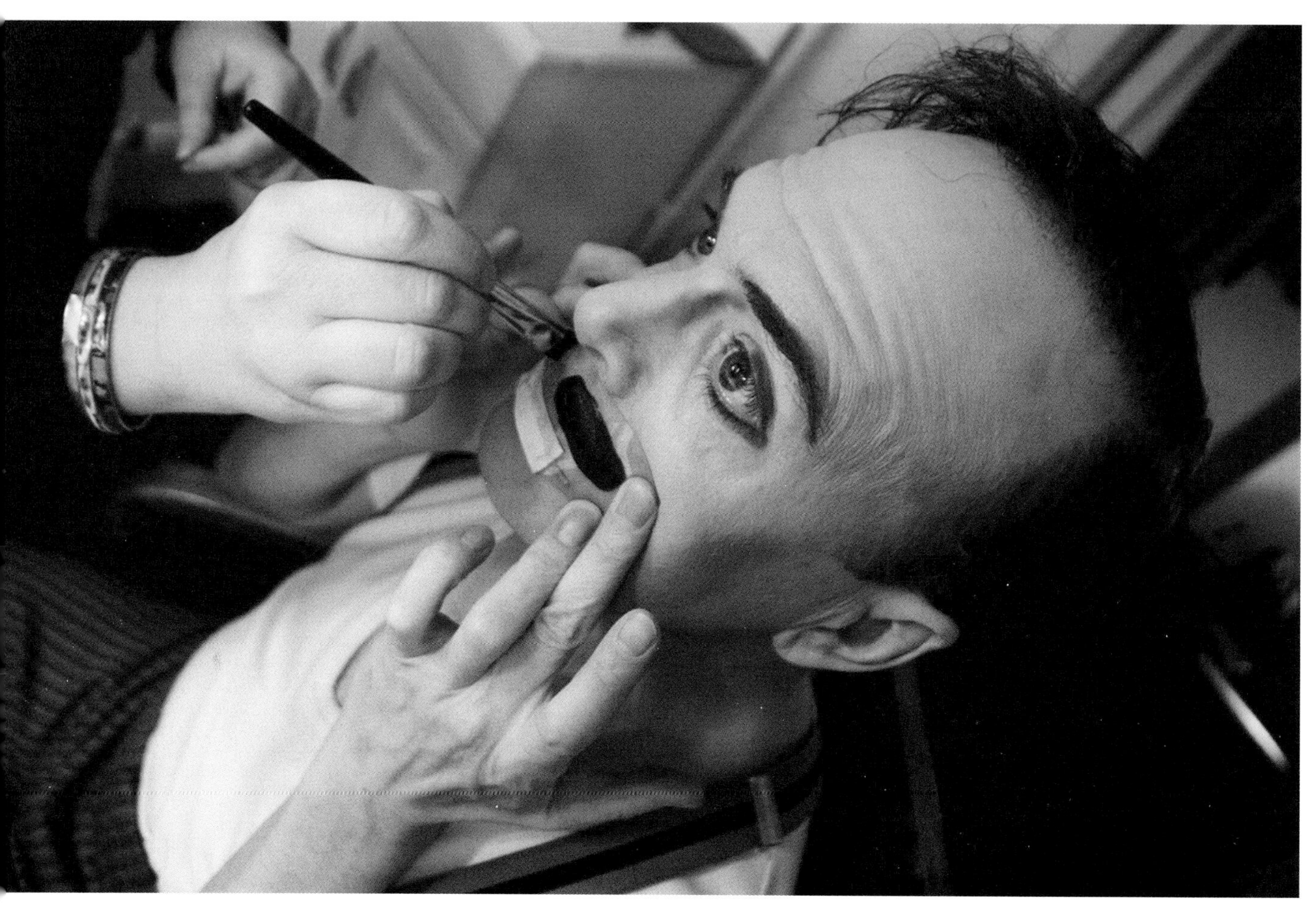

Jefferson Mays
A Gentleman's Guide to Love and Murder
Walter Kerr Theatre
2013

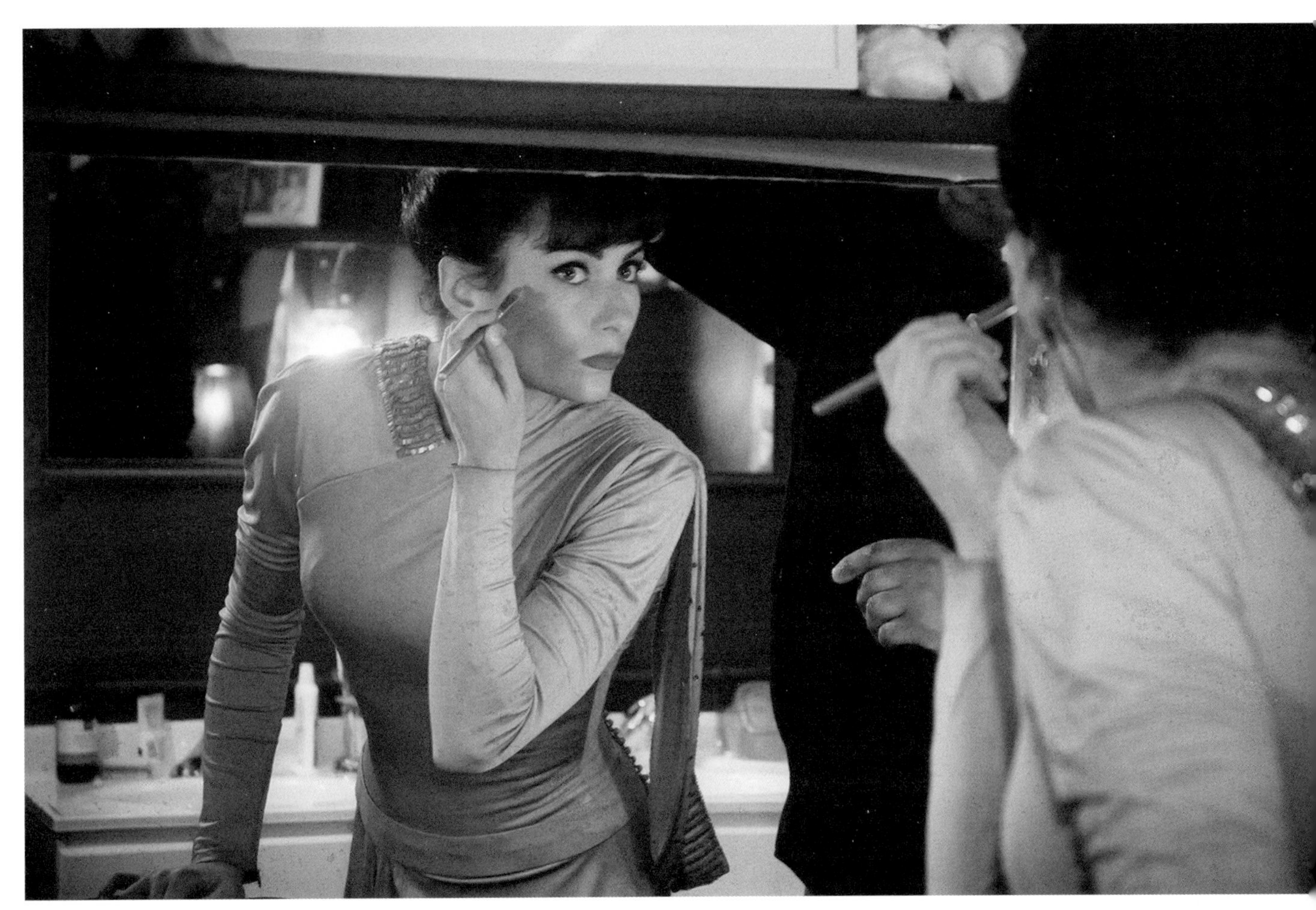

Laura Benanti
Gypsy
St. James Theatre
2008

Glenn Close
Sunset Boulevard
Palace Theatre
2017

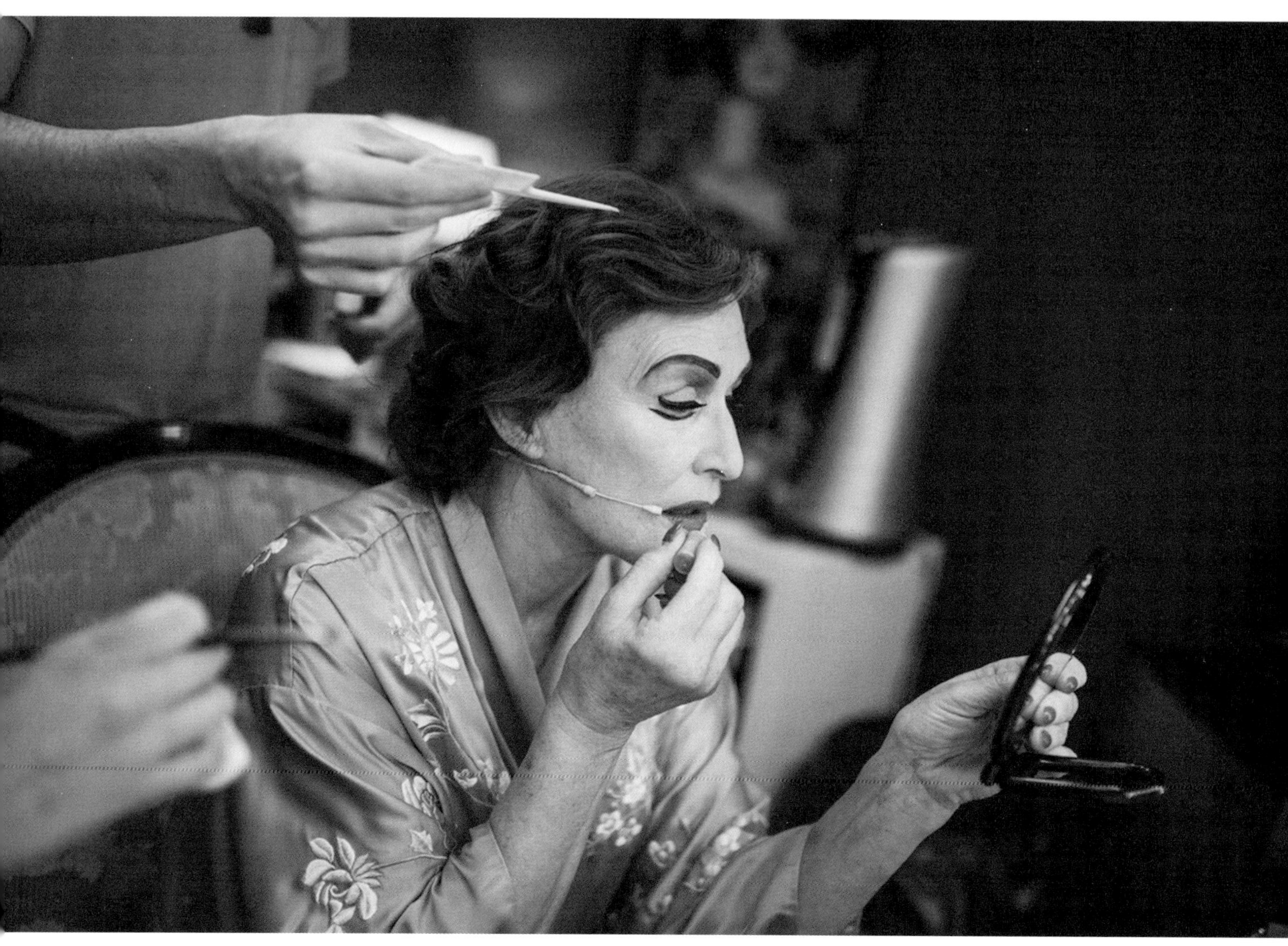

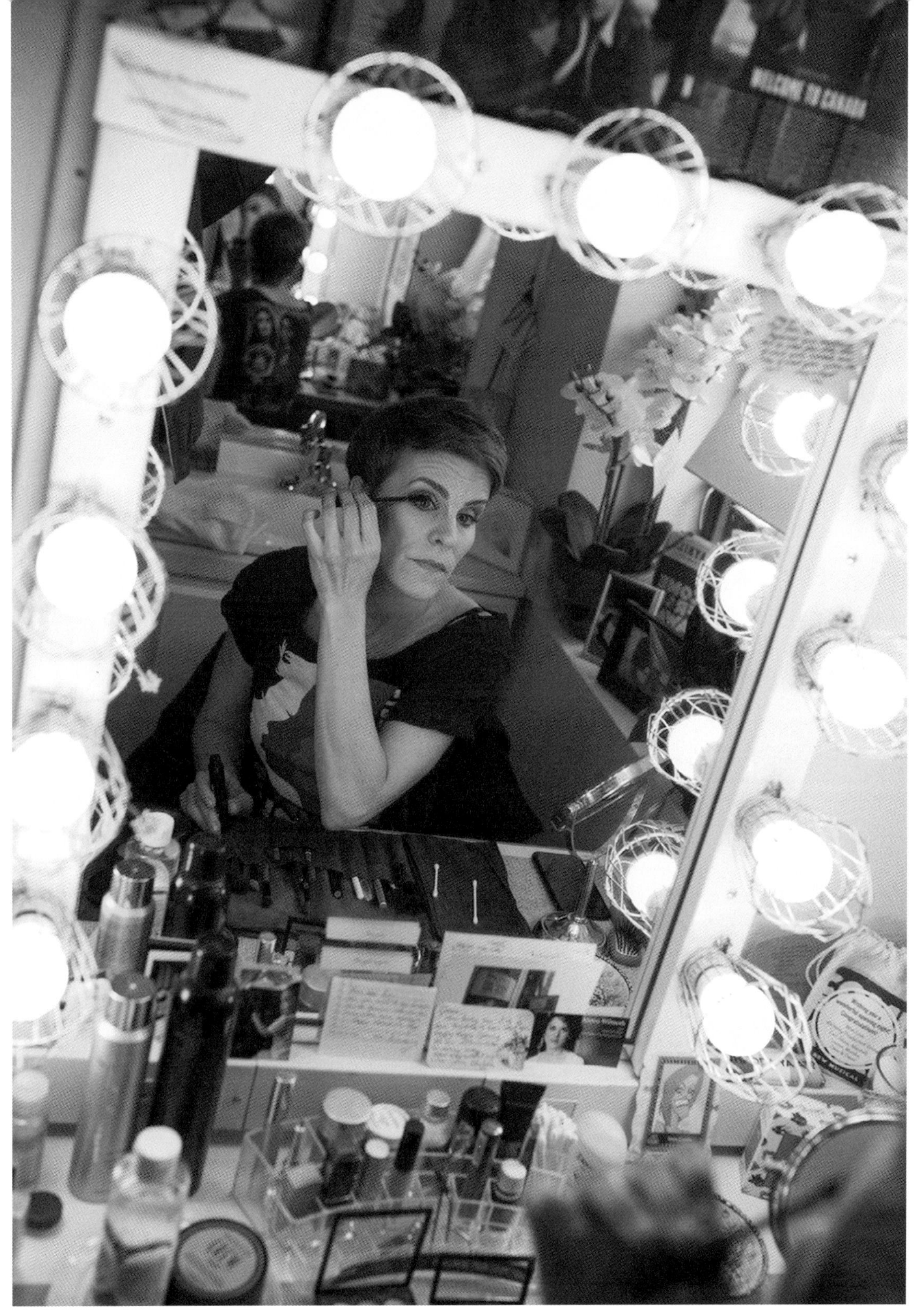

Jenn Colella
Come from Away
Gerald Schoenfeld Theatre
2017

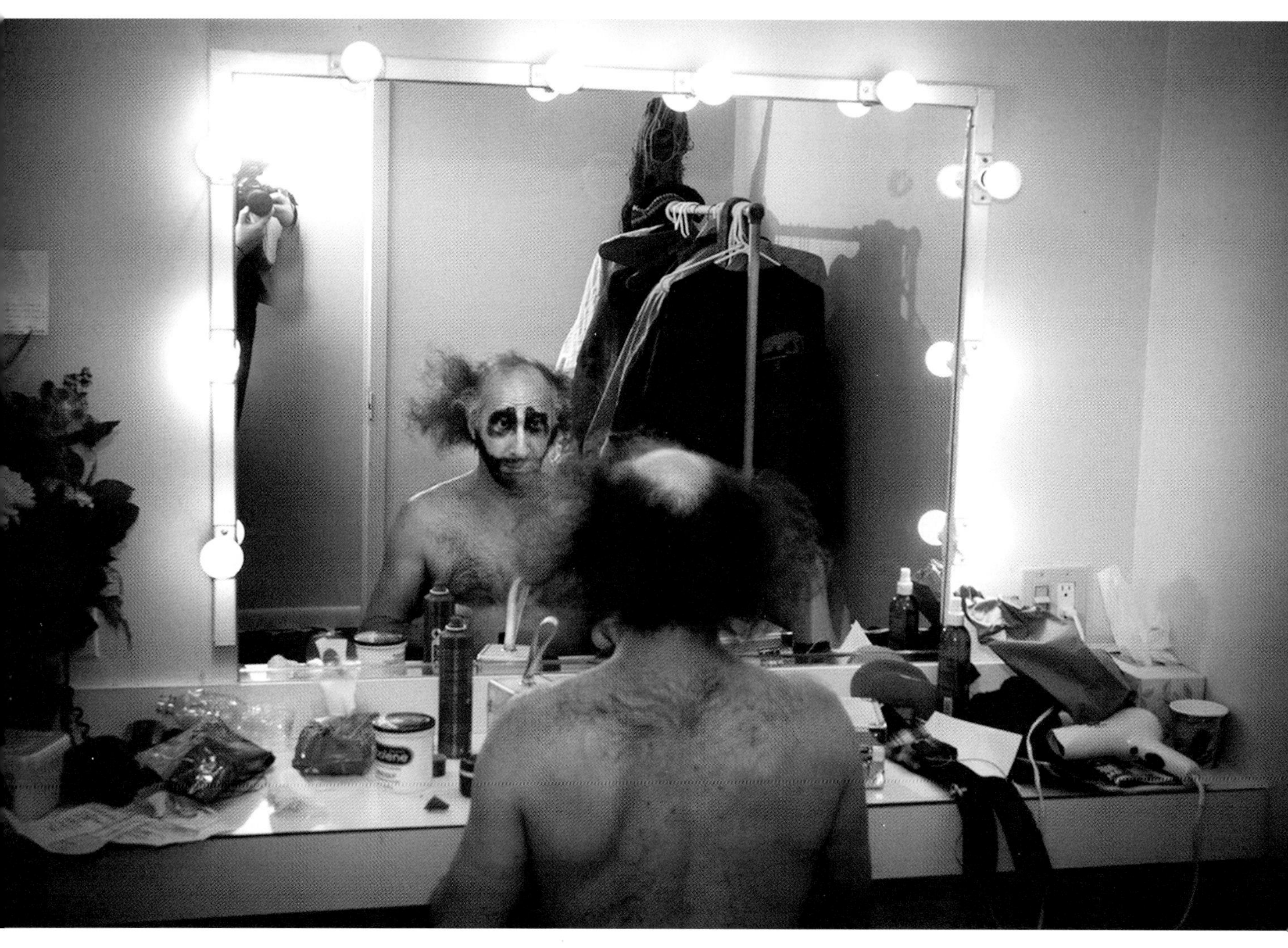

Slava's Snowshow
The Hayes Theater
2008

Elizabeth Ashley
August: Osage County
Music Box Theatre
2009

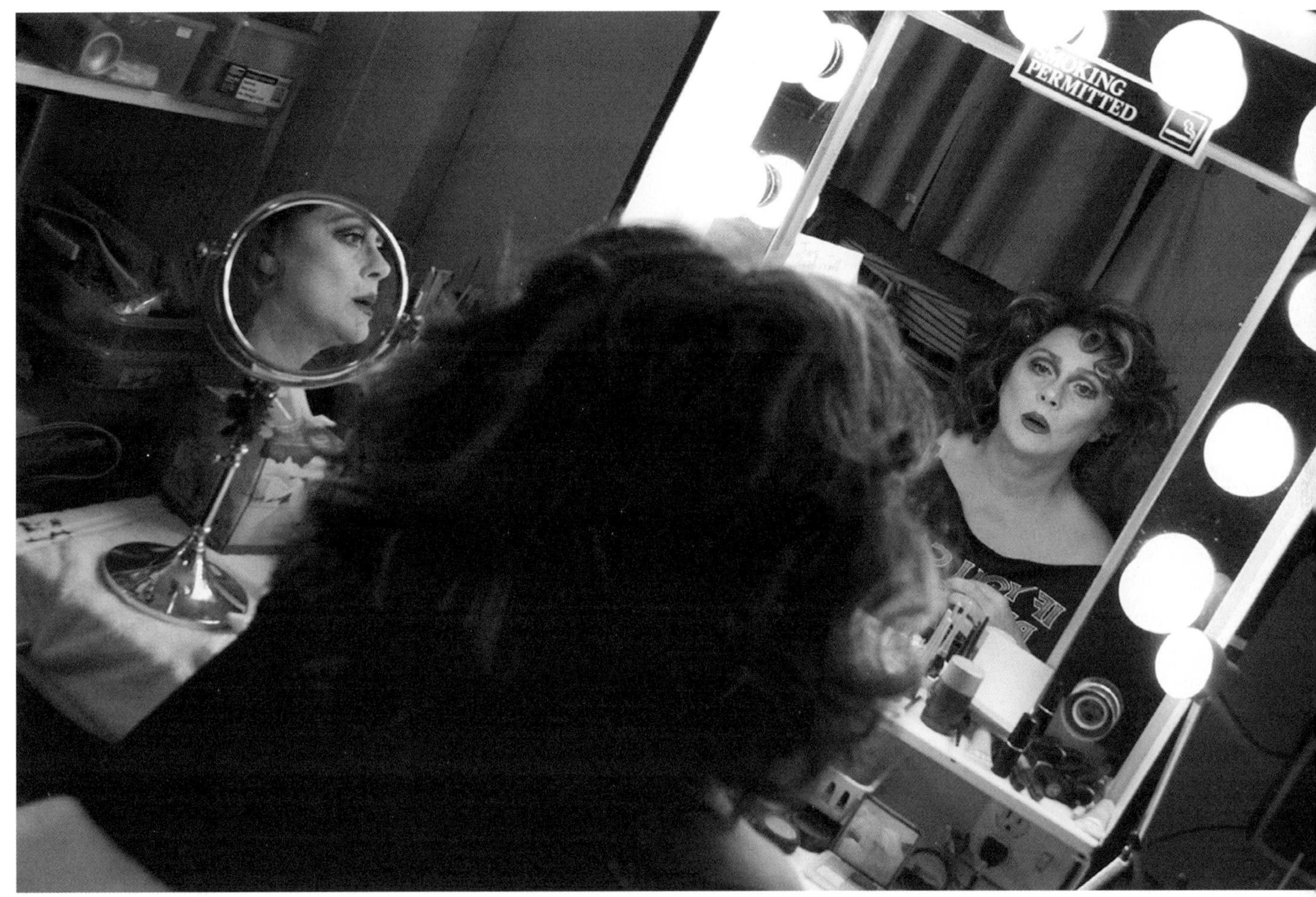

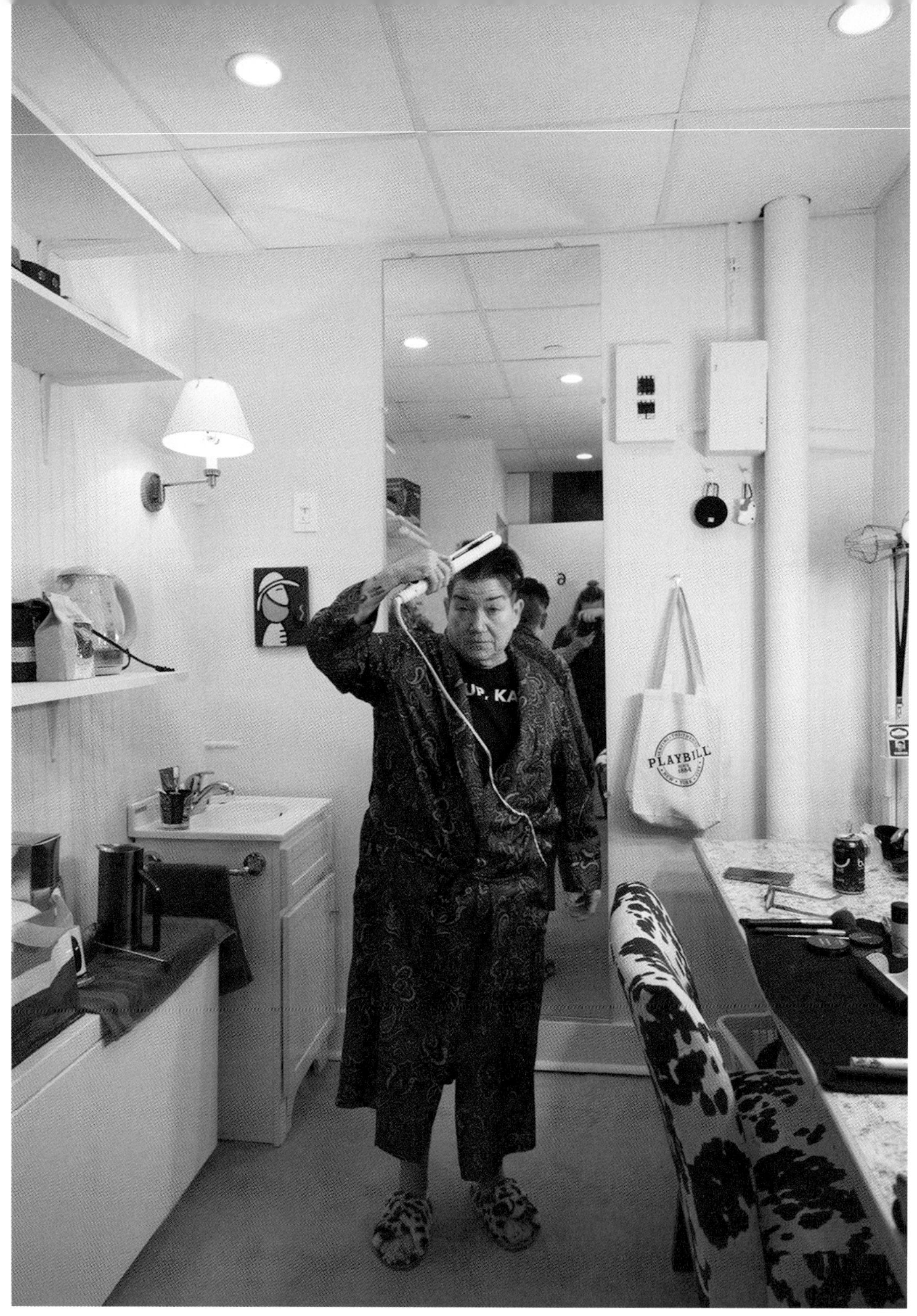

Lea DeLaria

POTUS: Or, Behind Every Great Dumbass Are Seven Women Trying to Keep Him Alive

Shubert Theatre

2022

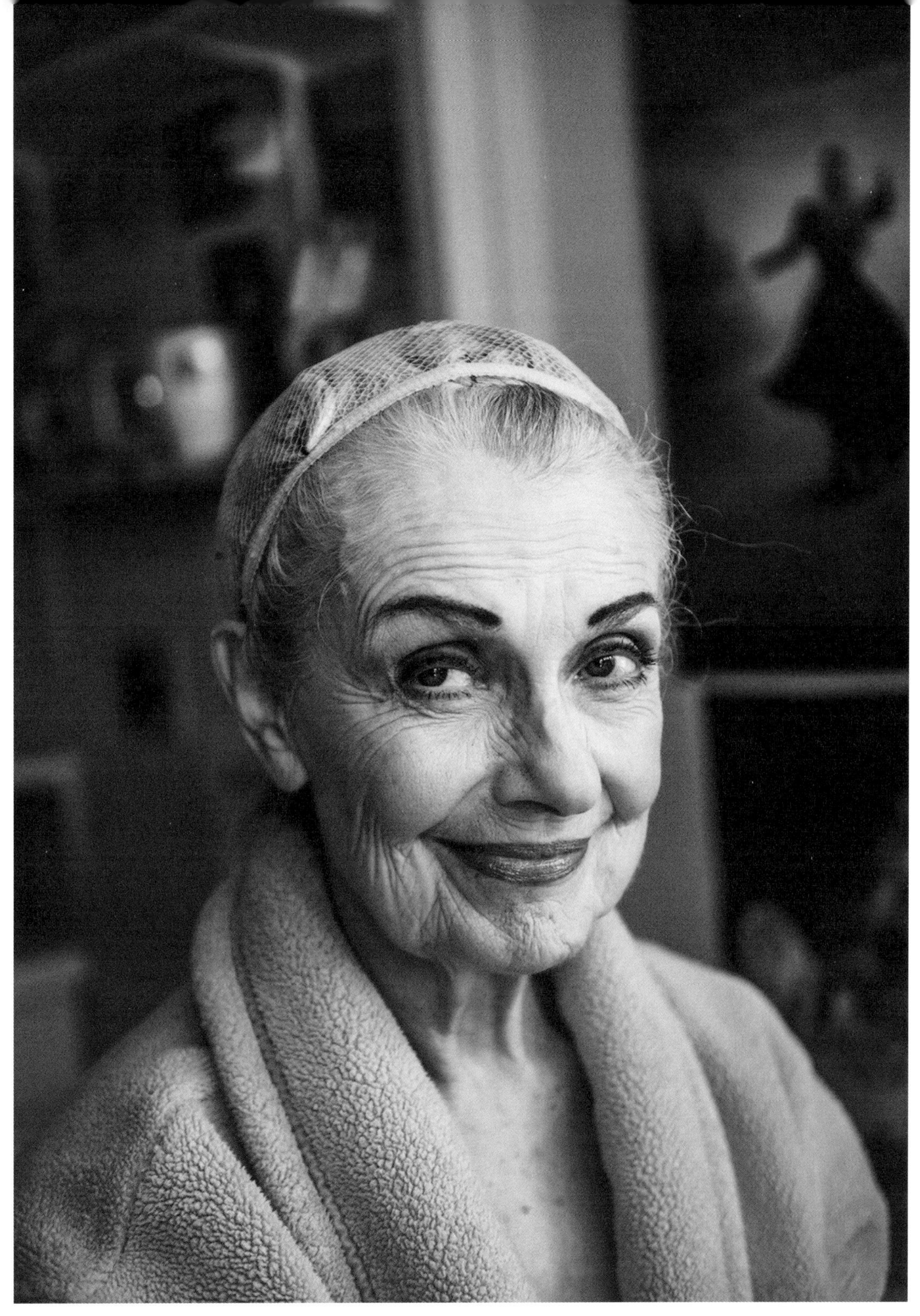

Mary Beth Peil
Anastasia
Broadhurst Theatre
2017

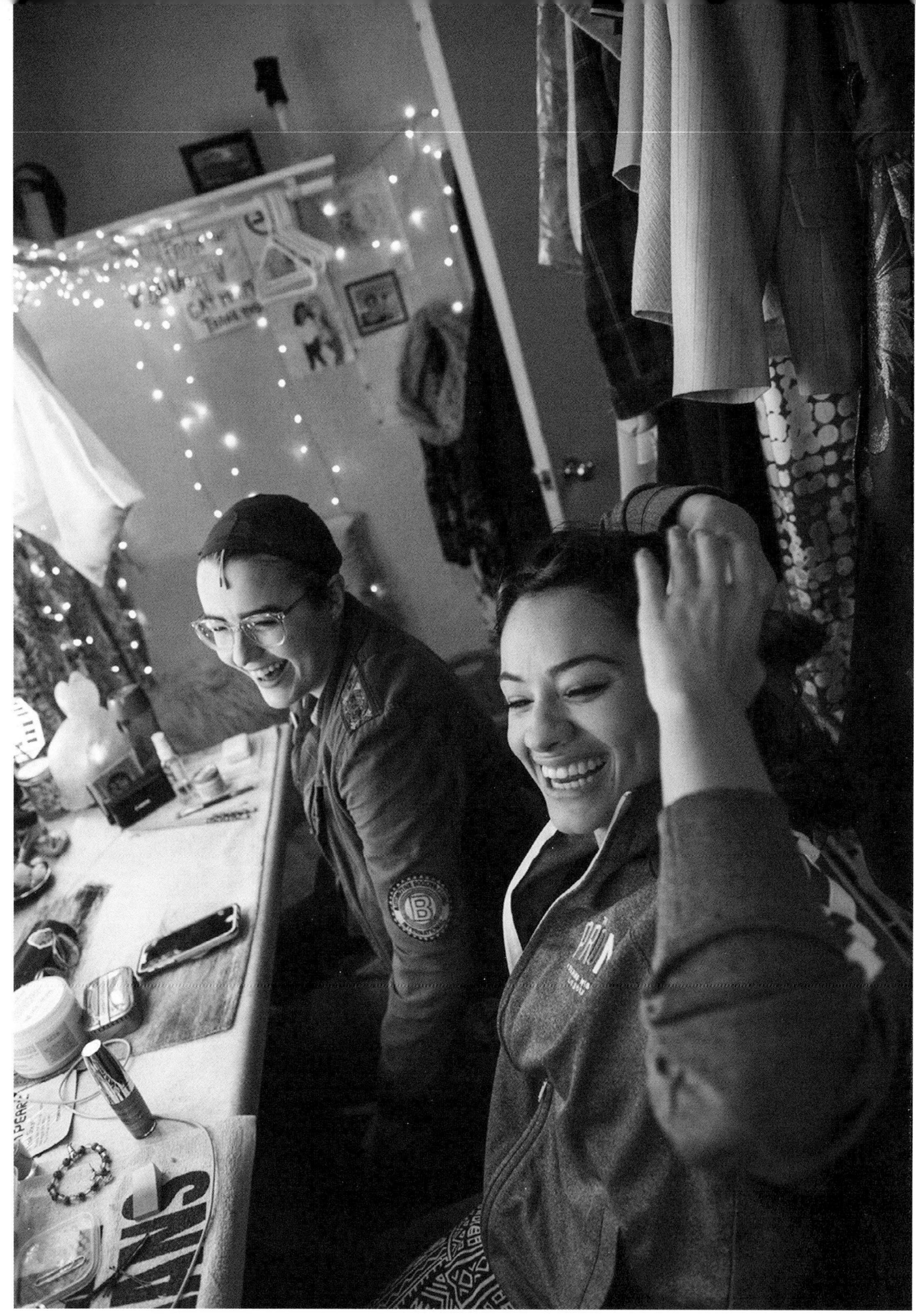

Caitlin Kinnunen and Isabelle McCalla
The Prom
Longacre Theatre
2019

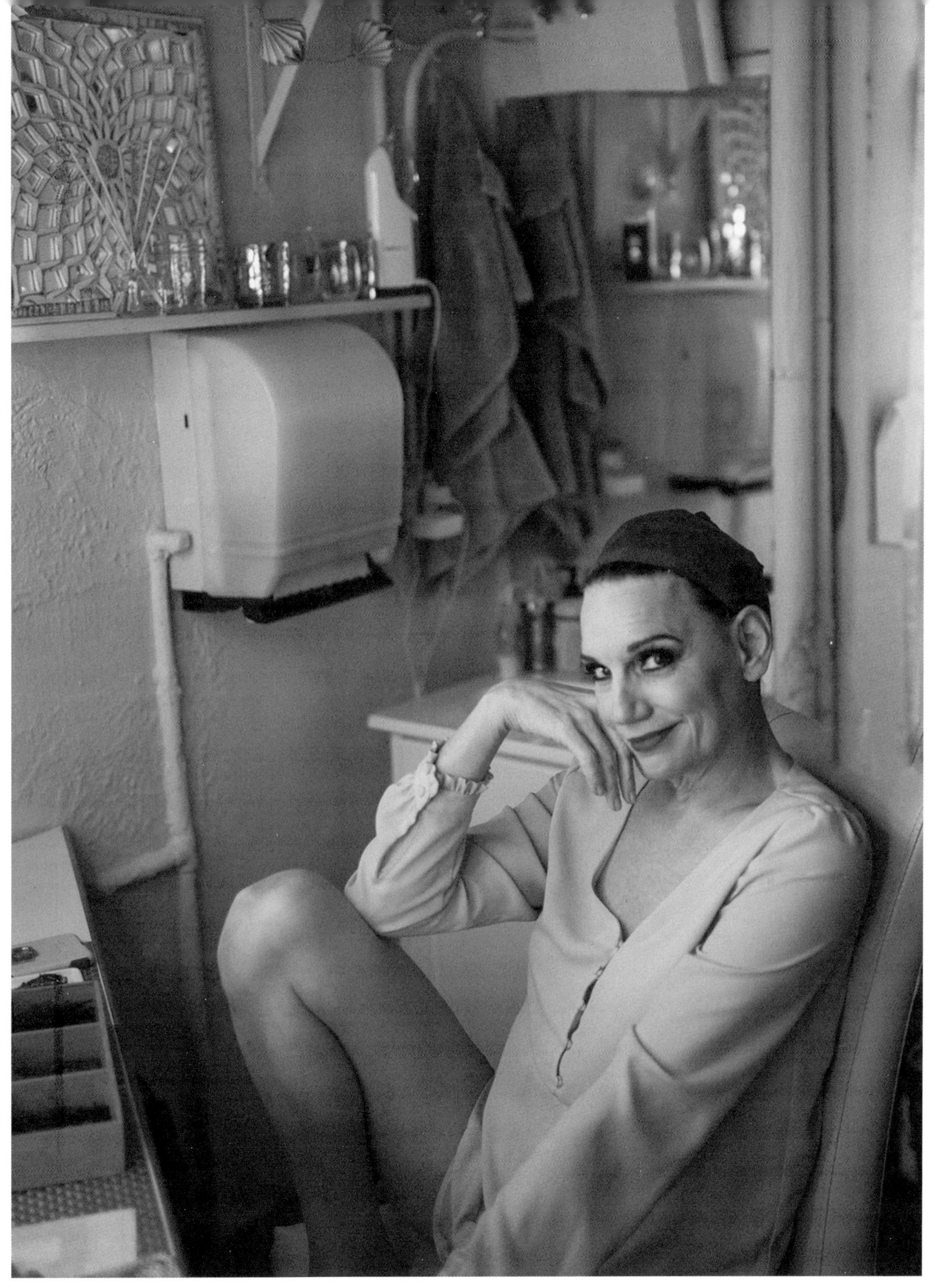

Beth Leavel
The Prom
Longacre Theatre
2018

Alex Newell
Shucked
Nederlander Theatre
2023

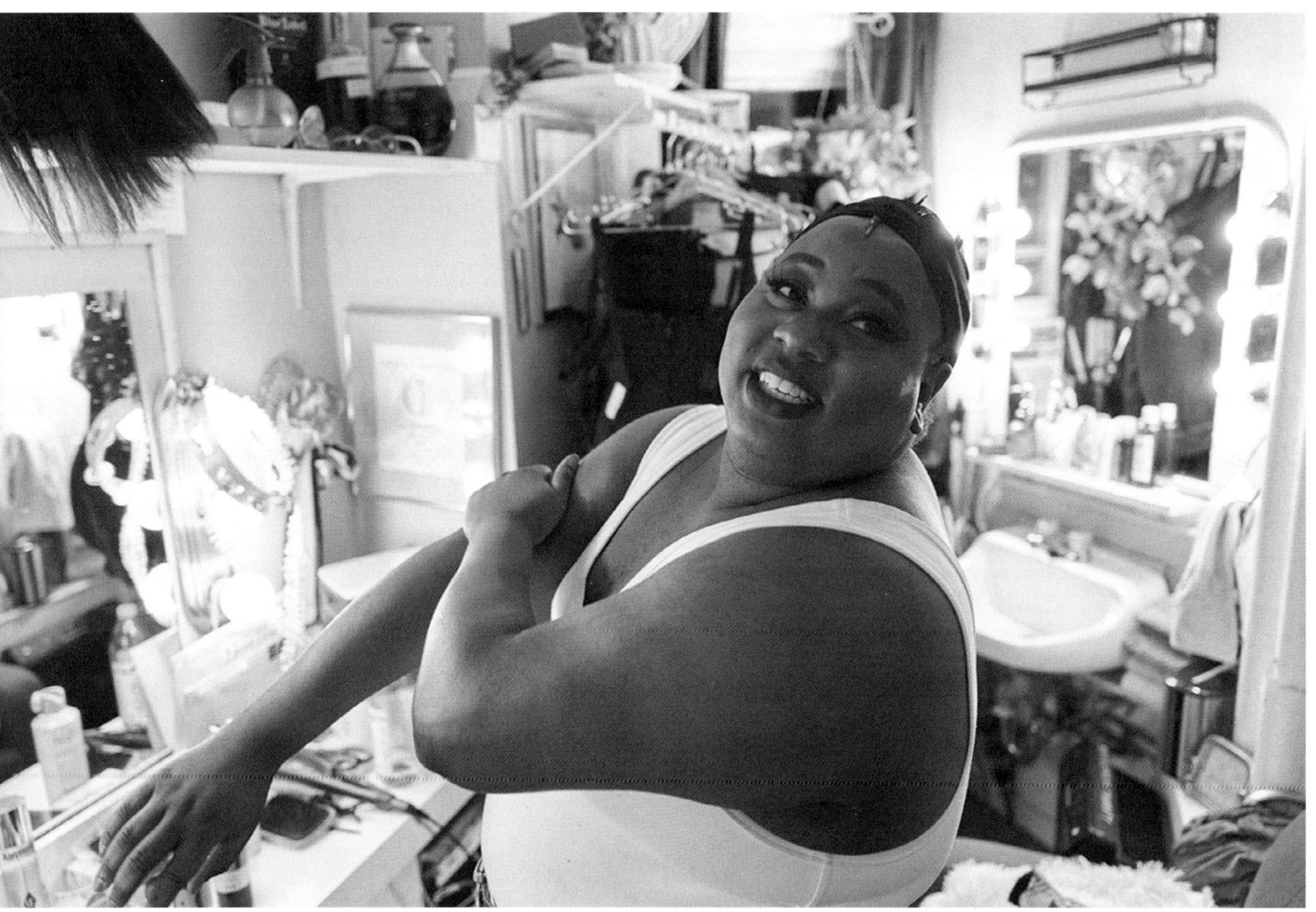

Kate Baldwin
Big Fish
Neil Simon Theatre
2013

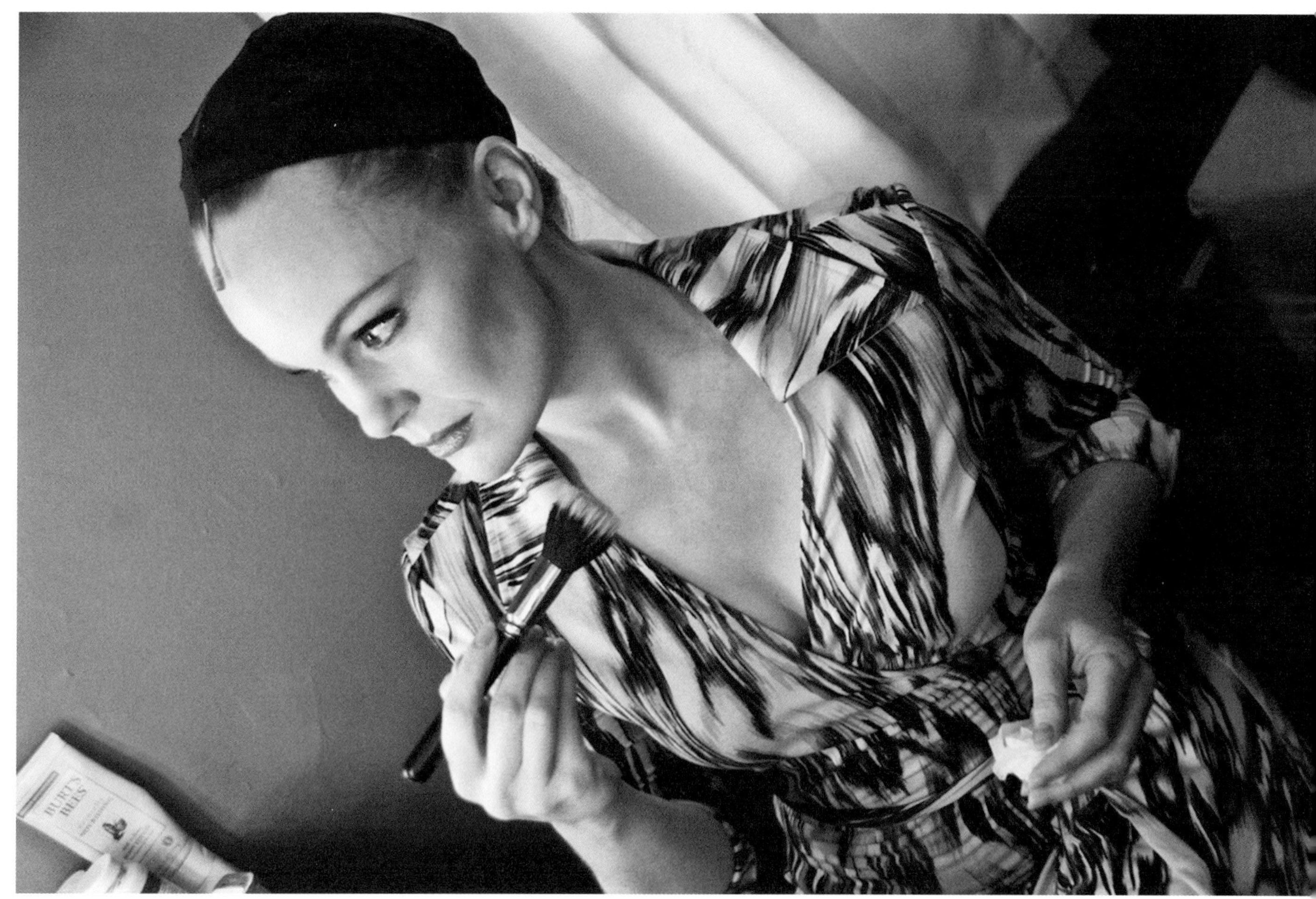

Annaleigh Ashford
Kinky Boots
Al Hirschfeld Theatre
2014

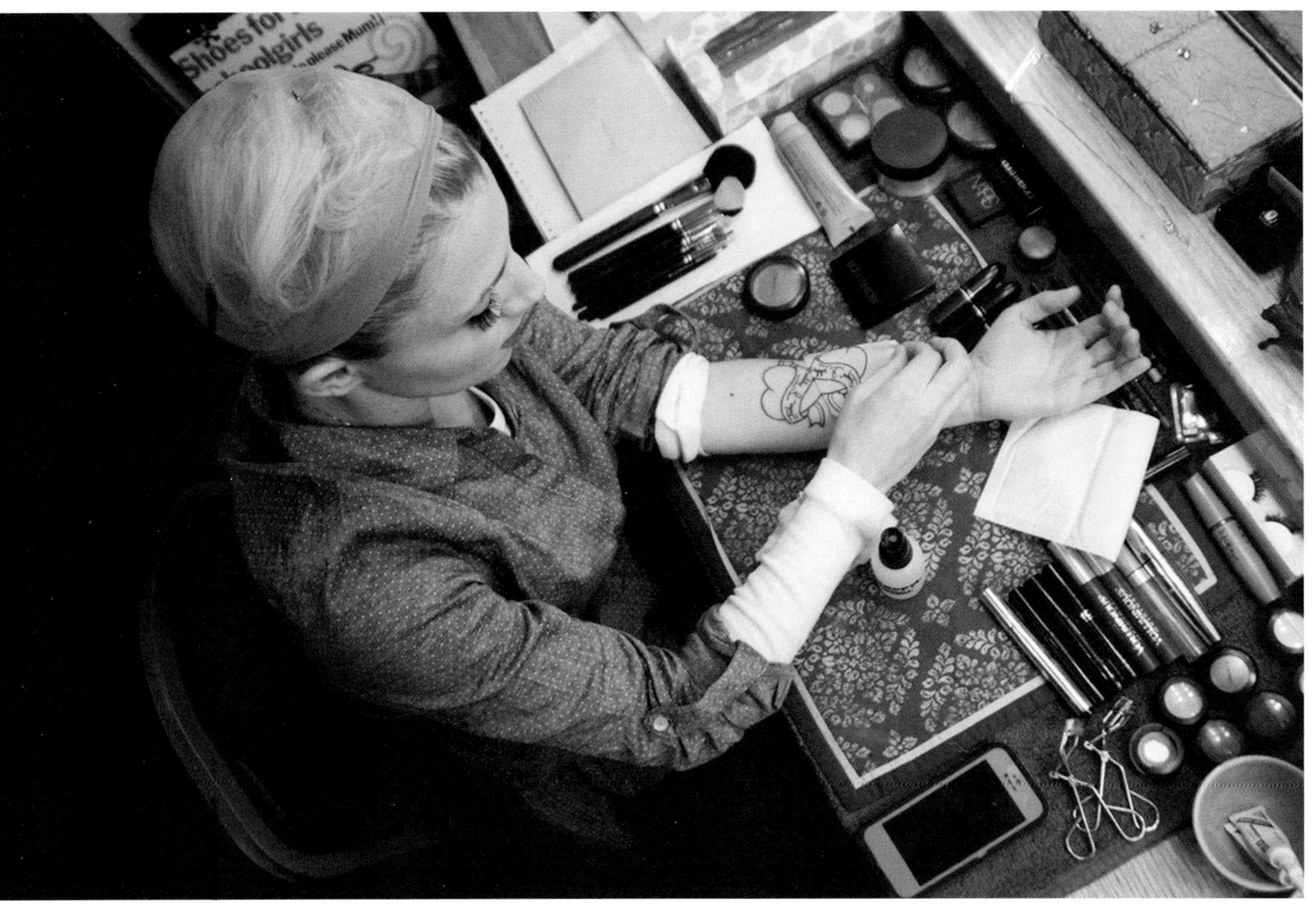

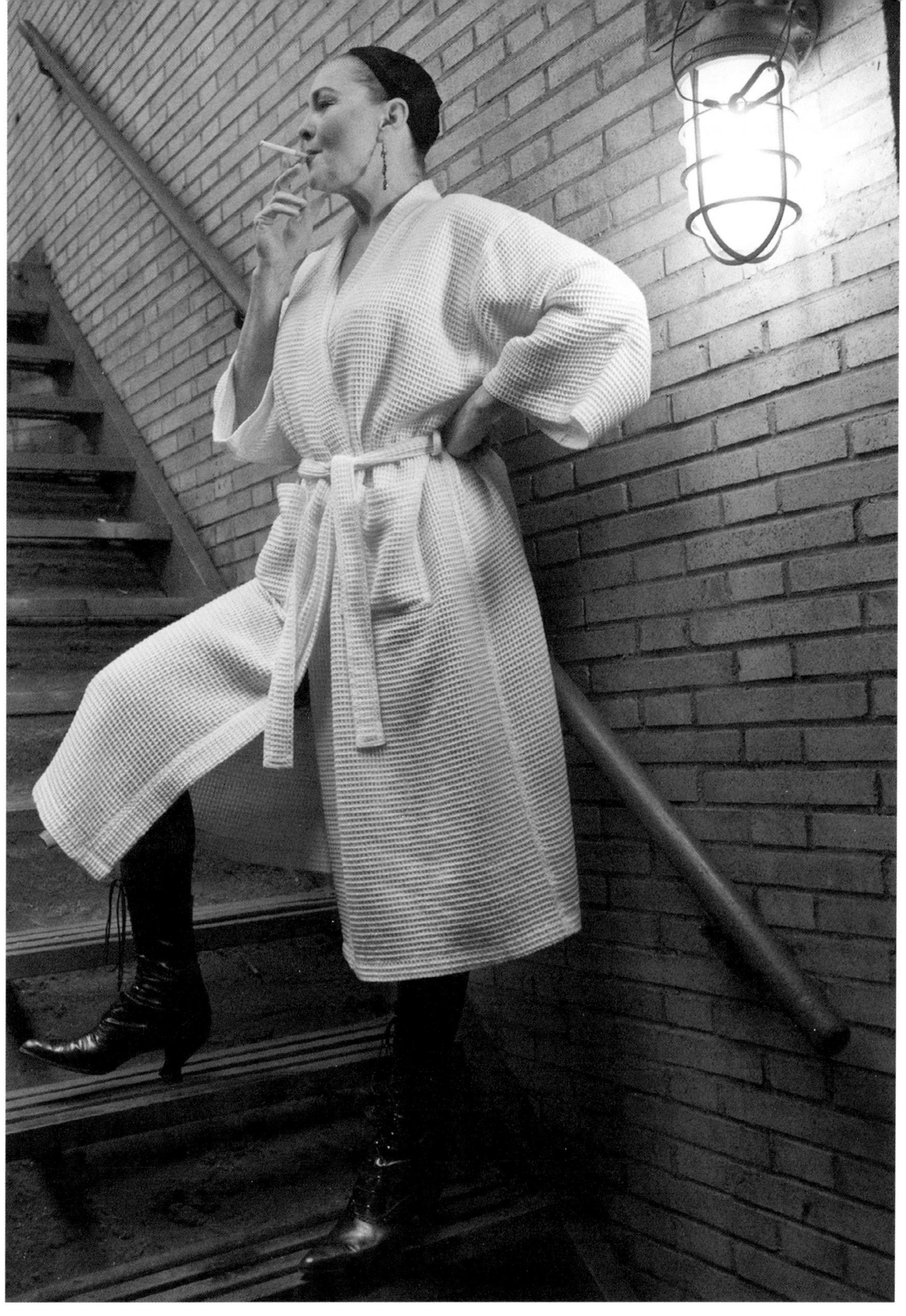

Cherry Jones
Mrs. Warren's Profession
American Airlines Theatre (now Todd Haimes Theatre)
2010

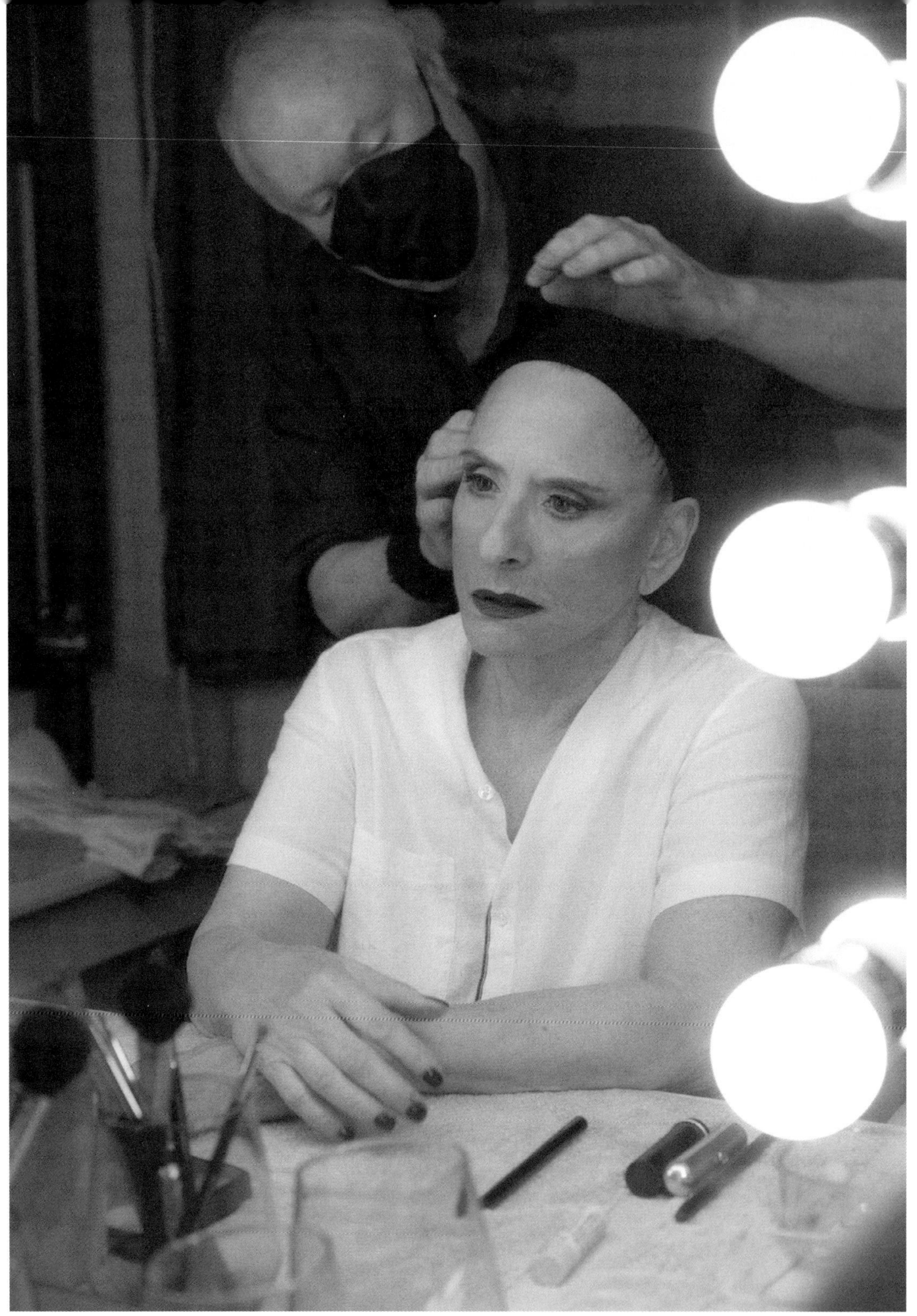

Patti LuPone
Company
Bernard B. Jacobs Theatre
2022

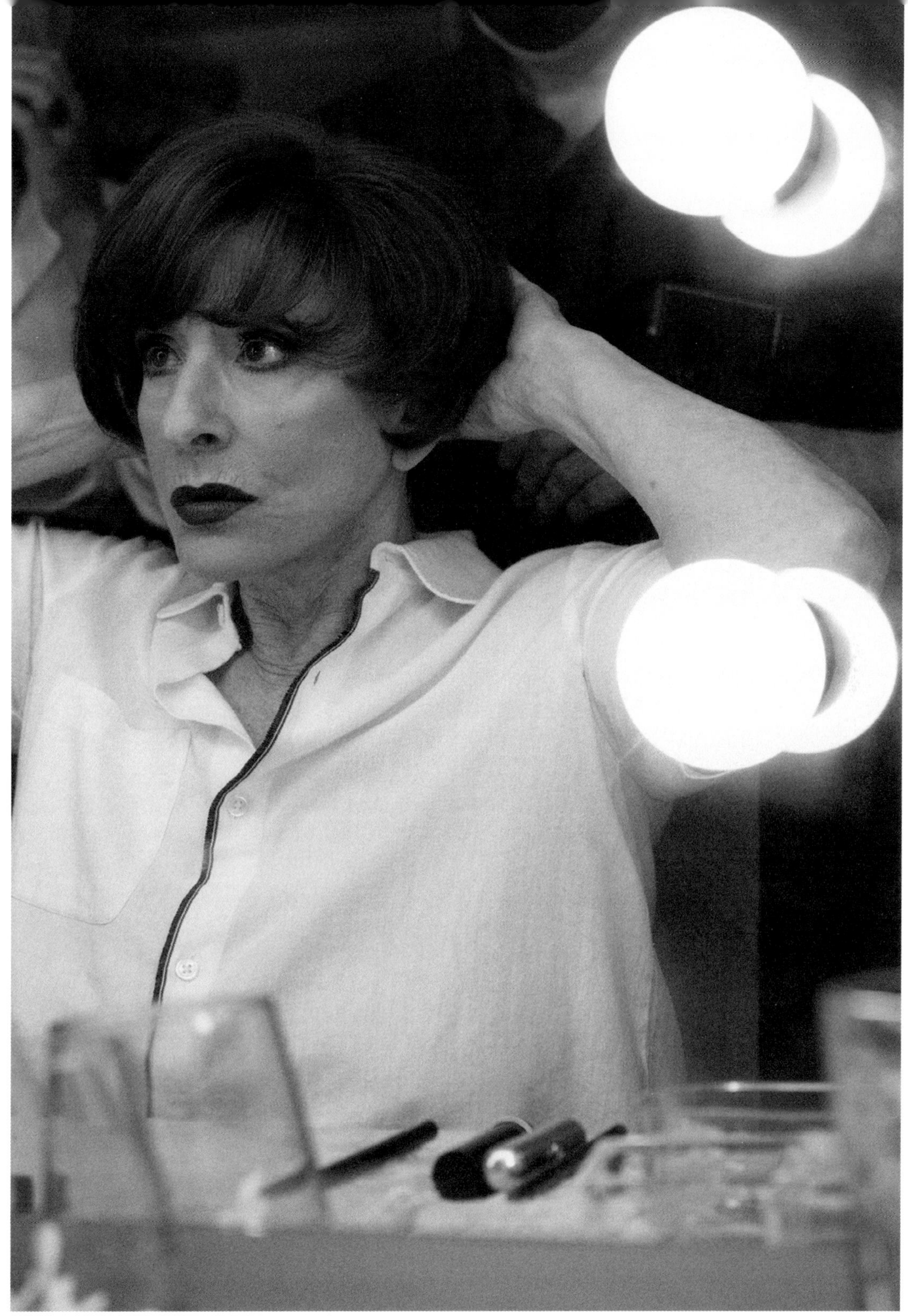

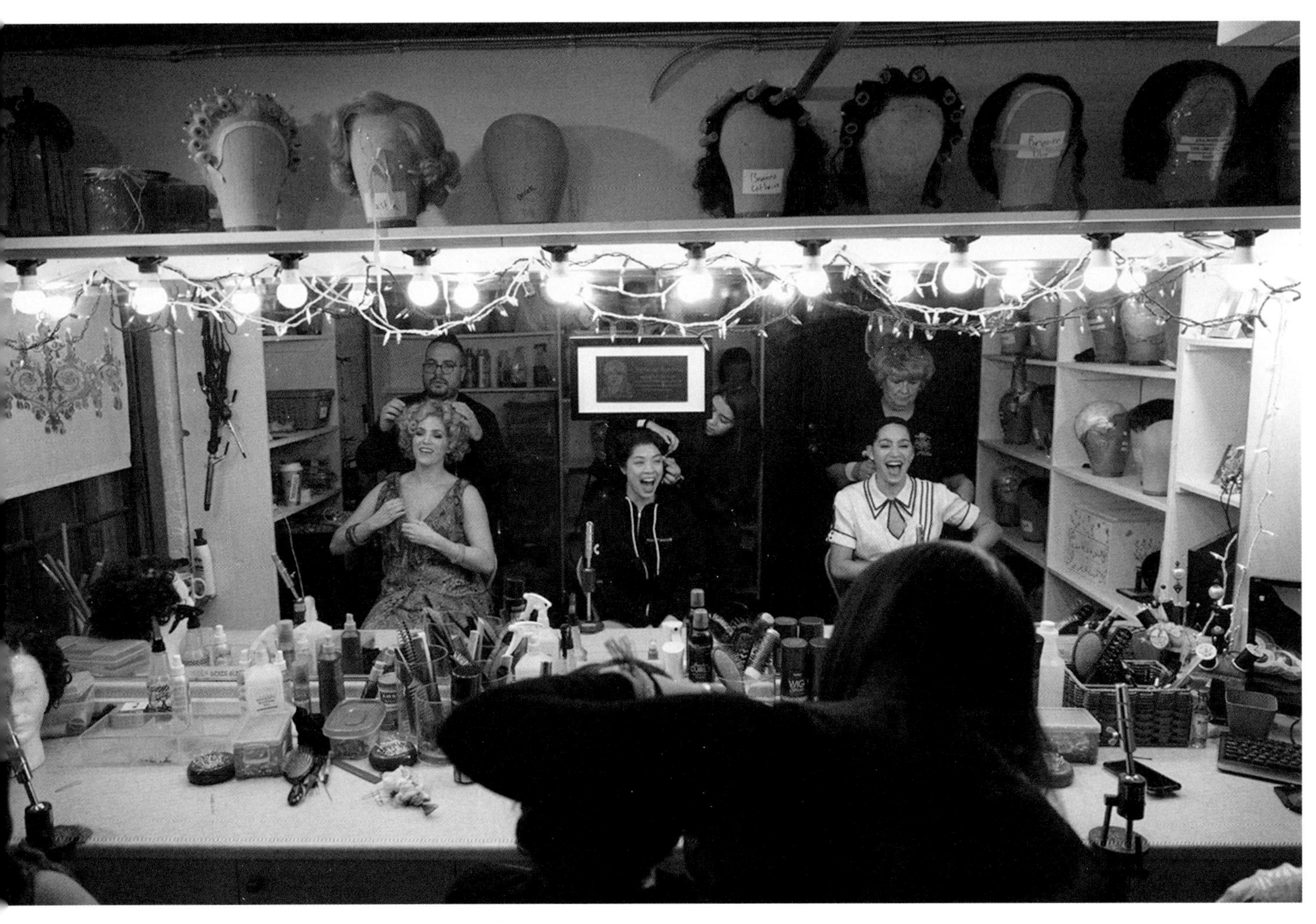

Sara Chase, Eva Noblezada, and Samantha Pauly
The Great Gatsby
Paper Mill Playhouse
2023

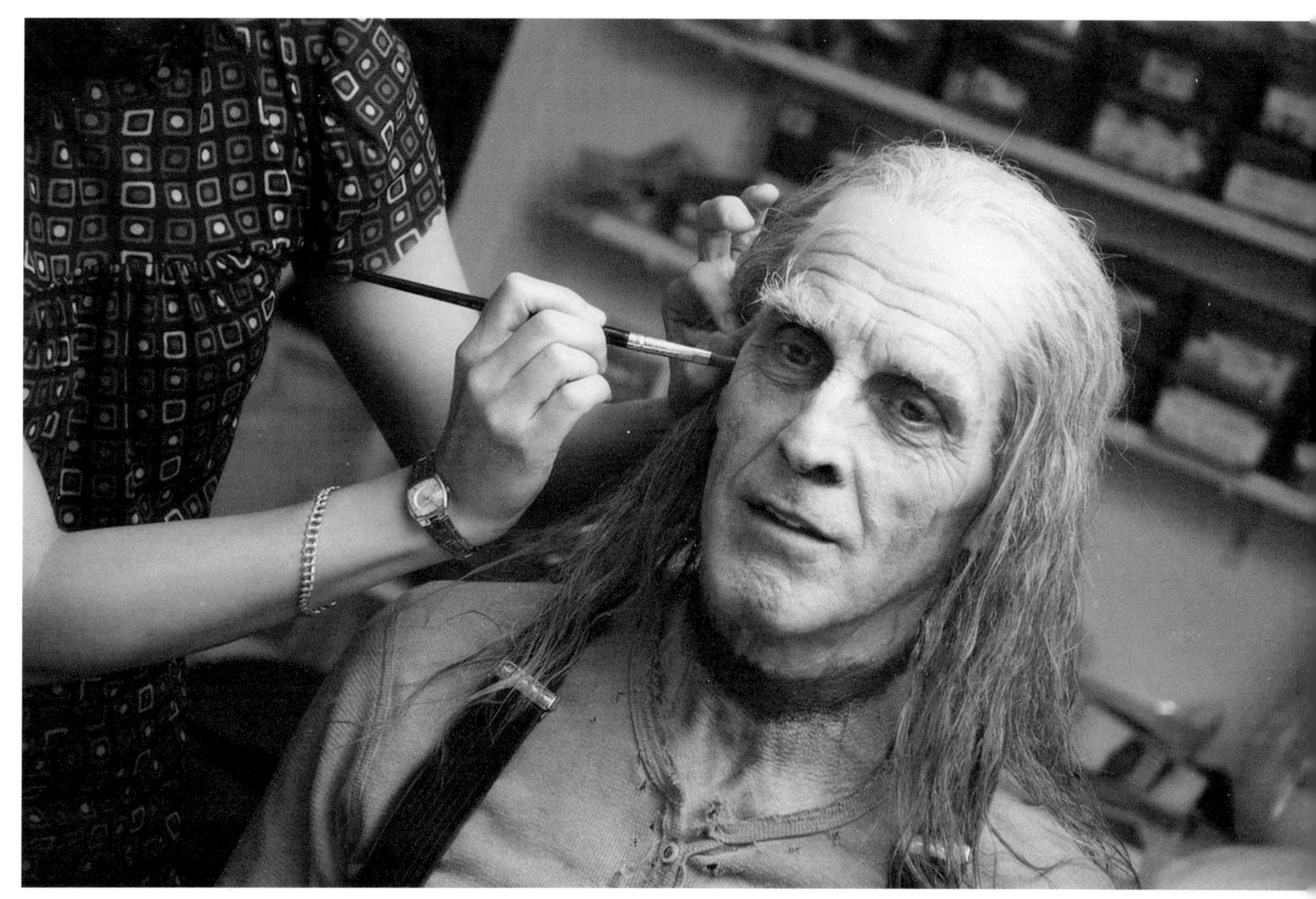

John Glover
Waiting for Godot
Studio 54
2009

Nicolette Robinson
Waitress
Brooks Atkinson Theatre (now Lena Horne Theatre)
2018

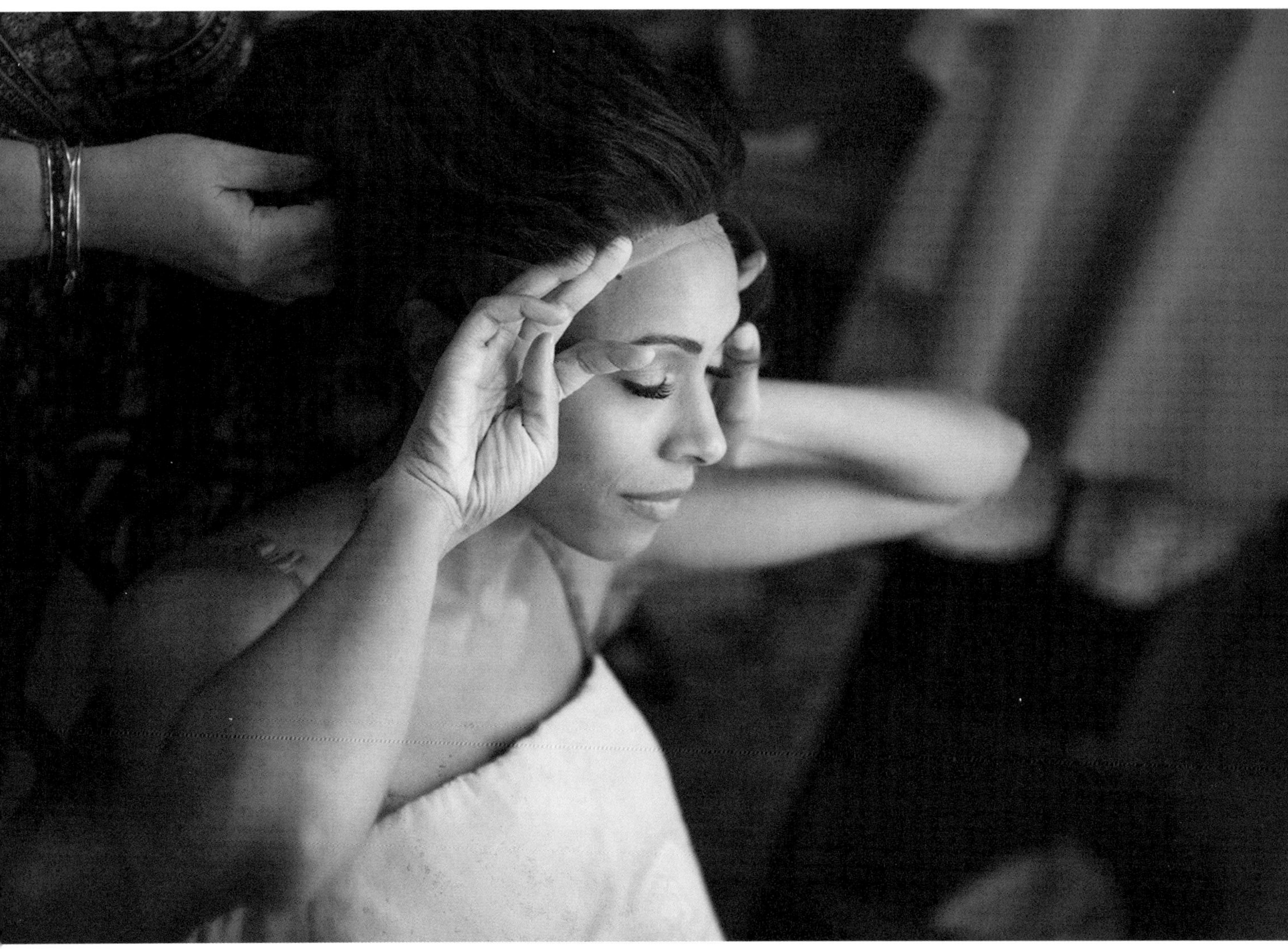

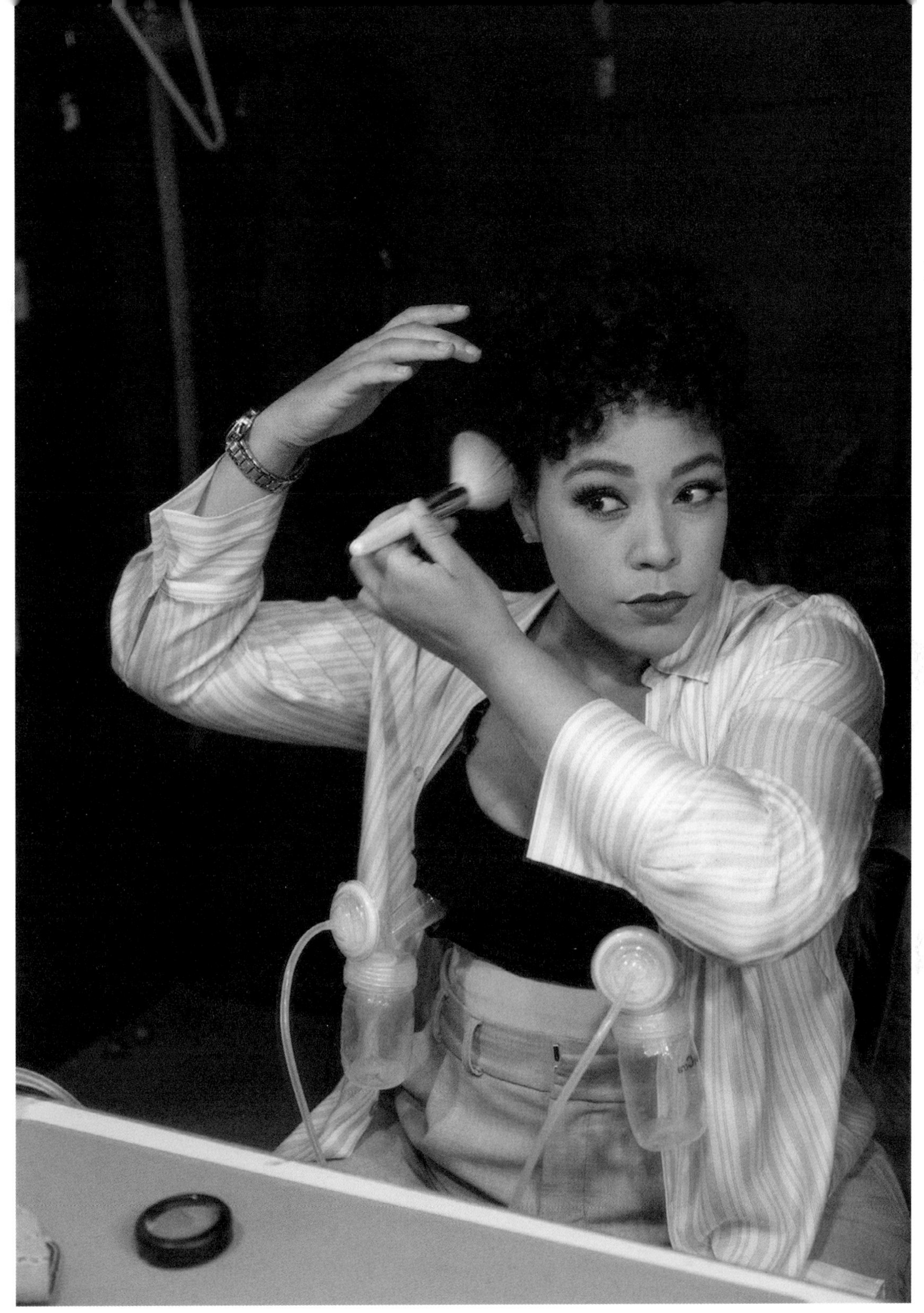

Lilli Cooper
POTUS: Or, Behind Every Great Dumbass Are Seven Women Trying to Keep Him Alive
Shubert Theatre
2022

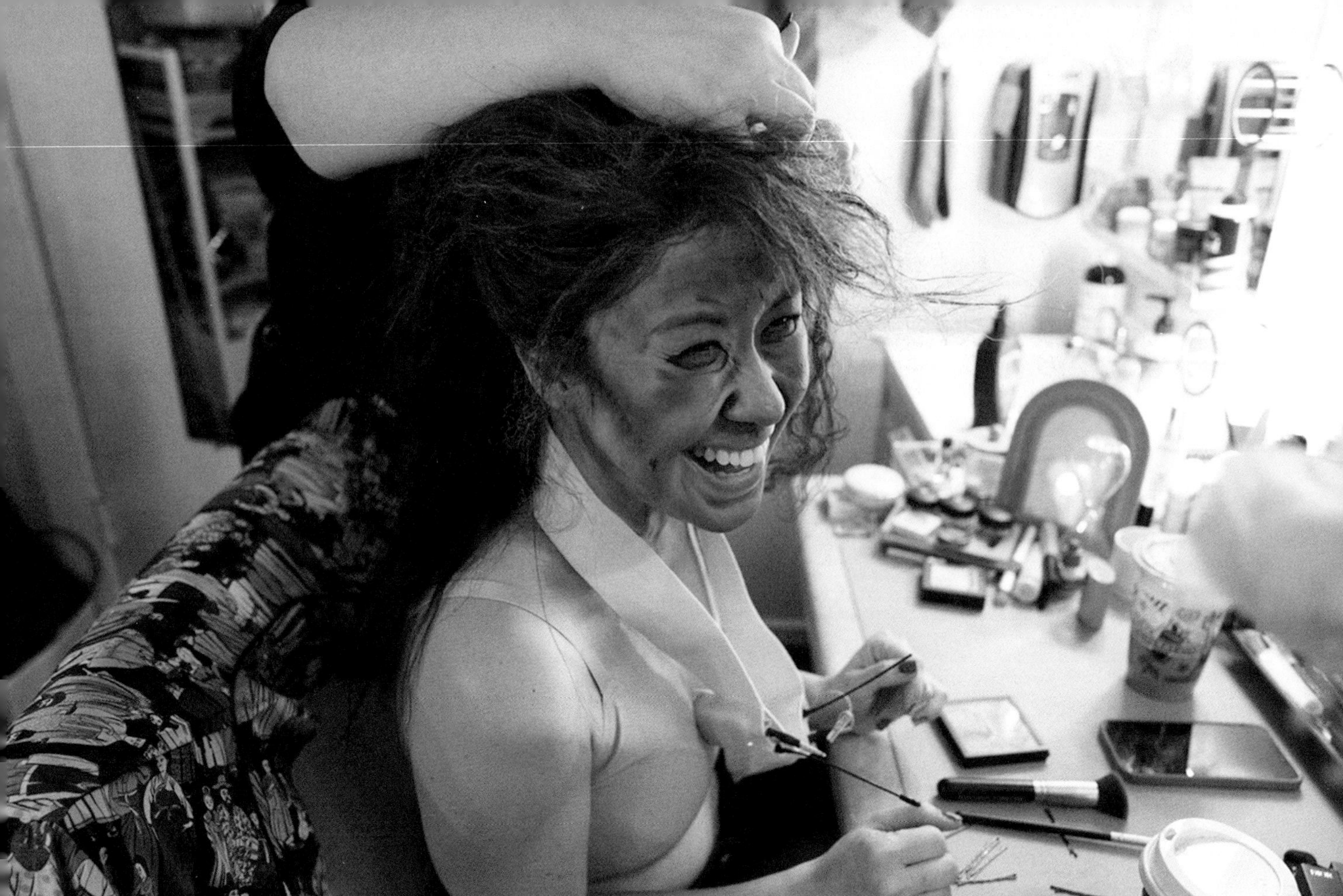

Ruthie Ann Miles
Sweeney Todd: The Demon Barber of Fleet Street
Lunt-Fontanne Theatre
2023

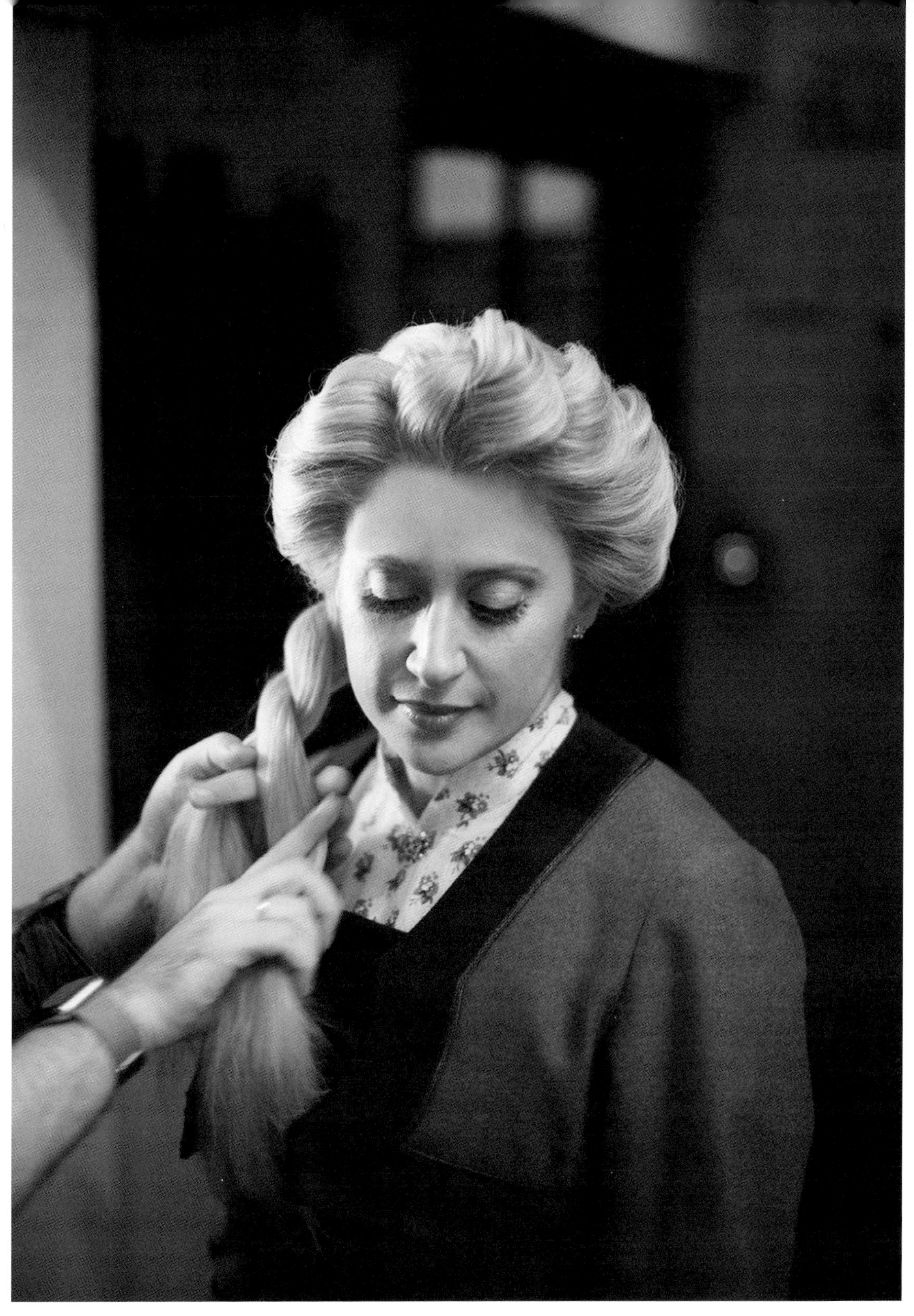

Caissie Levy
Frozen
St. James Theatre
2019

Storm Lever and Ariana DeBose
Summer: The Donna Summer Musical
Lunt-Fontanne Theatre
2018

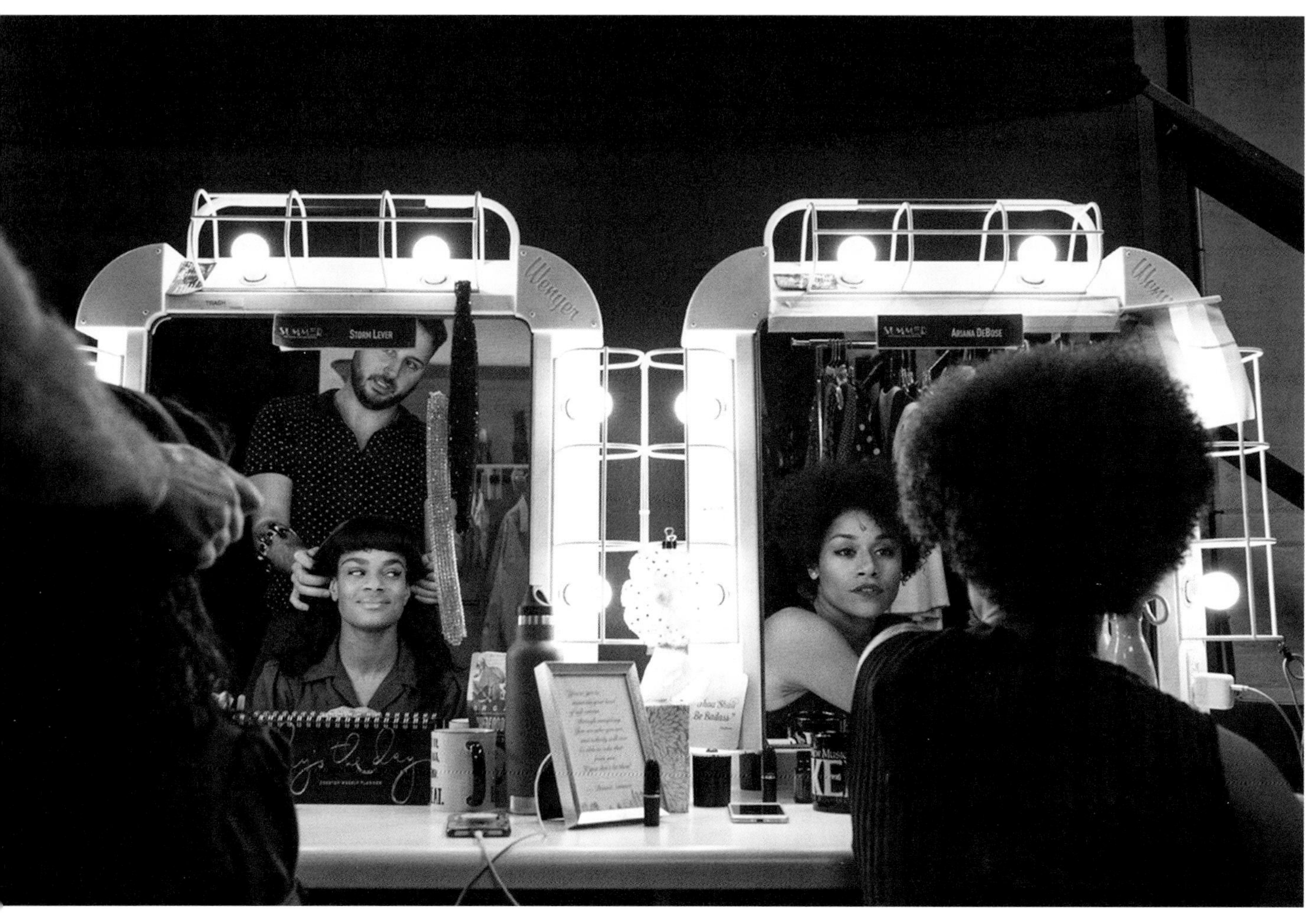

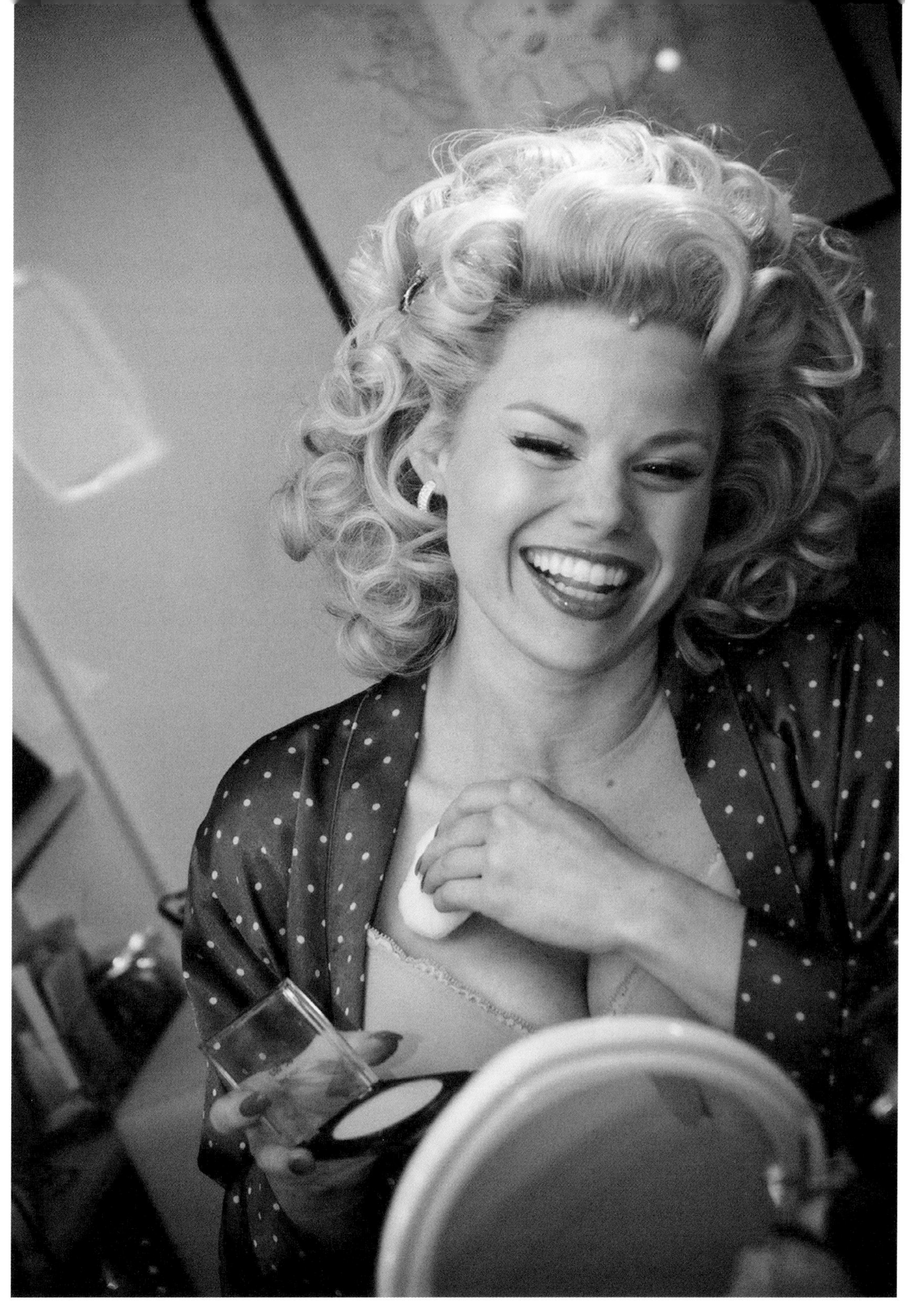

Megan Hilty
9 to 5
Marquis Theatre
2009

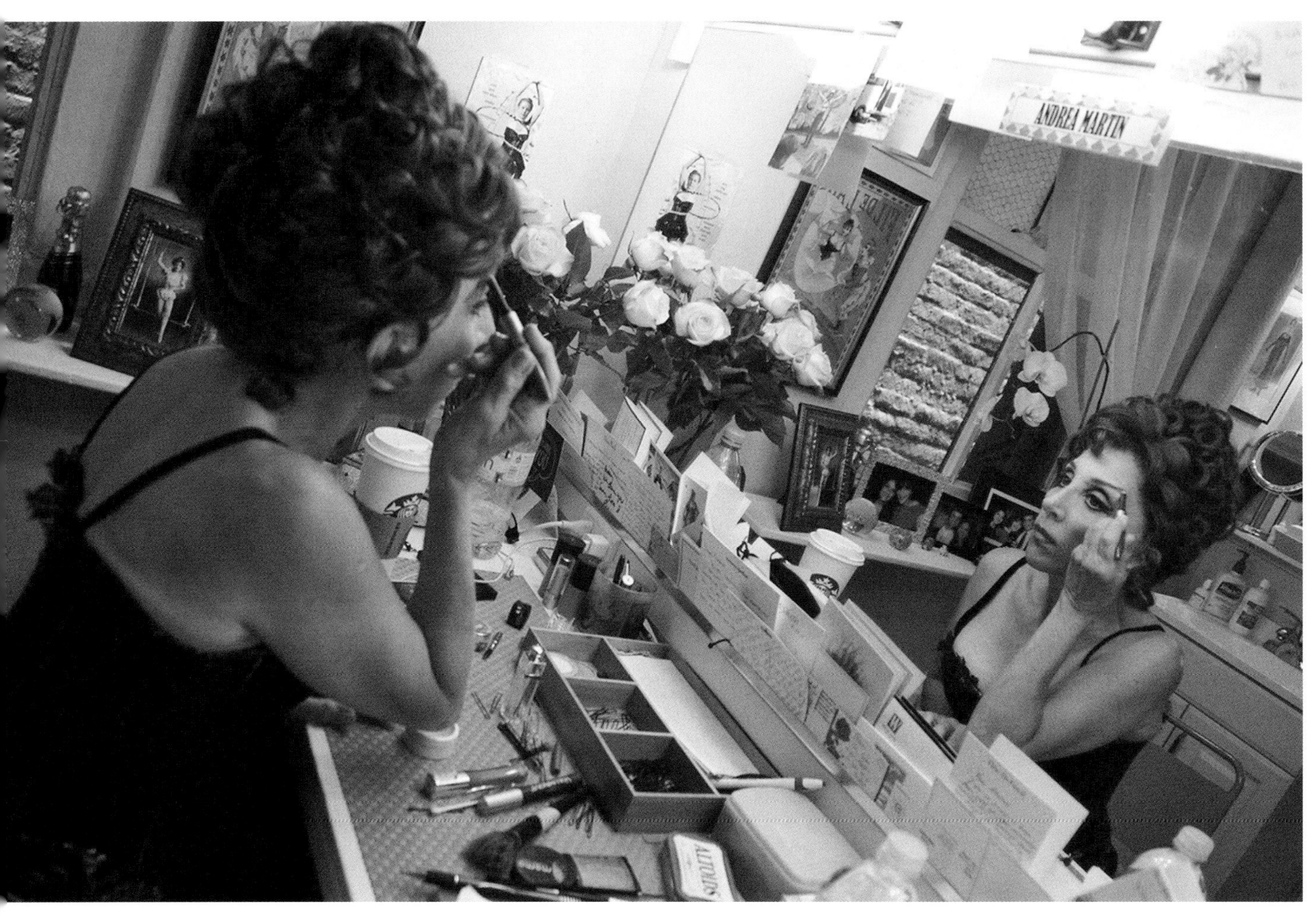

Andrea Martin
Pippin
Music Box Theatre
2013

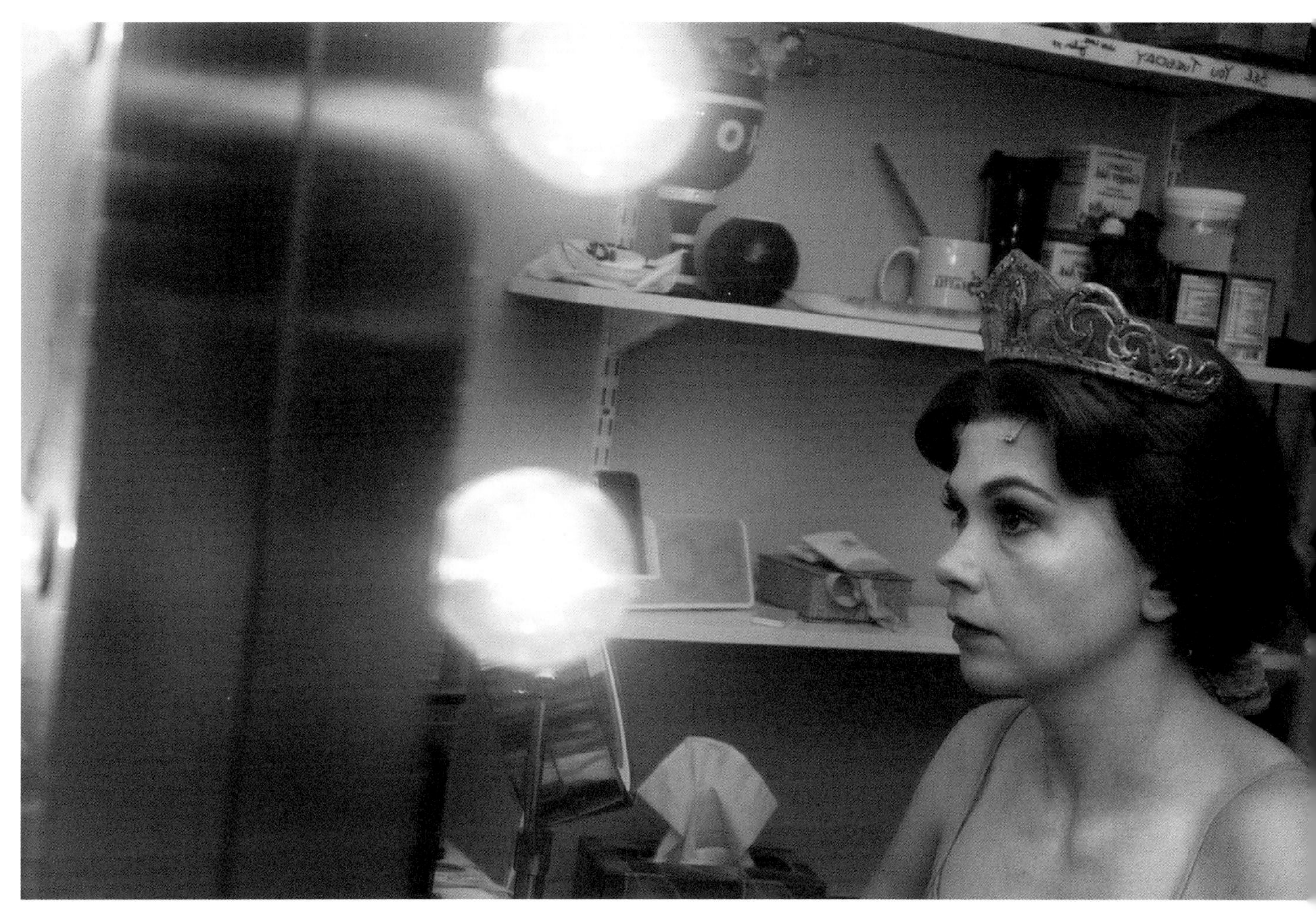

Sutton Foster
Shrek
Broadway Theatre
2009

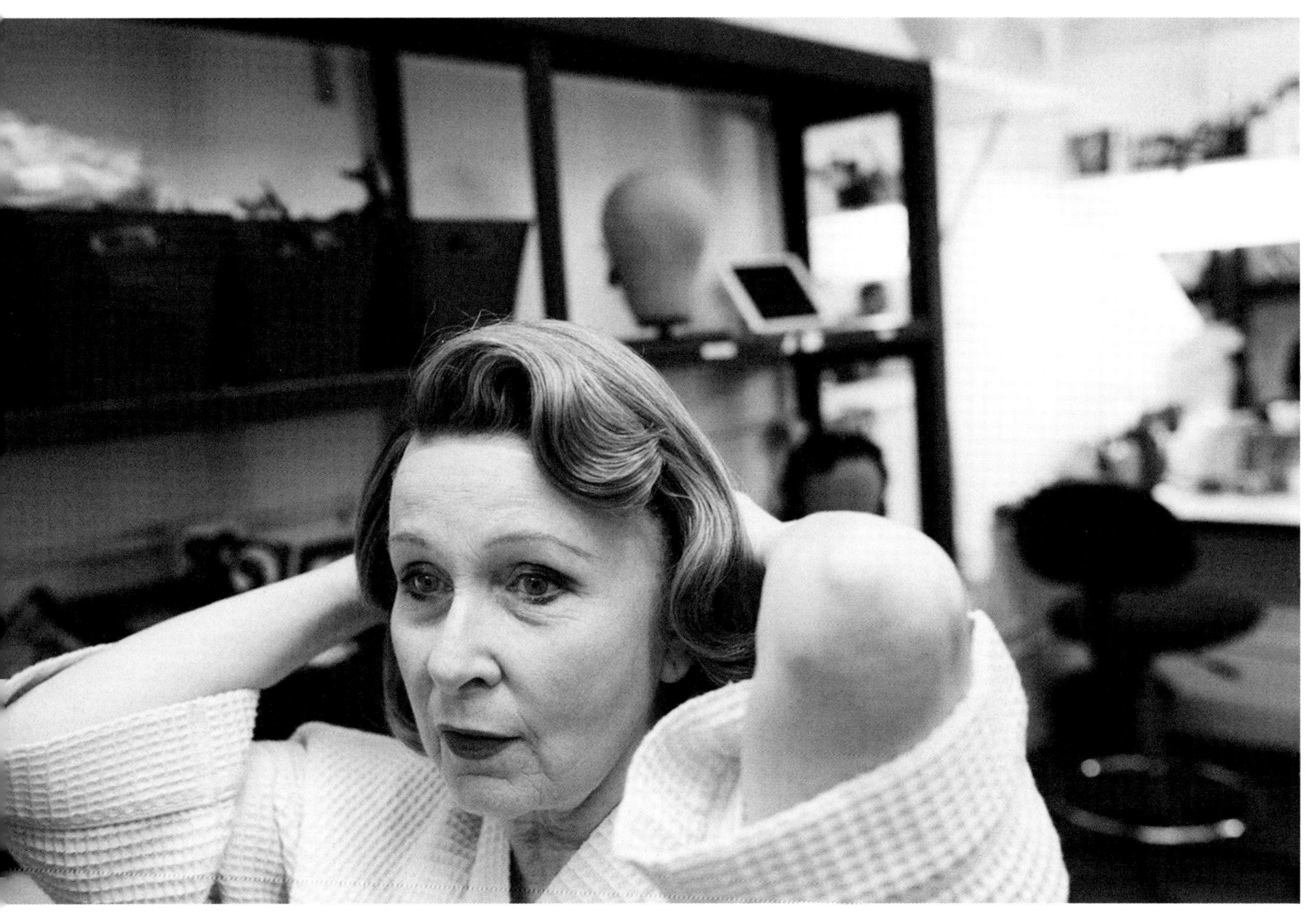

Kate Burton
Present Laughter
St. James Theatre
2017

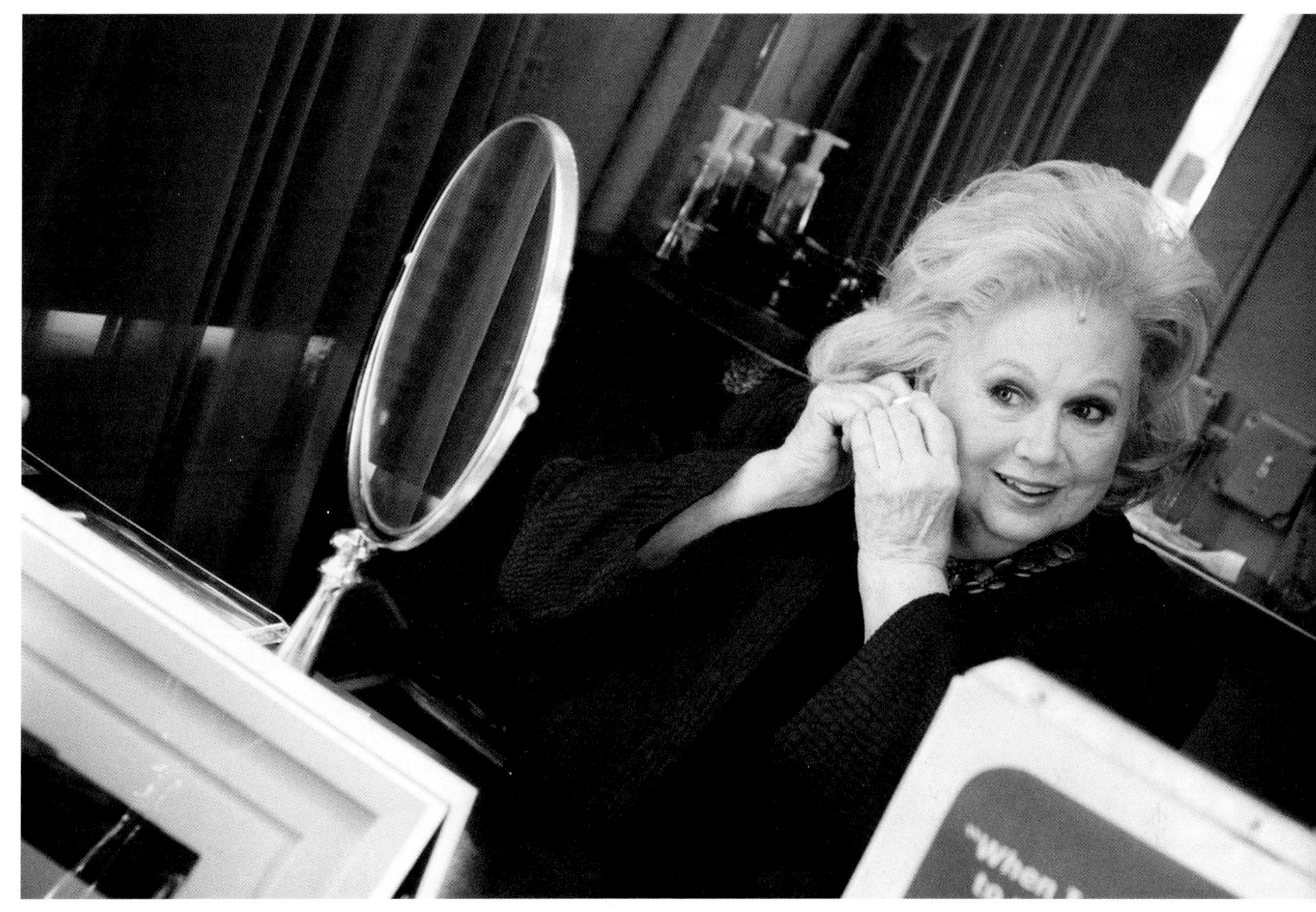

Barbara Cook
Sondheim on Sondheim
Studio 54
2010

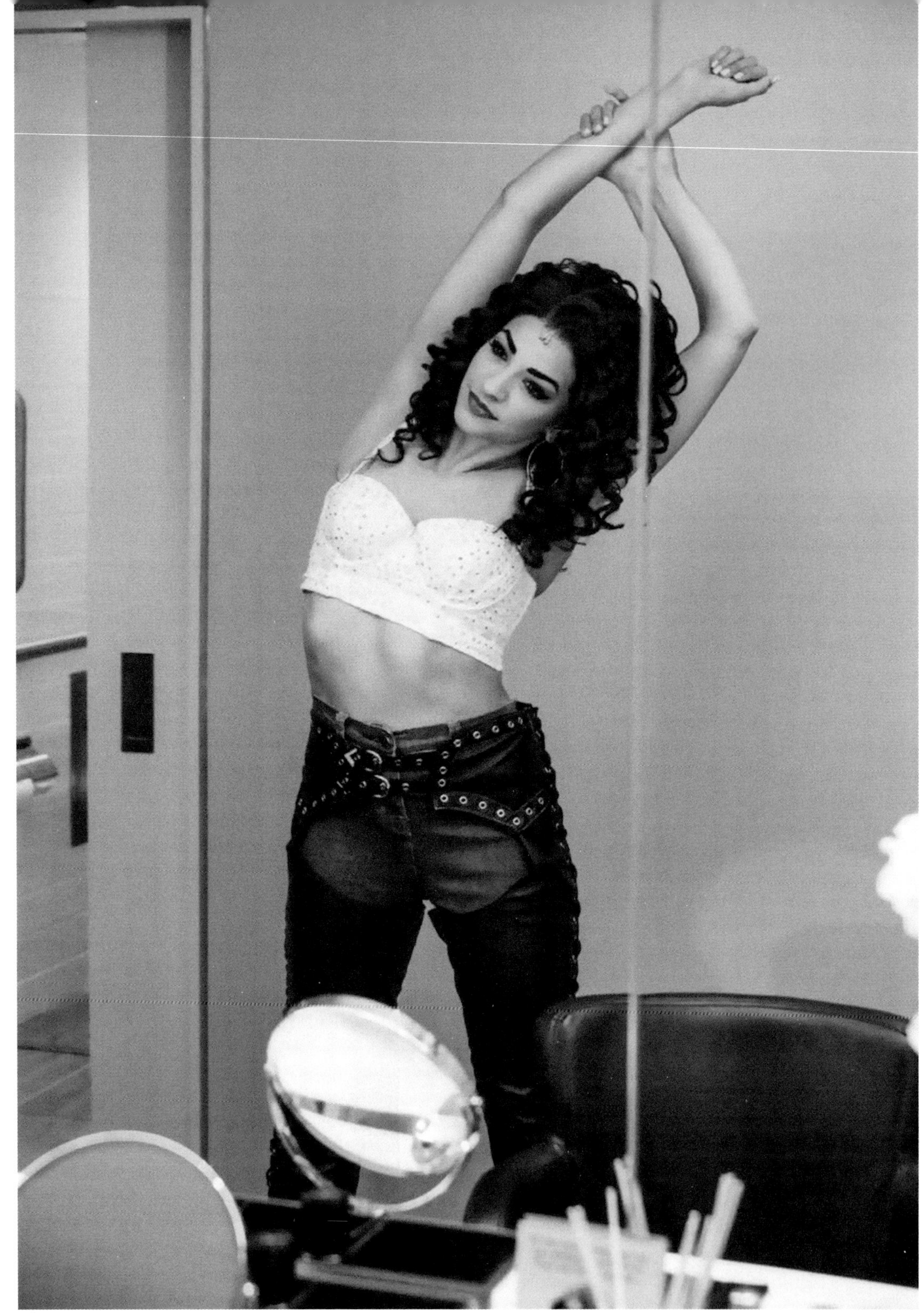

Ana Villafañe
On Your Feet! The Story of Emilio & Gloria Estefan
Marquis Theatre
2016

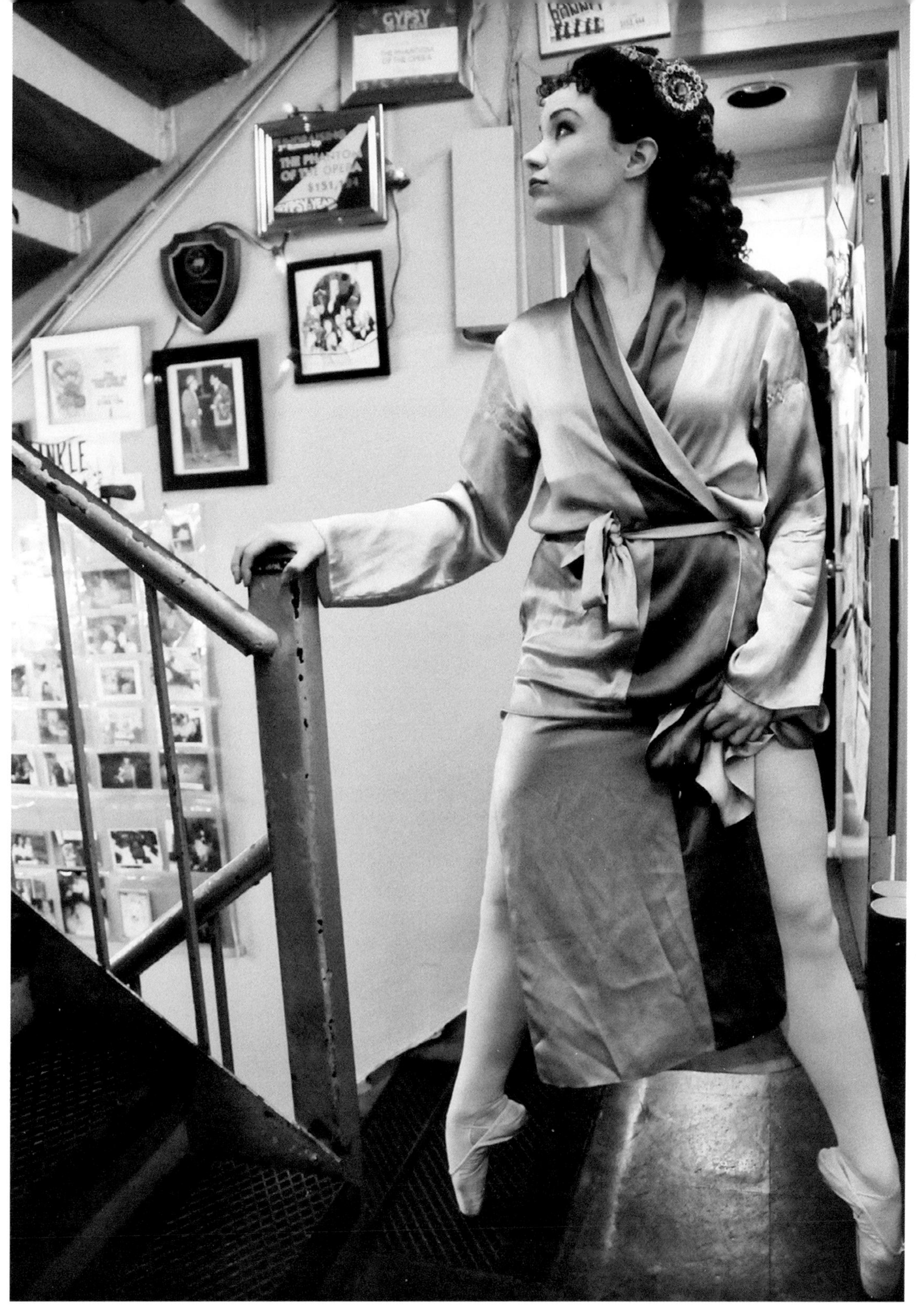

Sierra Boggess
The Phantom of the Opera
Majestic Theatre
2013

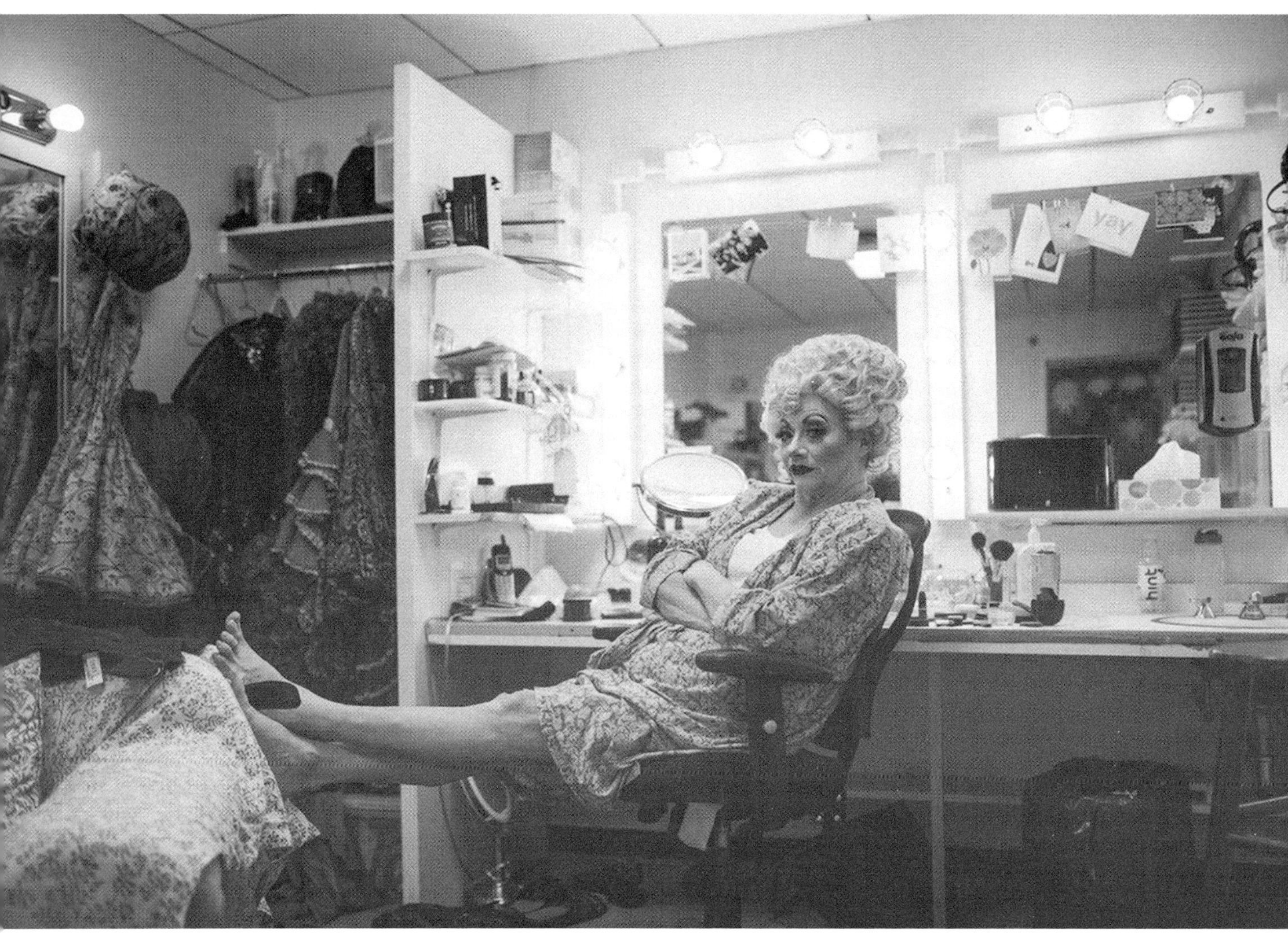

Rondi Reed
Wicked
Gershwin Theatre
2017

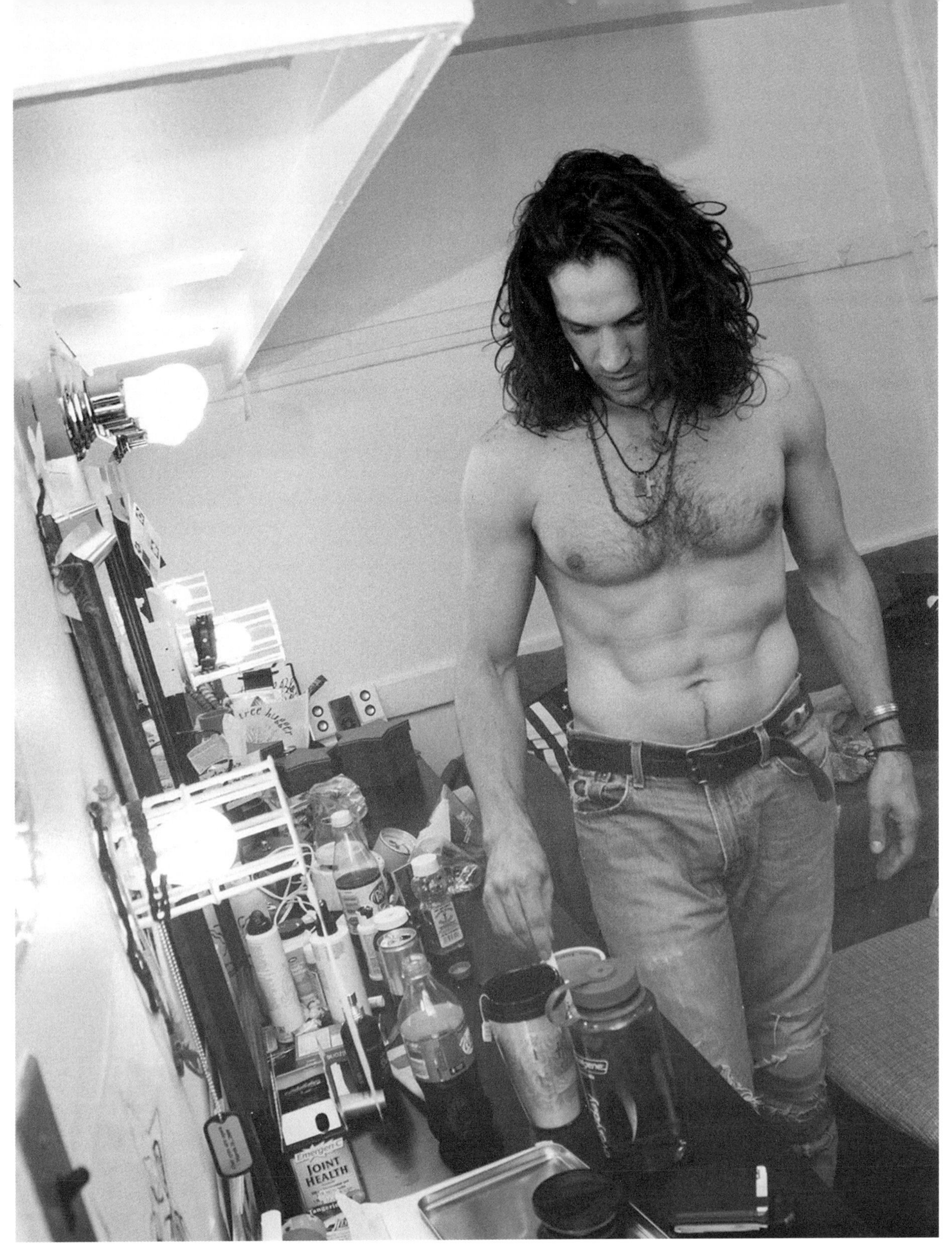

Will Swenson
Hair
Al Hirschfeld Theatre
2009

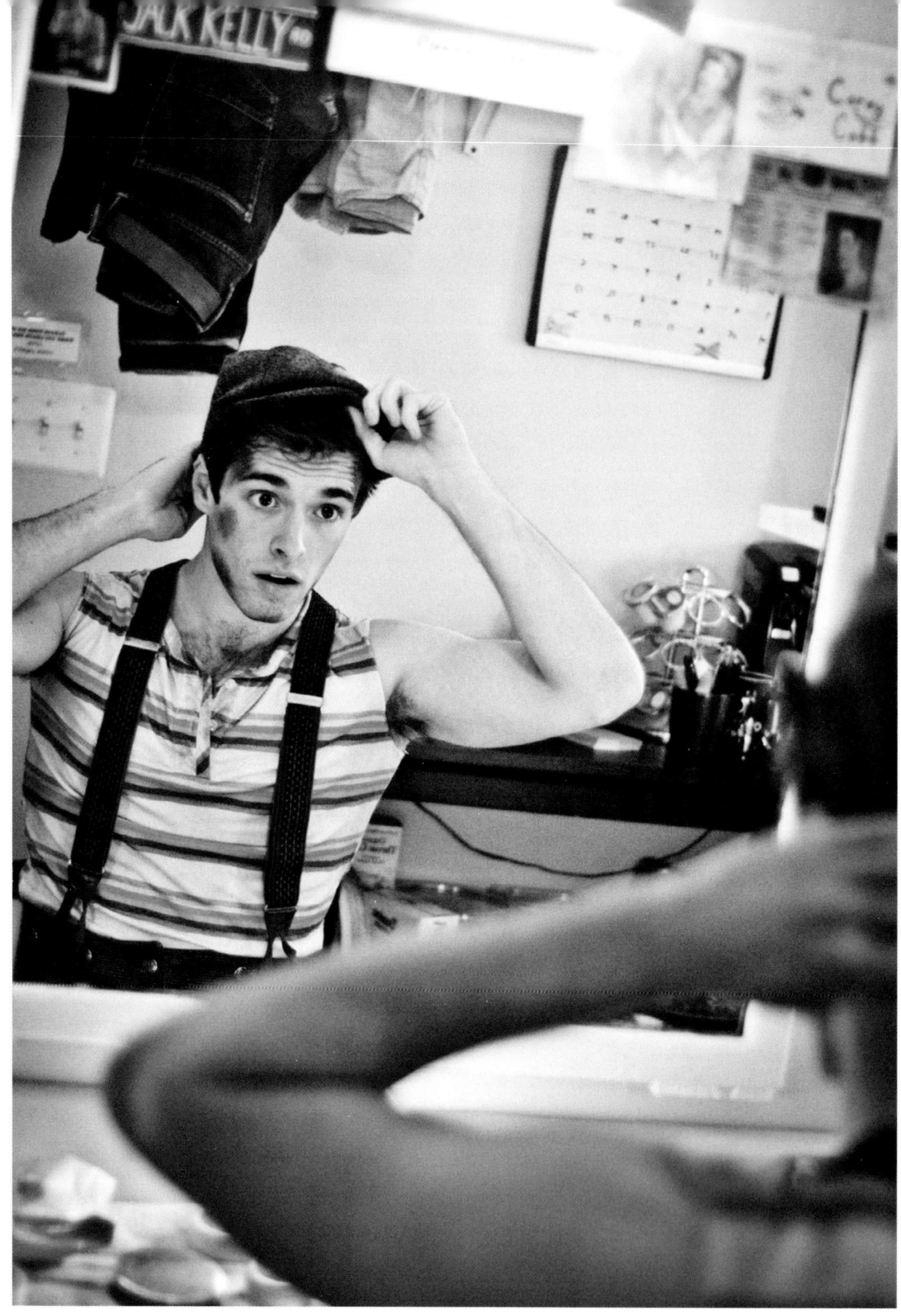

Corey Cott
Newsies
Nederlander Theatre
2013

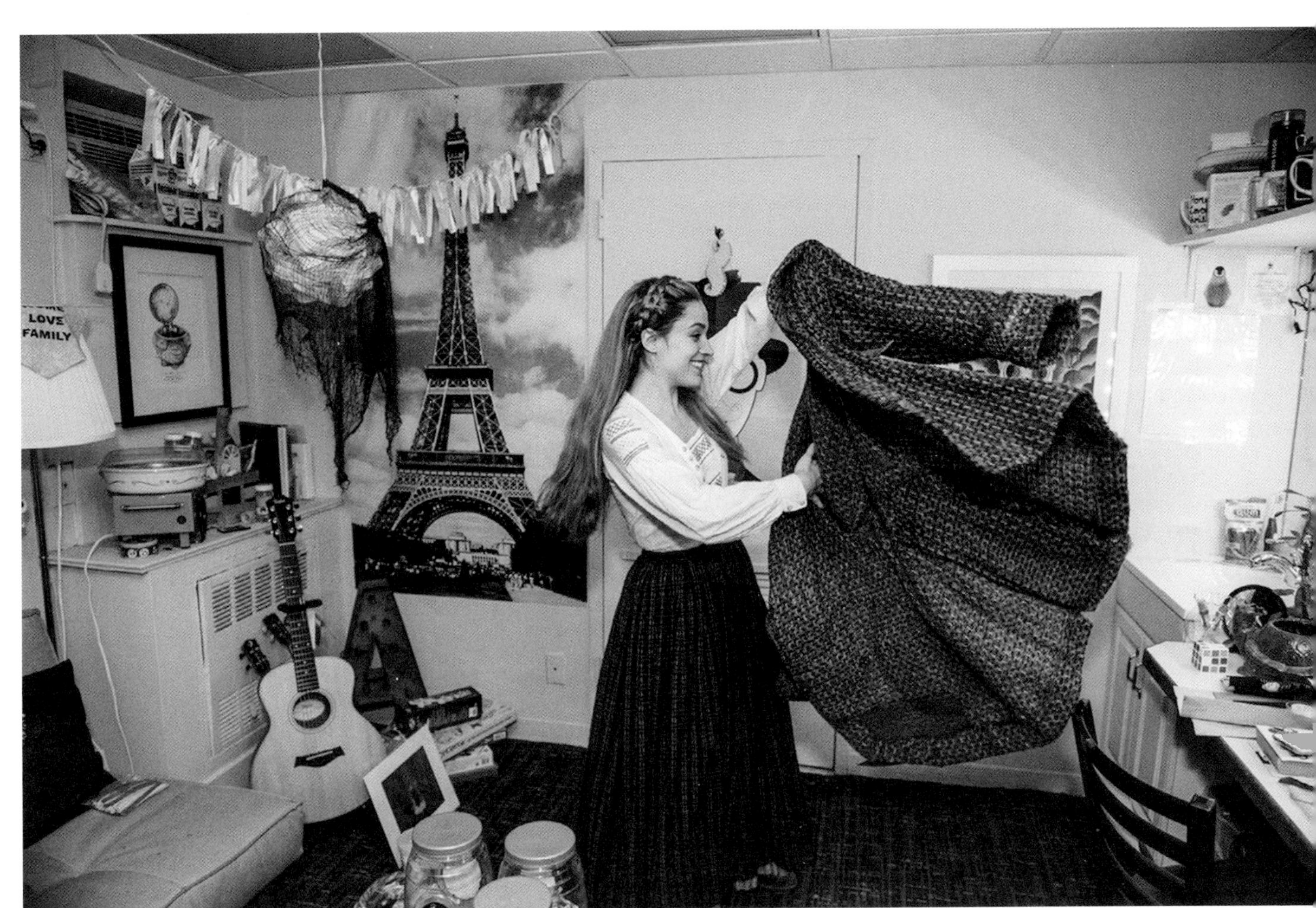

Christy Altomare
Anastasia
Broadhurst Theatre
2018

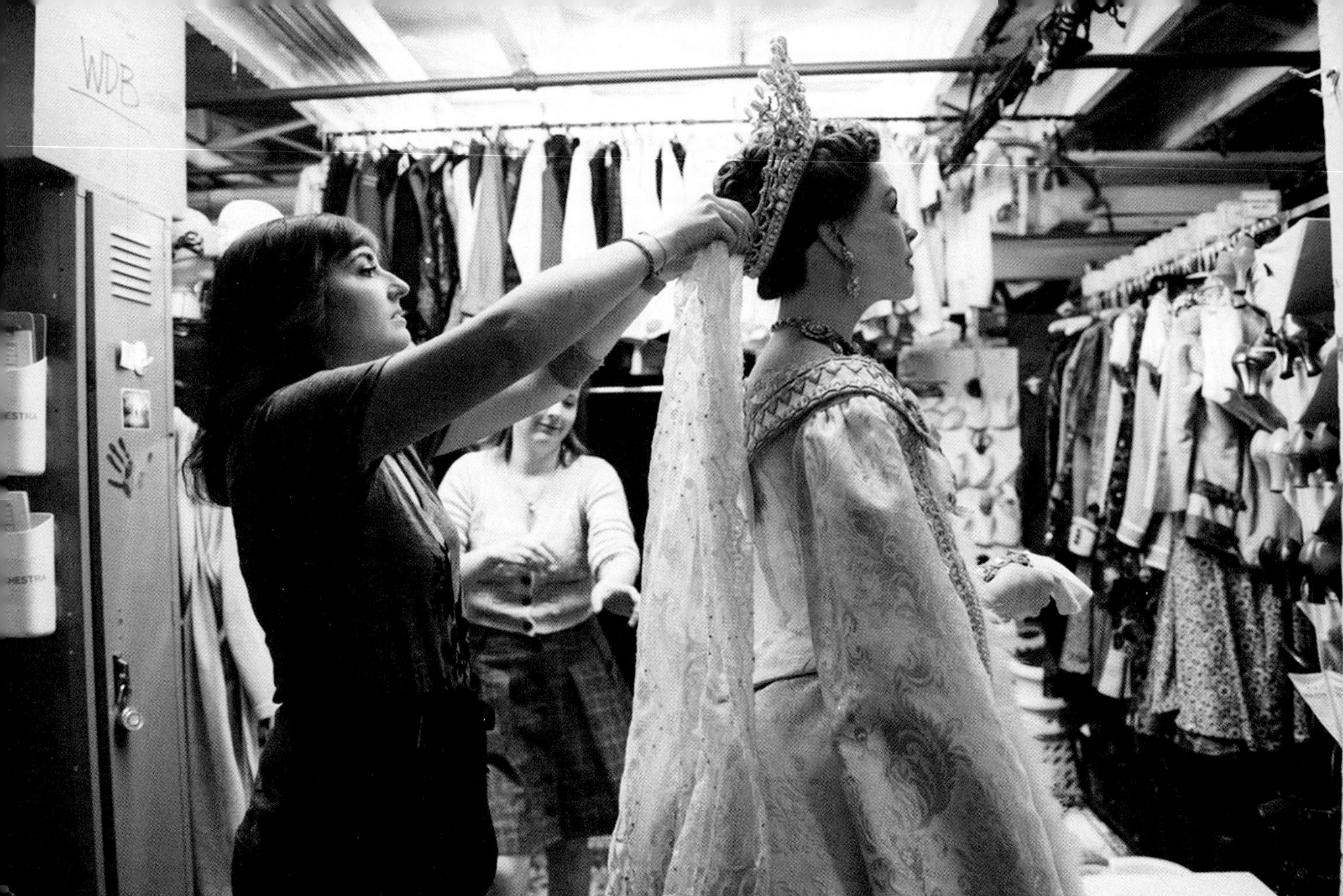

Lauren Blackman
Anastasia
Broadhurst Theatre
2018

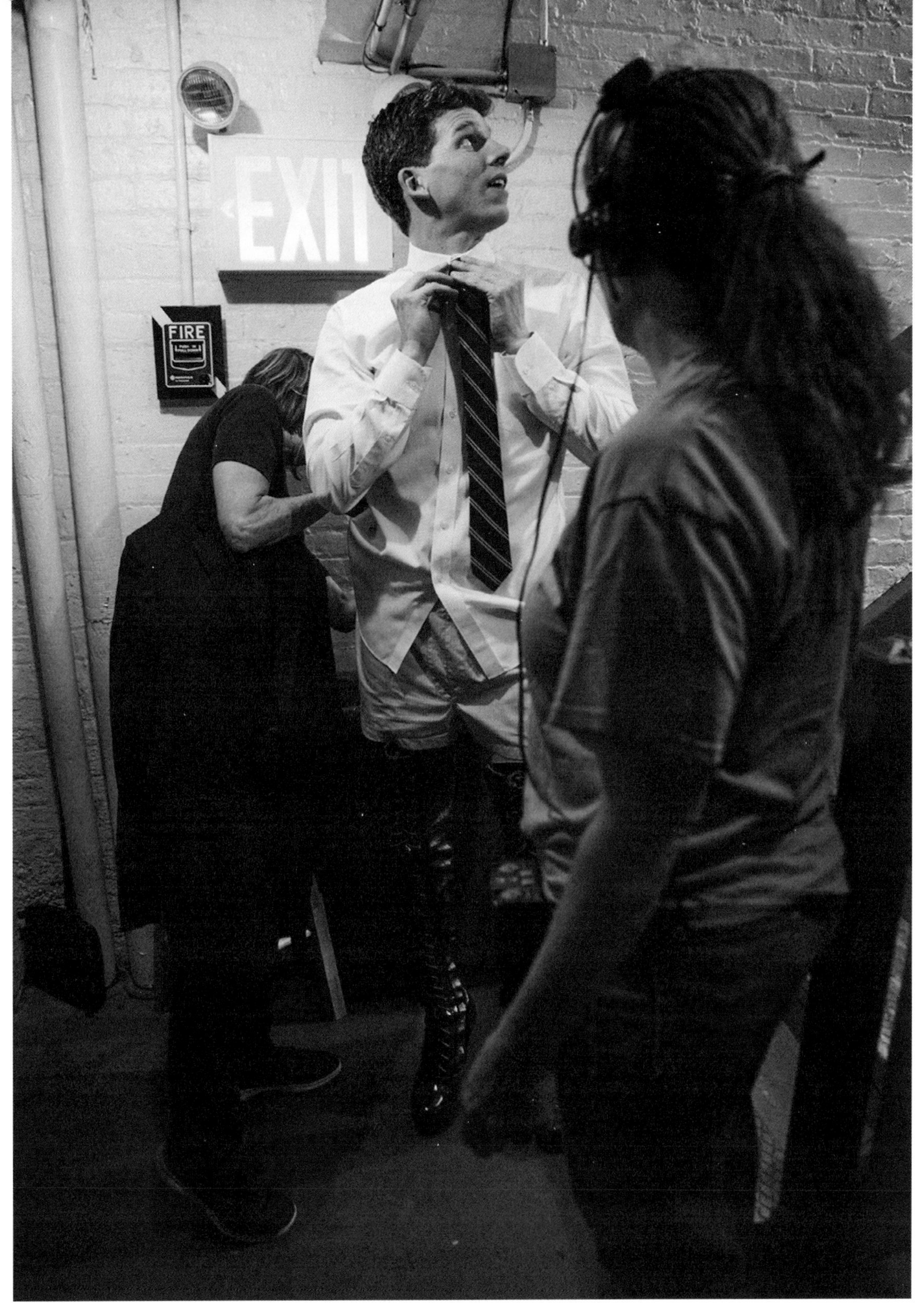

Stark Sands
Kinky Boots
Al Hirschfeld Theatre
2013

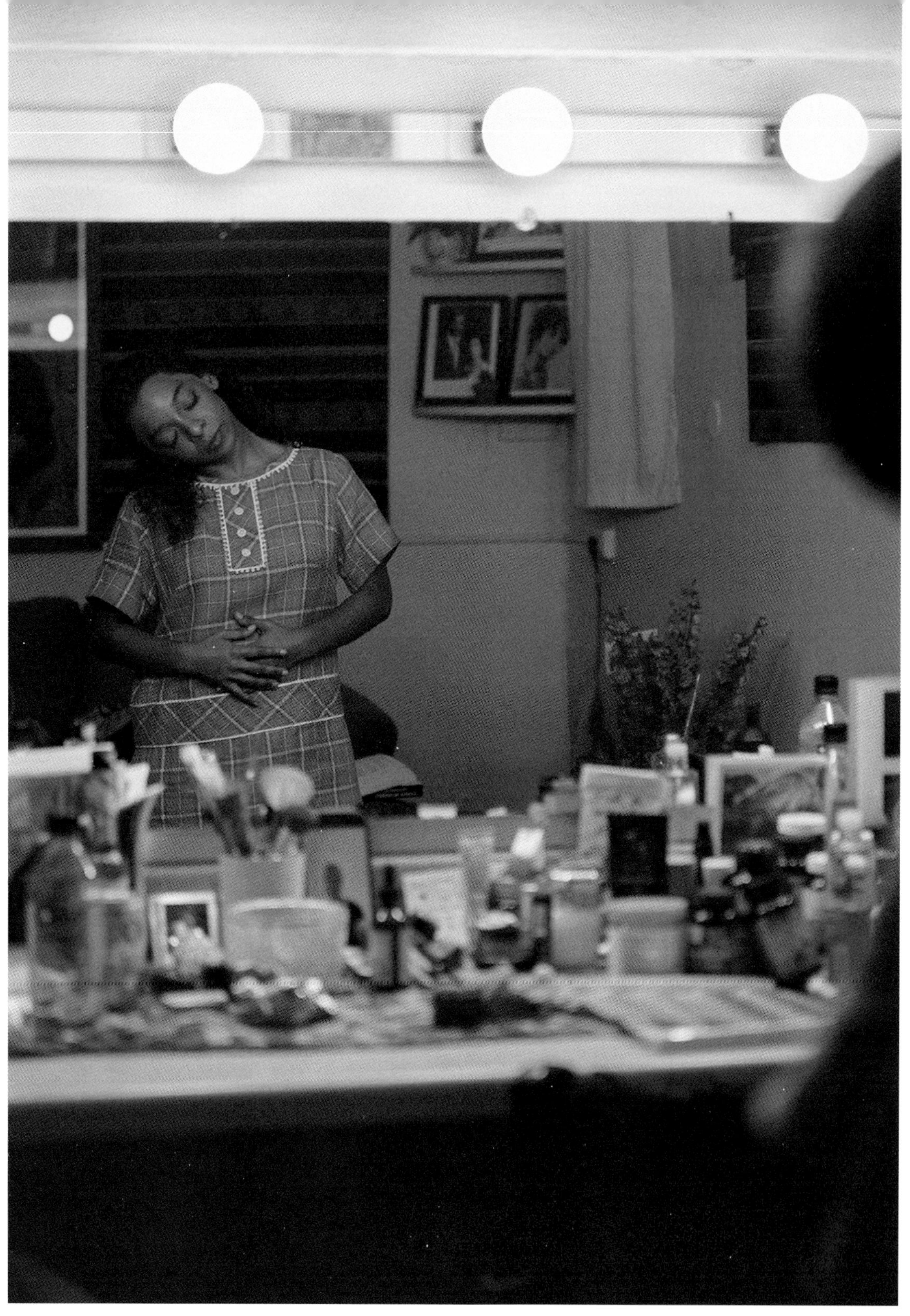

Kara Young
Purlie Victorious
Music Box Theatre
2023

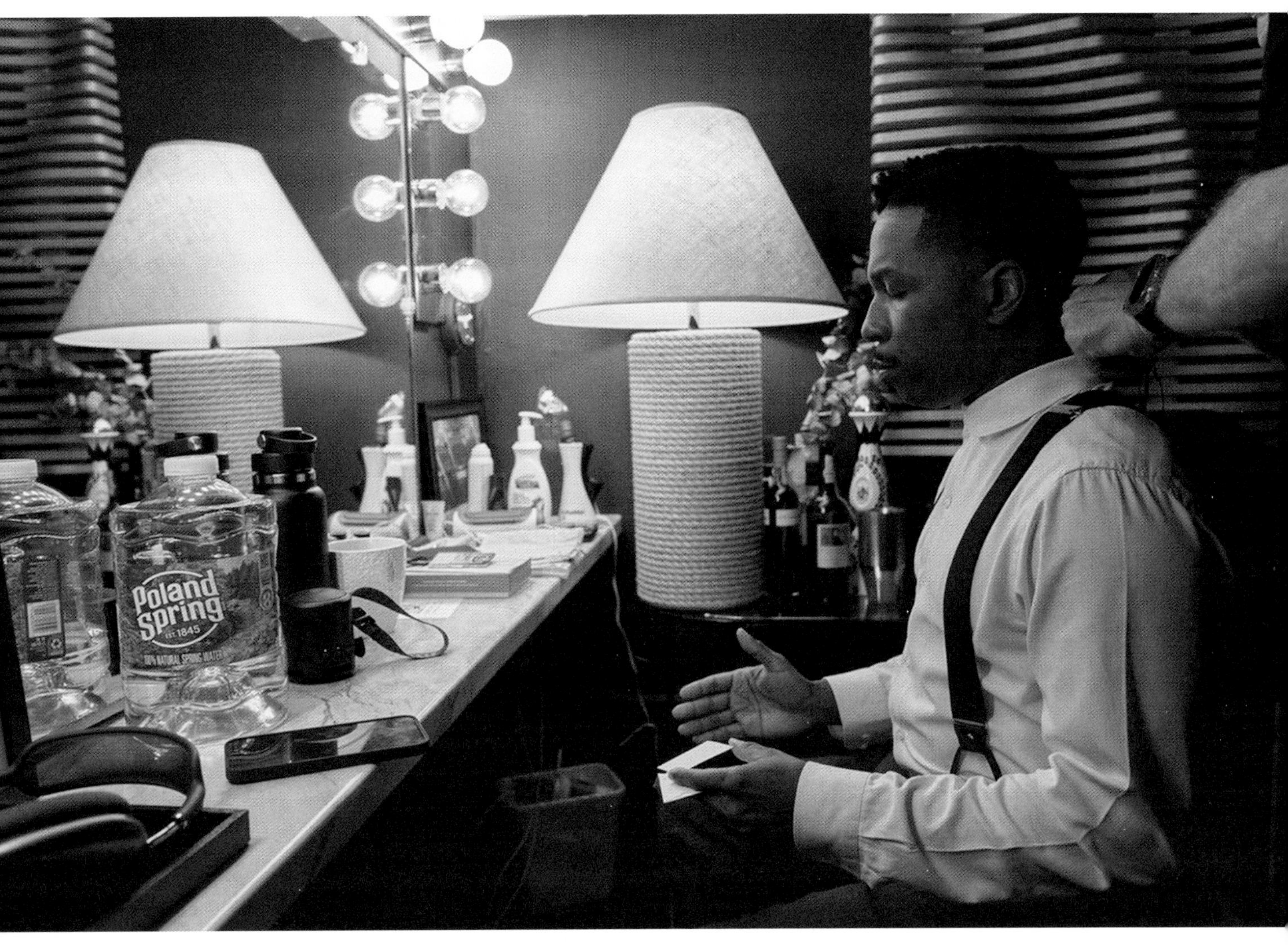

Leslie Odom Jr.
Purlie Victorious
Music Box Theatre
2023

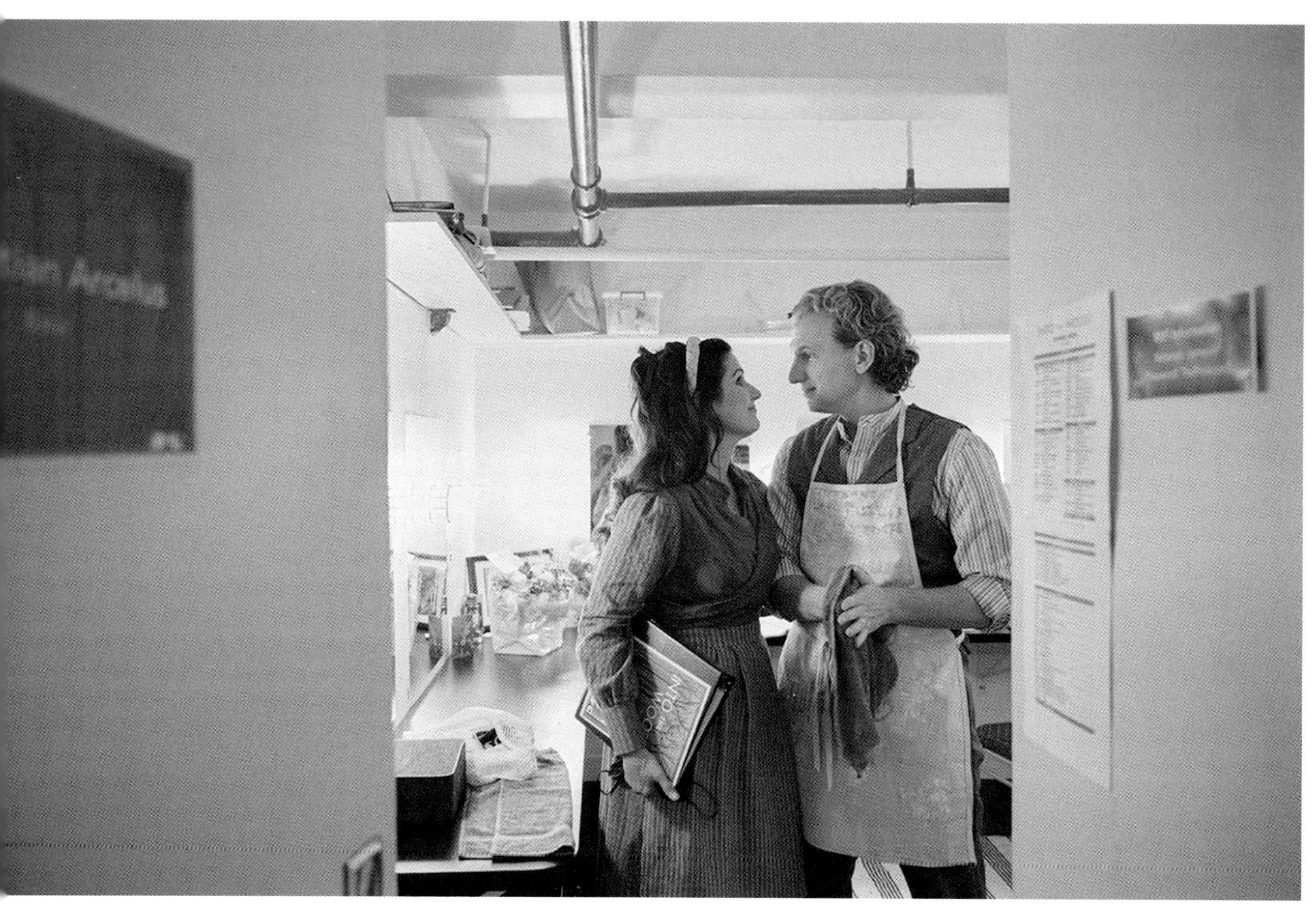

Stephanie J. Block and Sebastian Arcelus
Into the Woods
St. James Theatre
2022

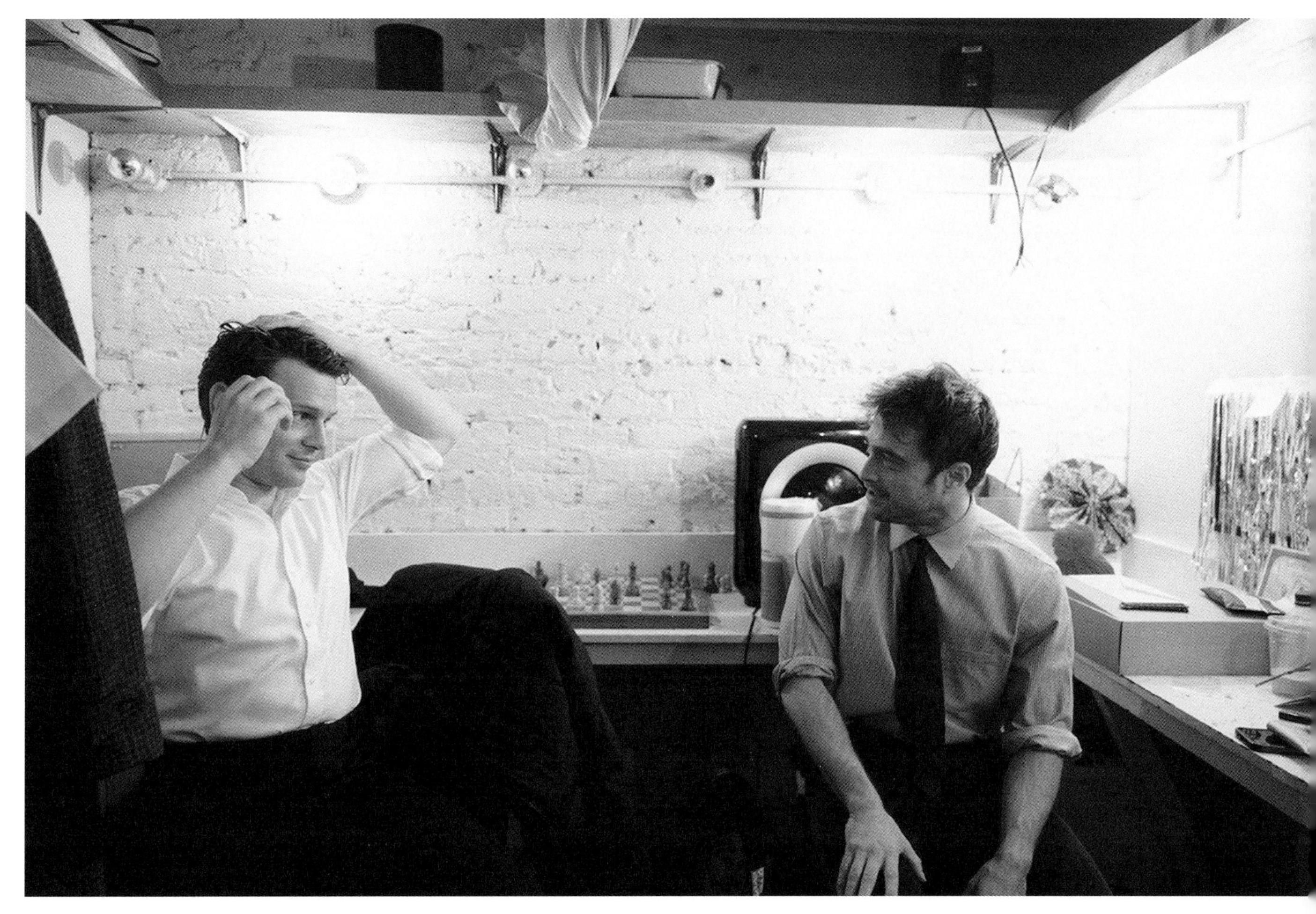

Jonathan Groff and Daniel Radcliffe
Merrily We Roll Along
New York Theatre Workshop
2023

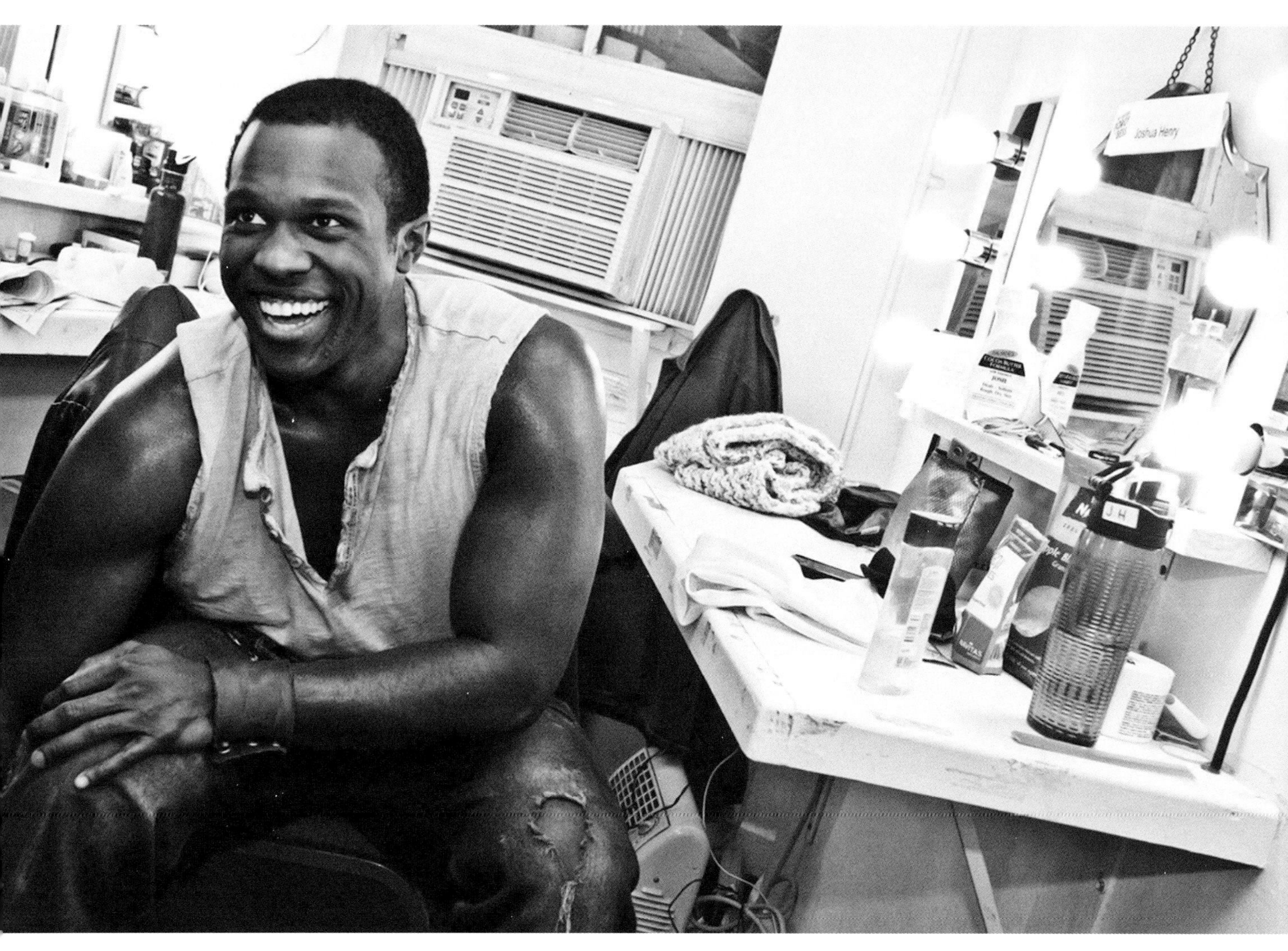

Joshua Henry
The Gershwins' Porgy and Bess
Richard Rodgers Theatre
2012

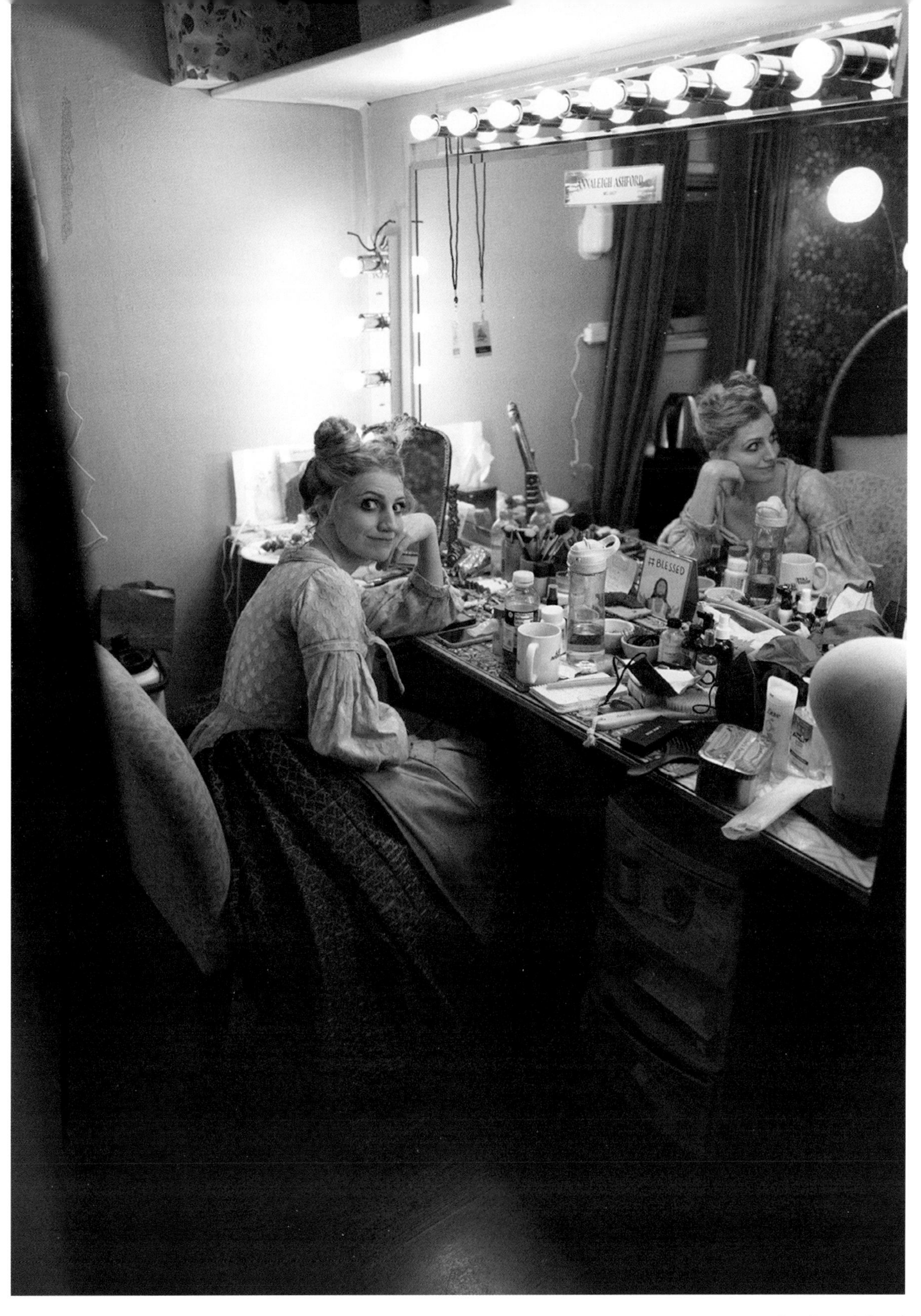

Annaleigh Ashford
Sweeney Todd: The Demon Barber of Fleet Street
Lunt-Fontanne Theatre
2023

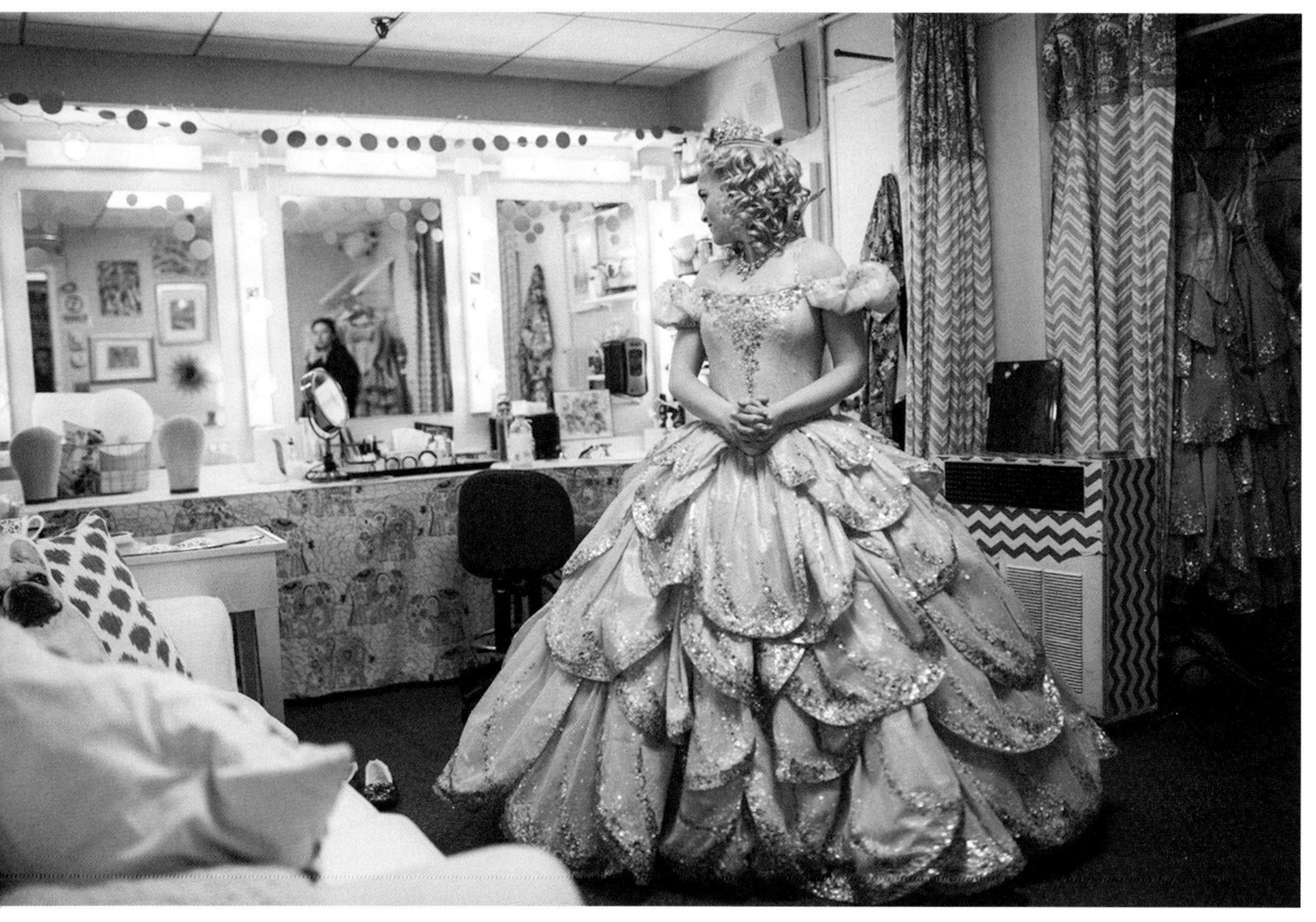

Amanda Jane Cooper
Wicked
Gershwin Theatre
2018

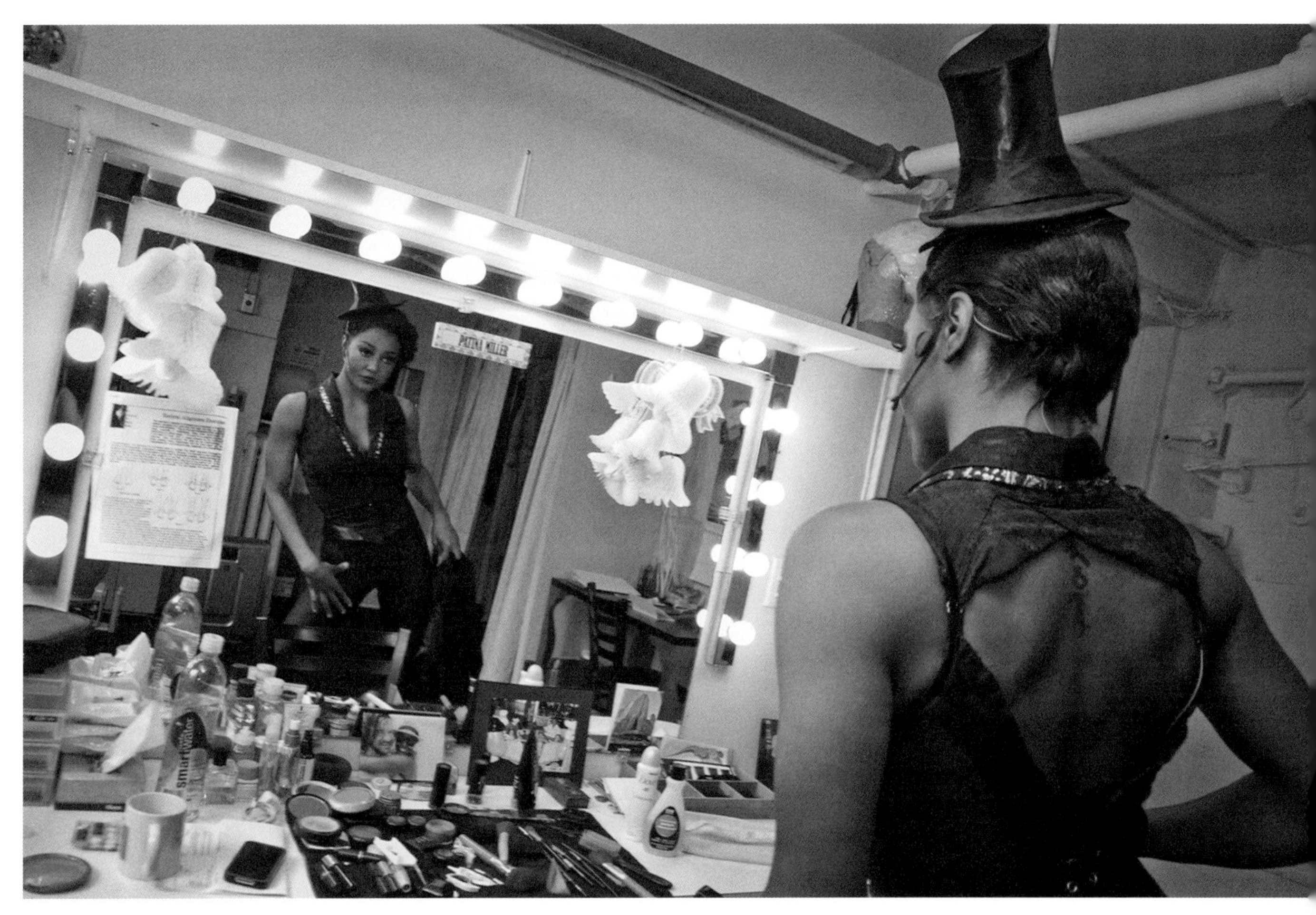

Patina Miller
Pippin
Music Box Theatre
2013

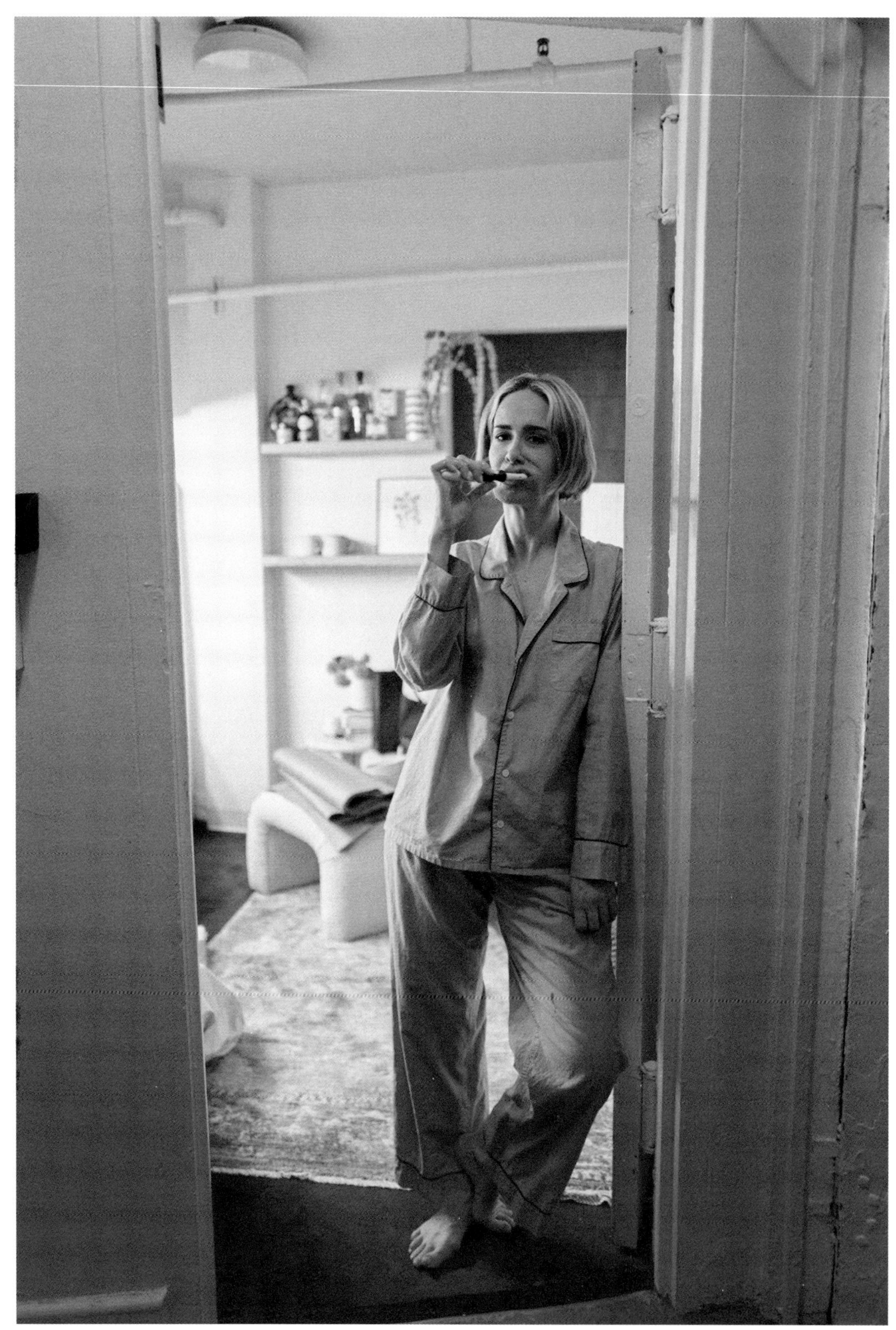

Sarah Paulson
Appropriate
Belasco Theatre
2024

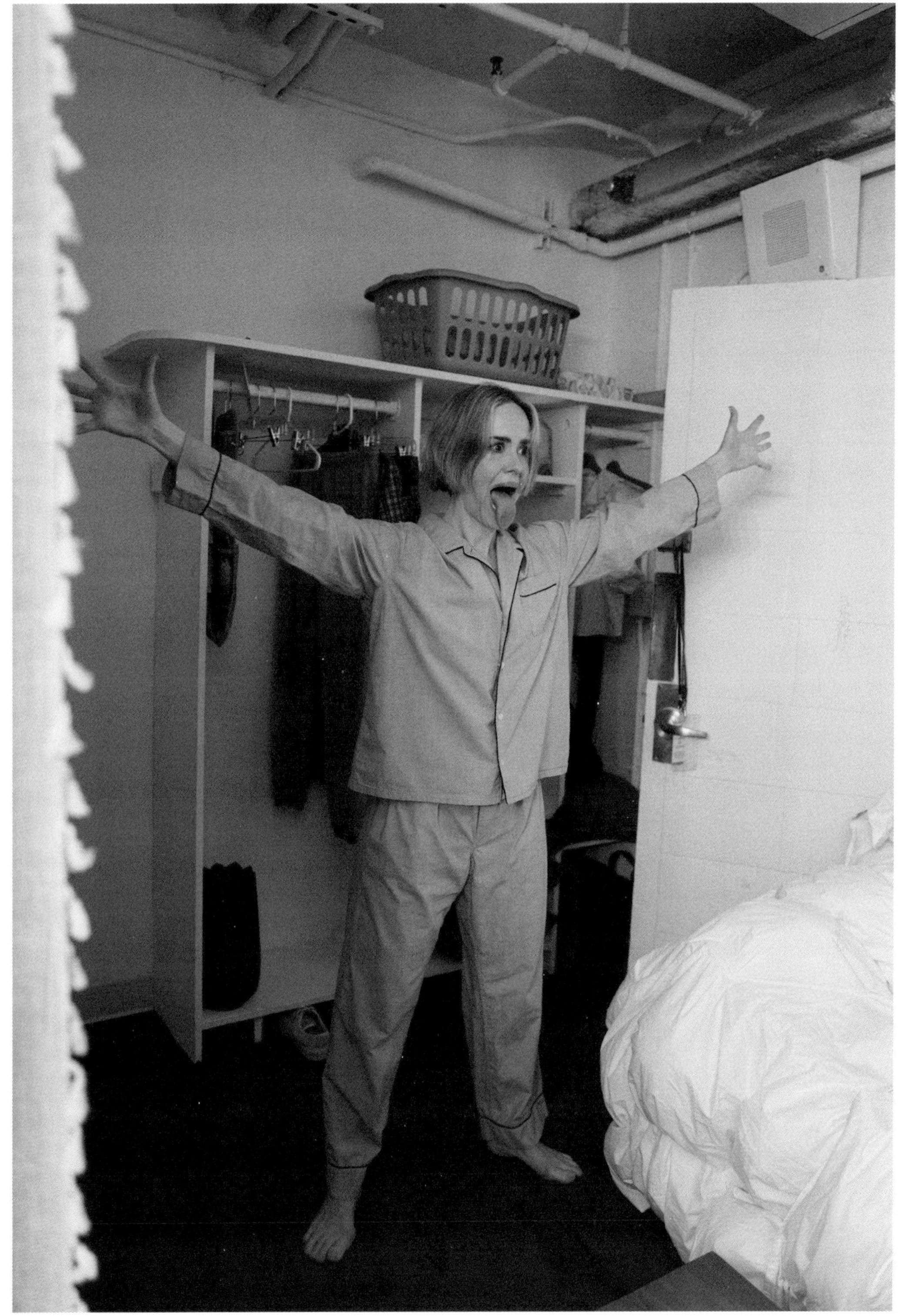

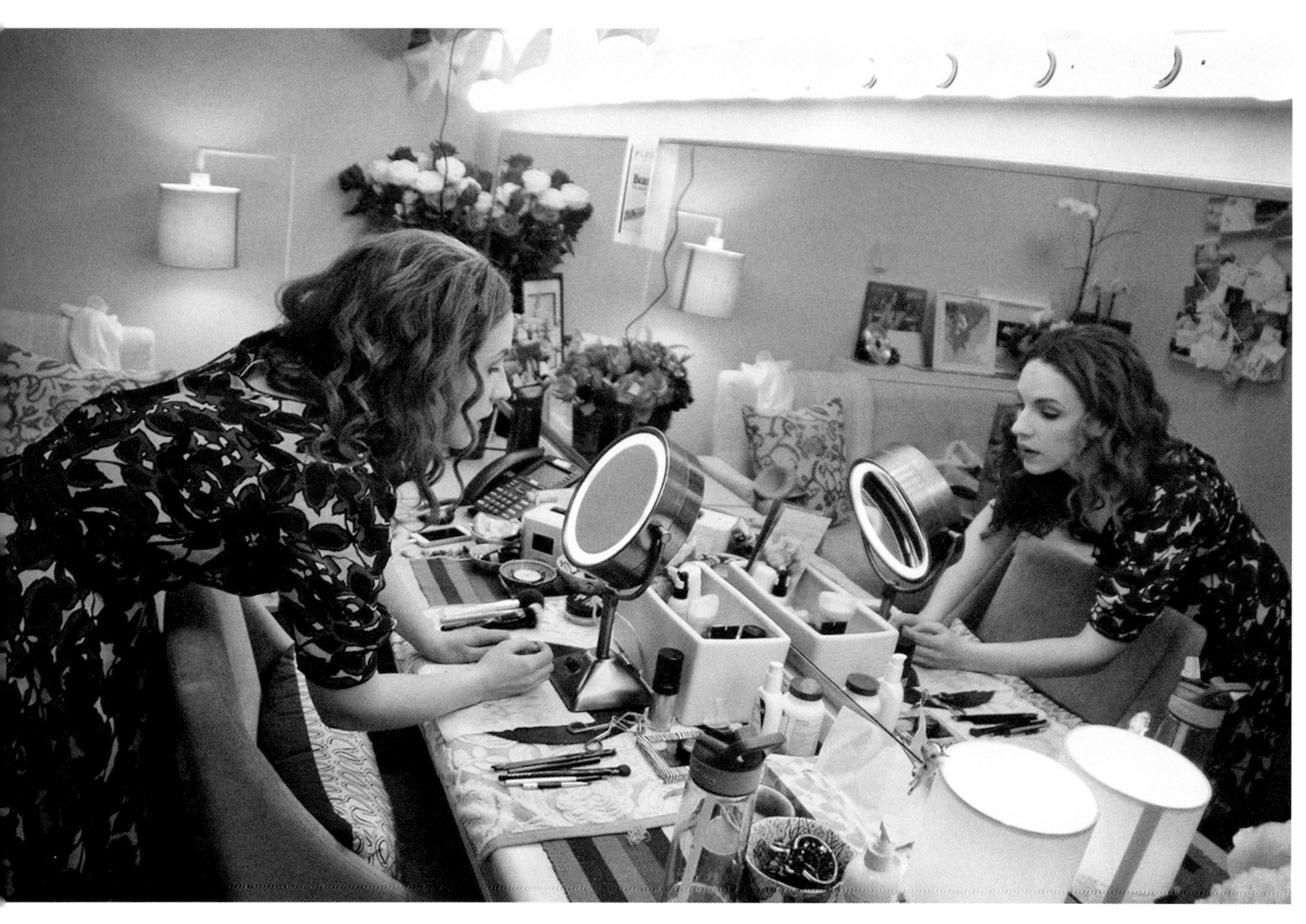

Jessie Mueller
Beautiful: The Carole King Musical
Stephen Sondheim Theatre
2015

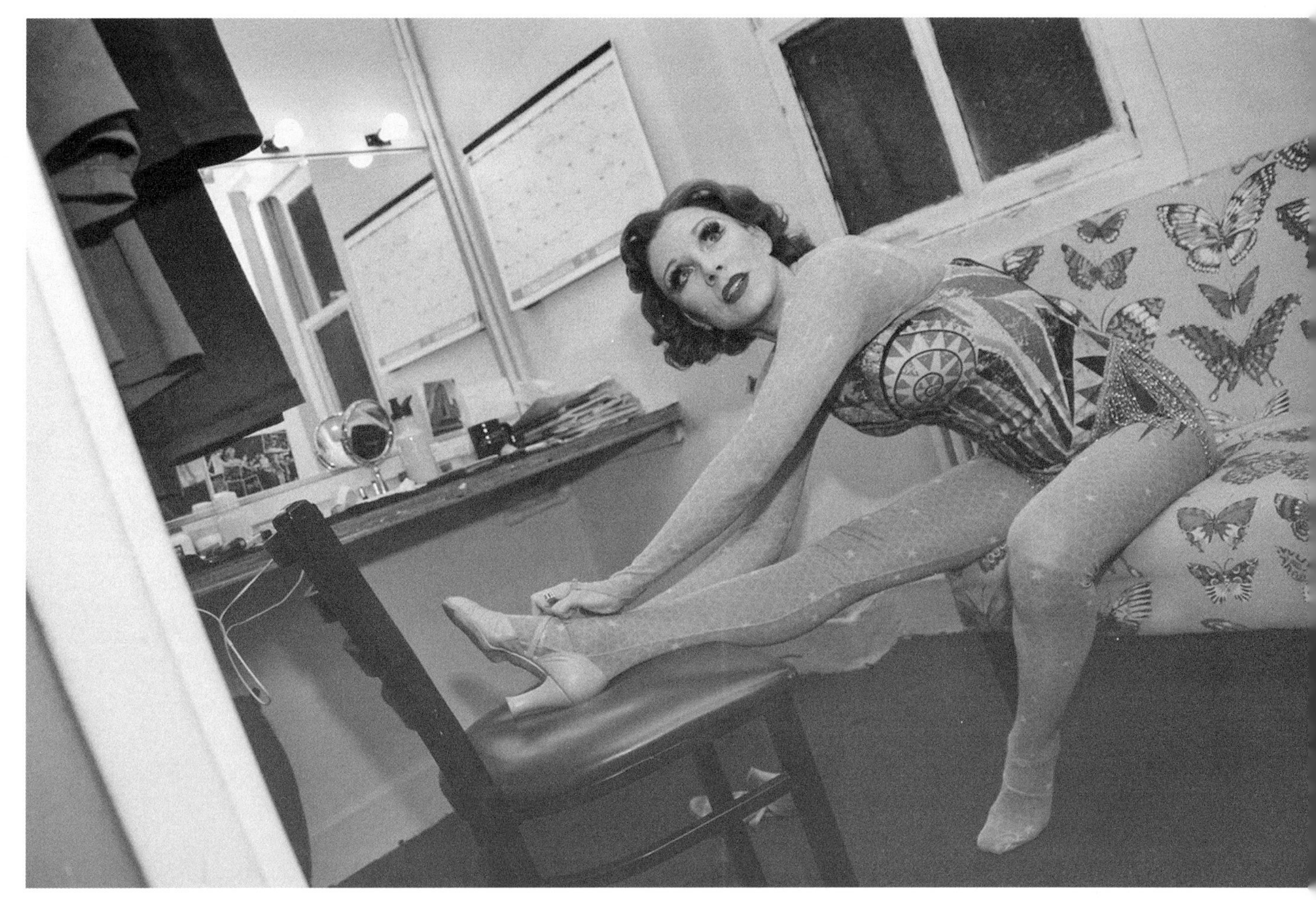

Charlotte d'Amboise
Pippin
Music Box Theatre
2013

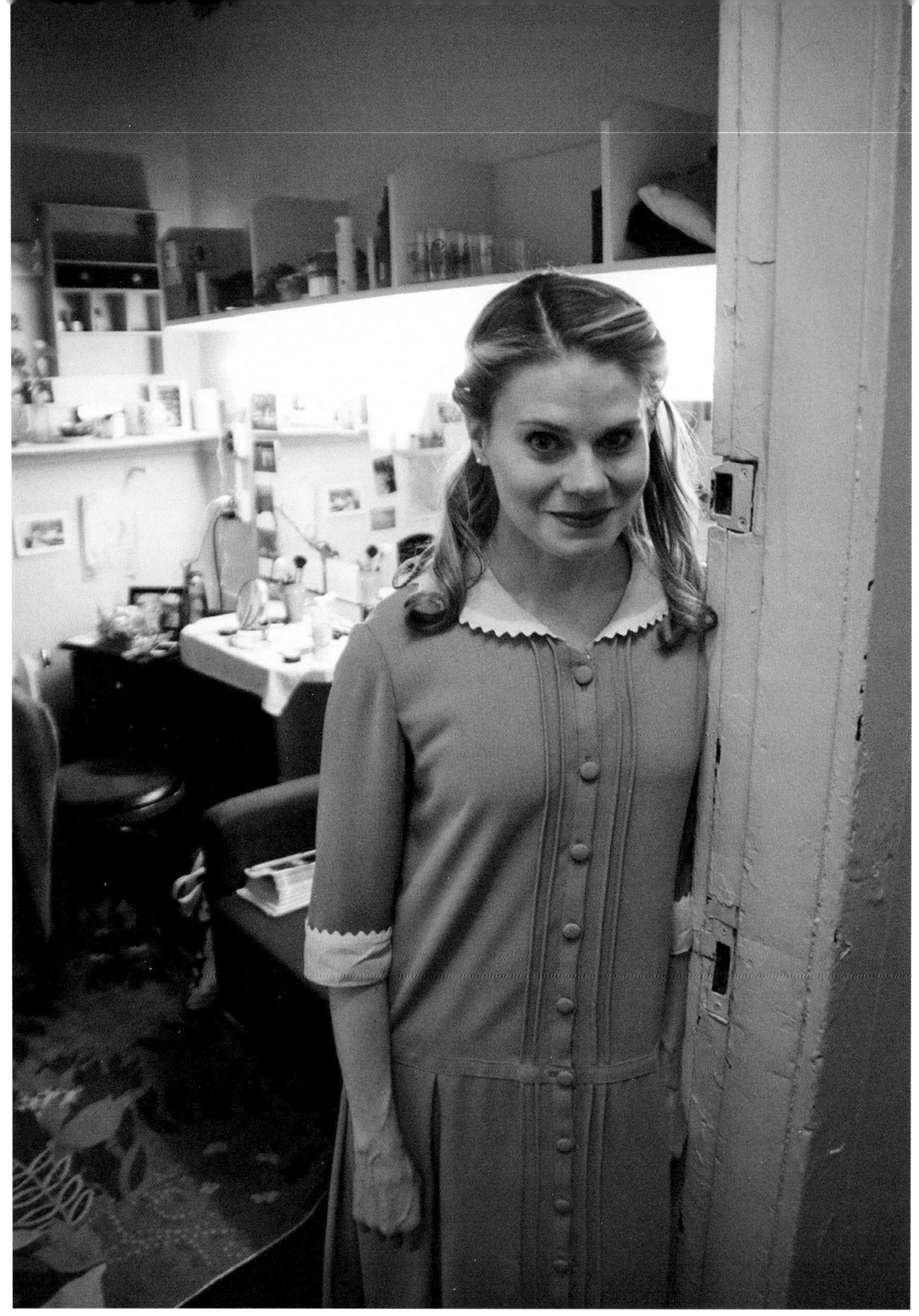

Celia Keenan-Bolger
The Glass Menagerie
Booth Theatre
2013

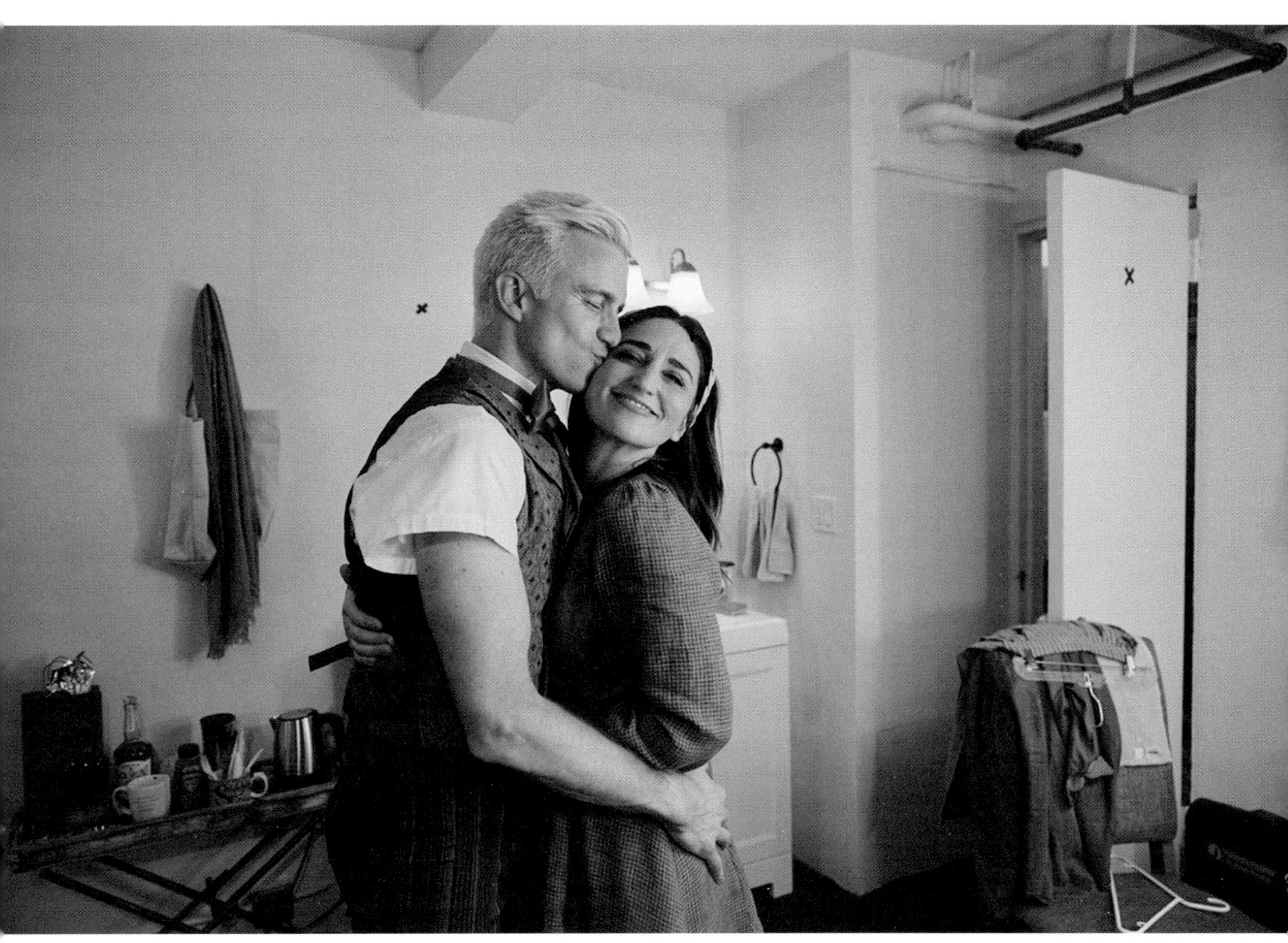

Gavin Creel and Sara Bareilles
Into the Woods
St. James Theatre
2022

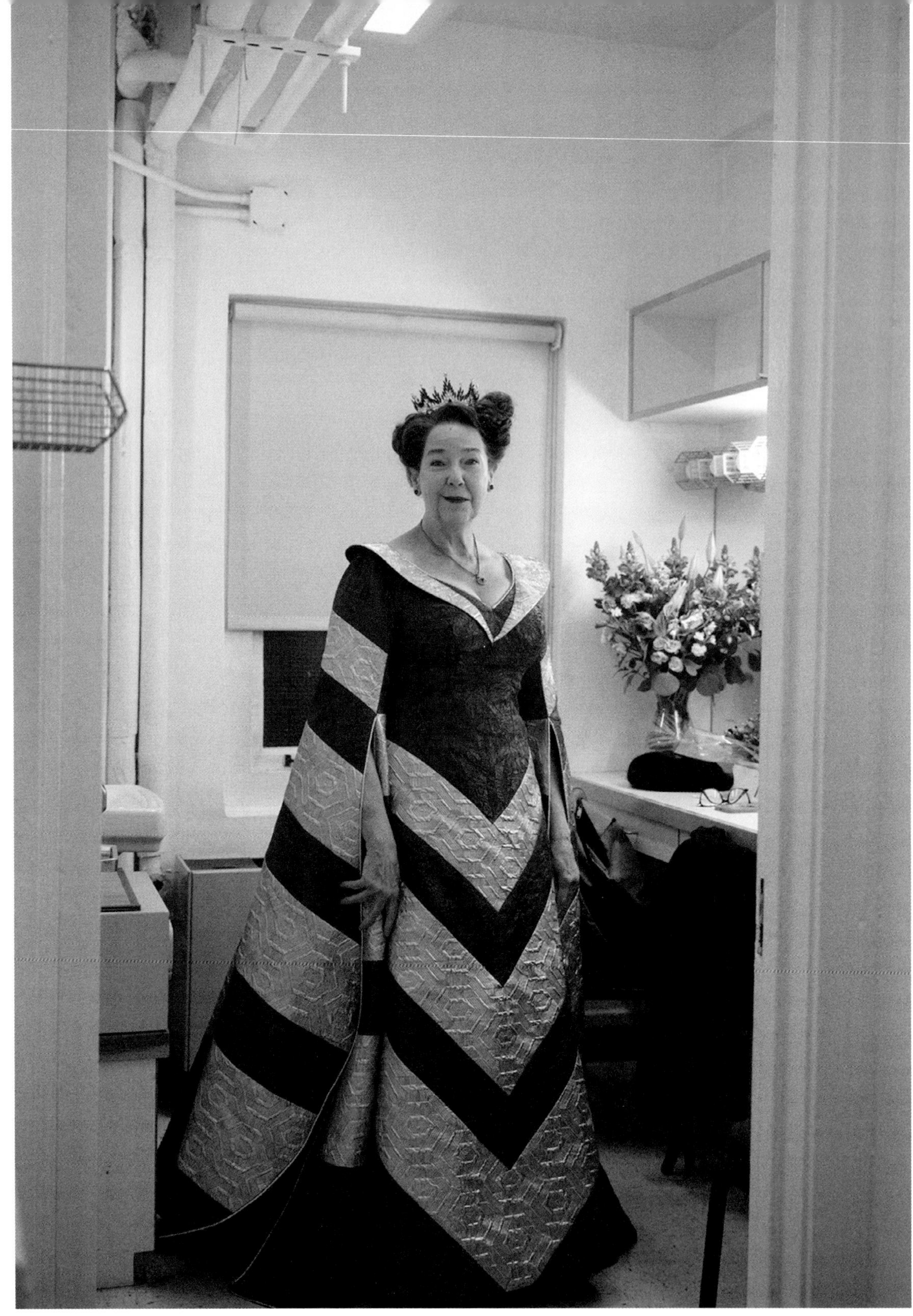

Harriet Harris
Once Upon a Mattress
New York City Center
2023

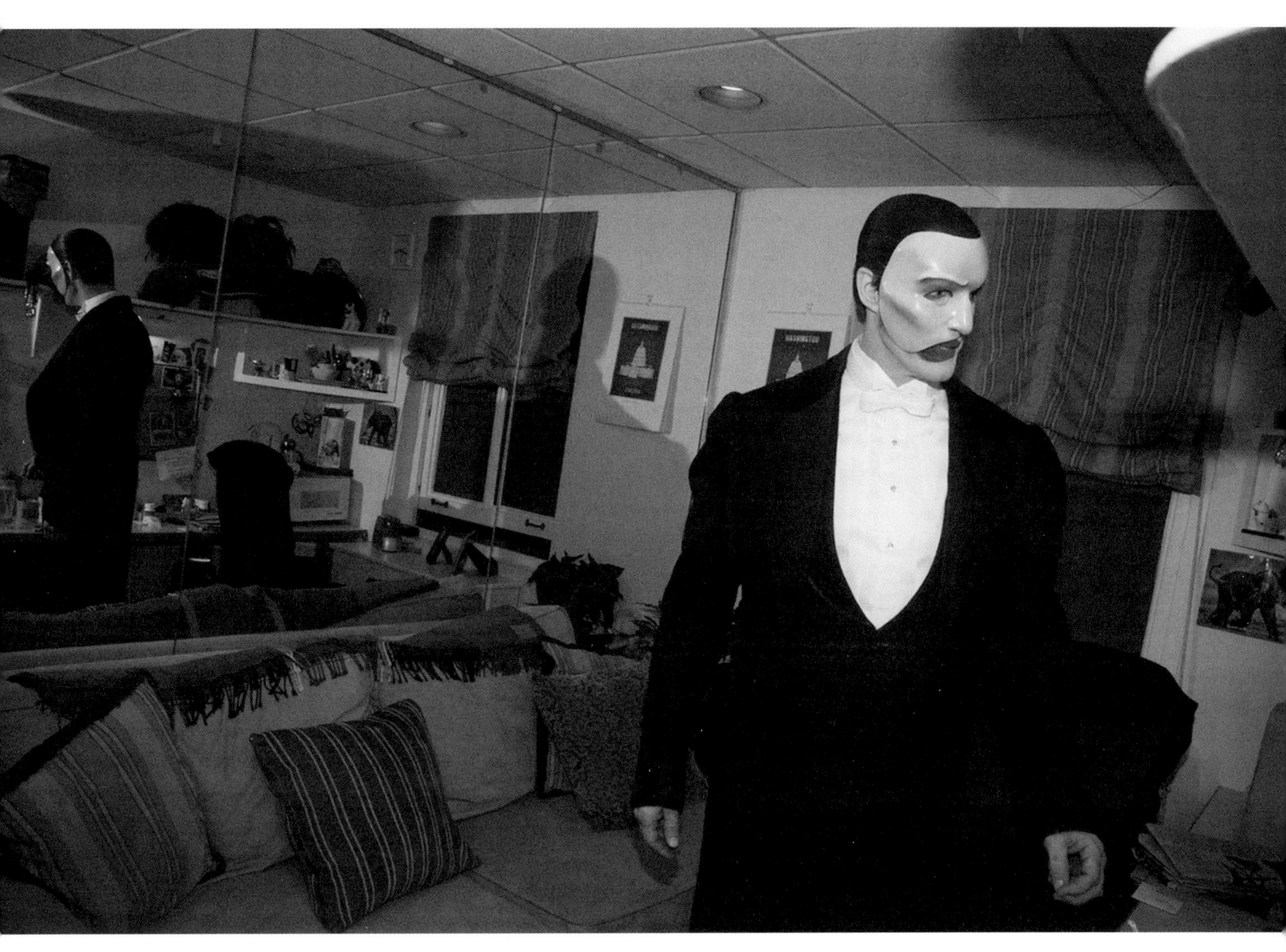

Howard McGillin
The Phantom of the Opera
Majestic Theatre
2009

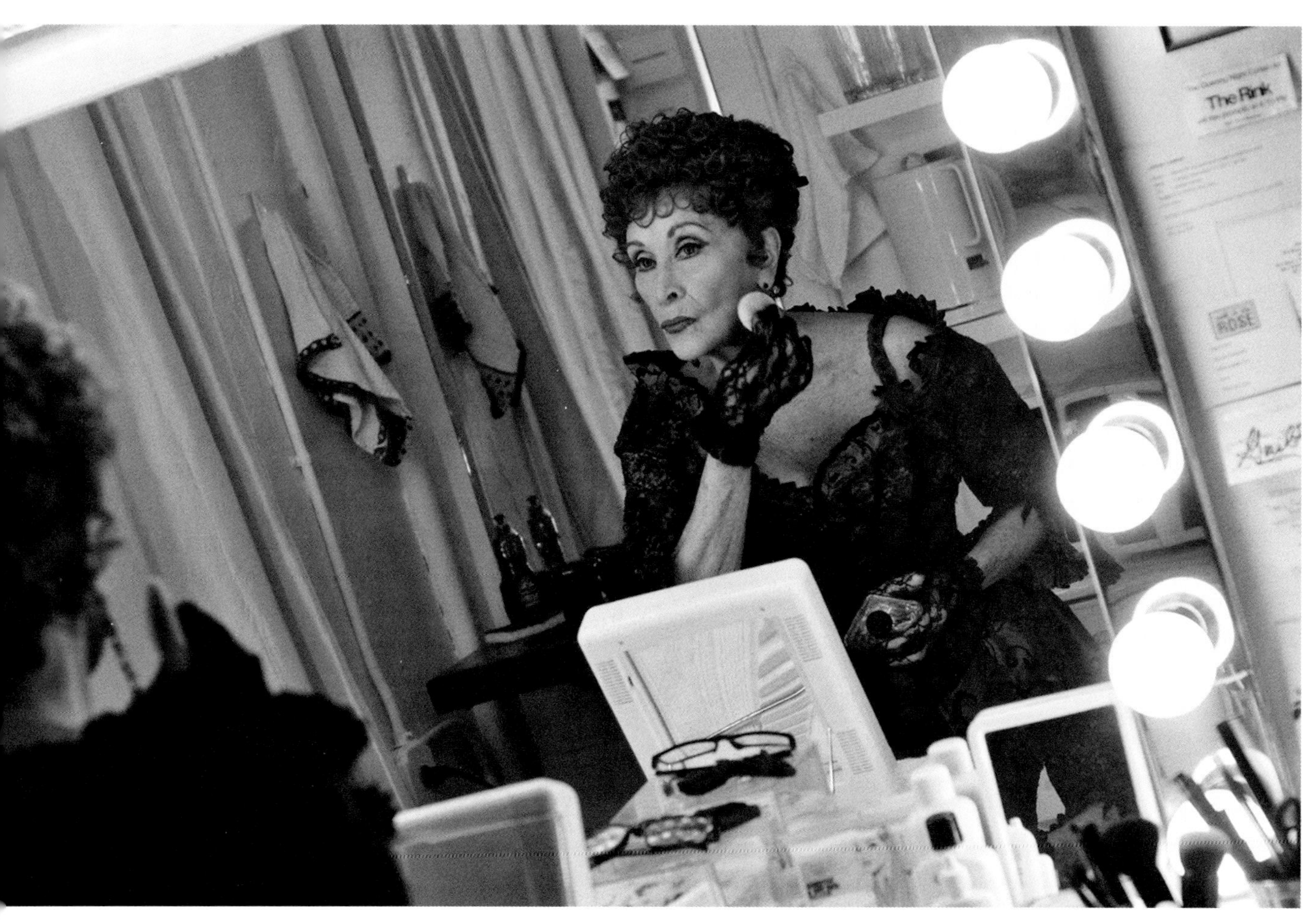

Chita Rivera
The Mystery of Edwin Drood
Studio 54
2012

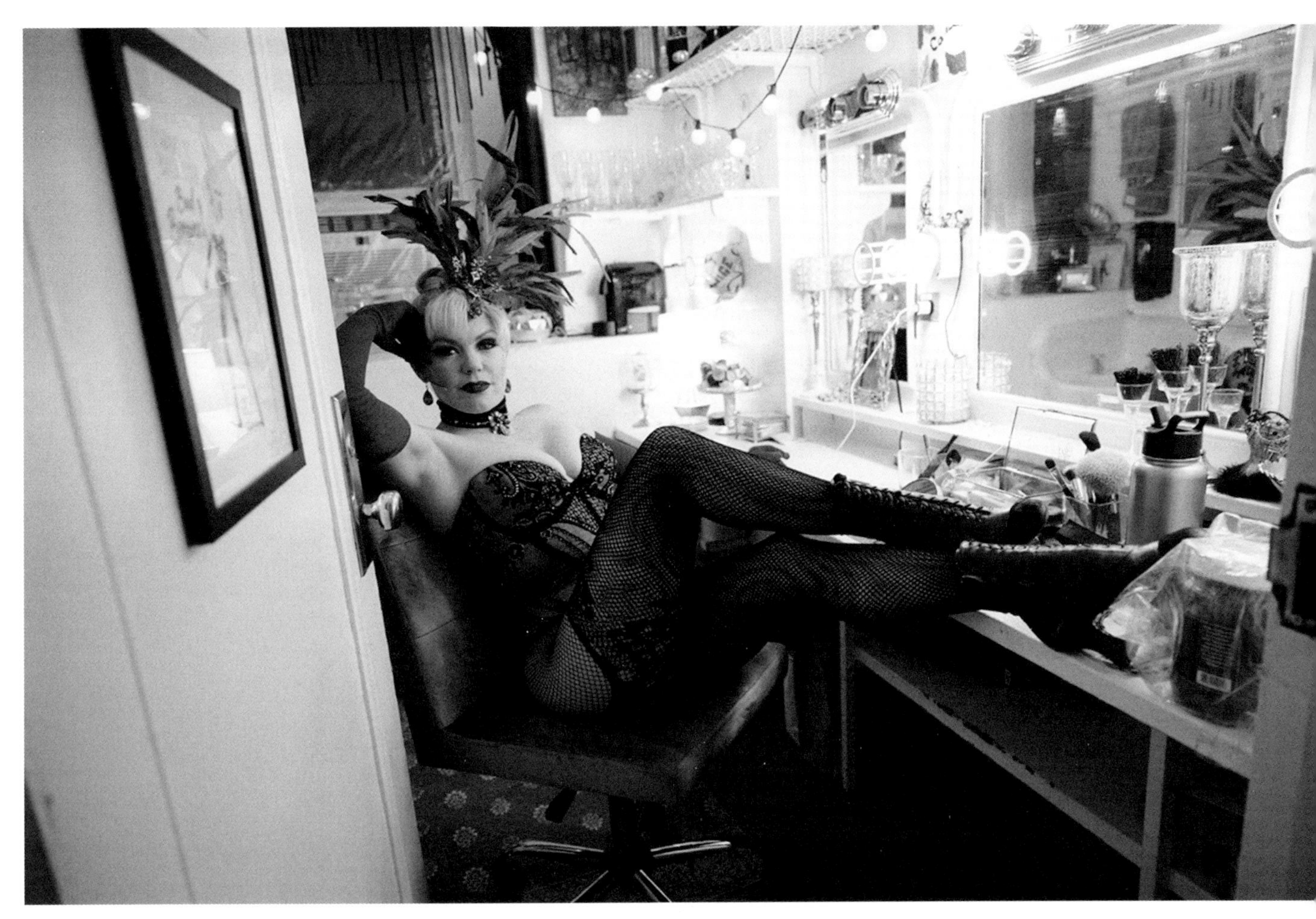

Robyn Hurder
Moulin Rouge!
Al Hirschfeld Theatre
2022

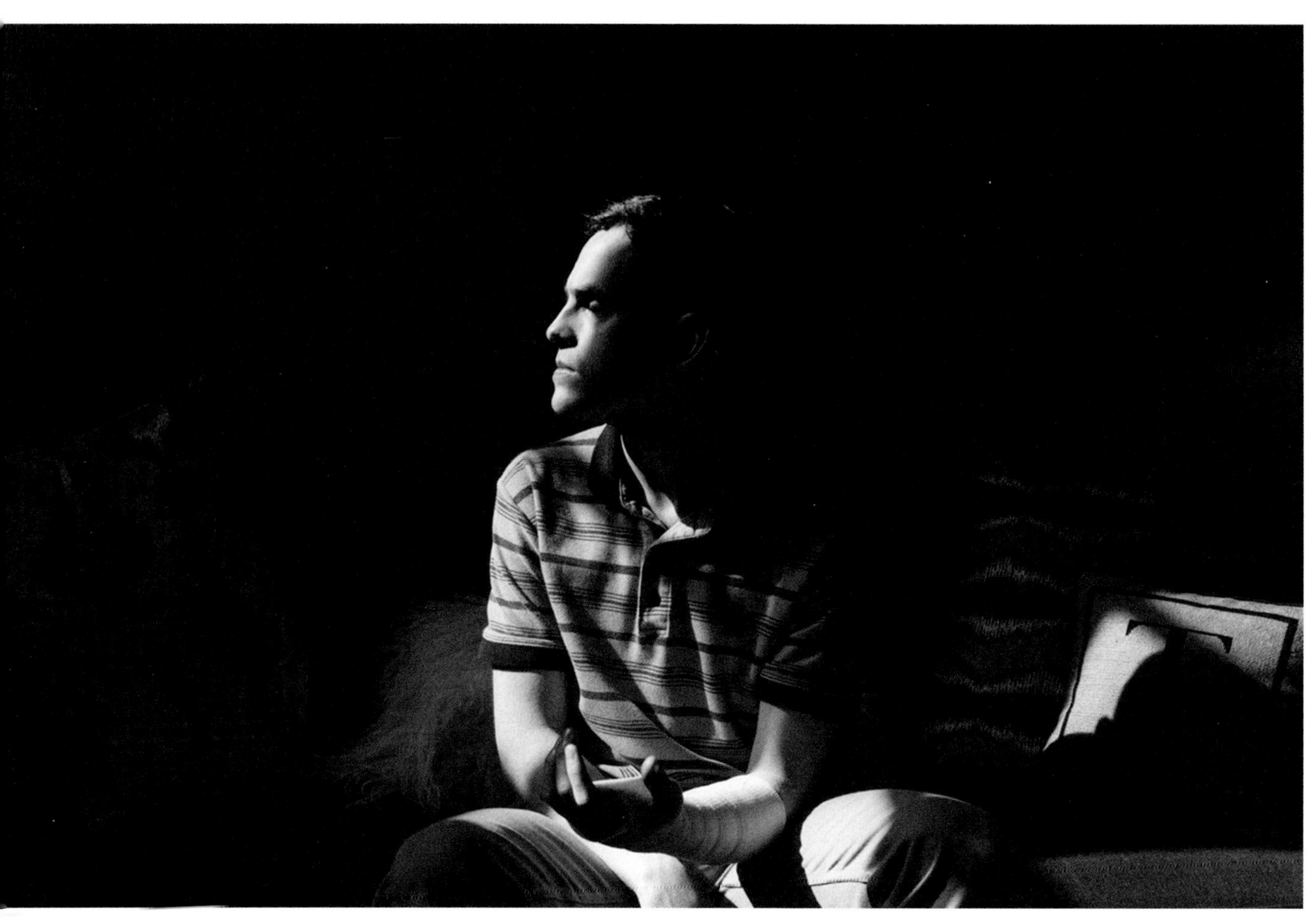

Taylor Trensch
Dear Evan Hansen
Music Box Theatre
2018

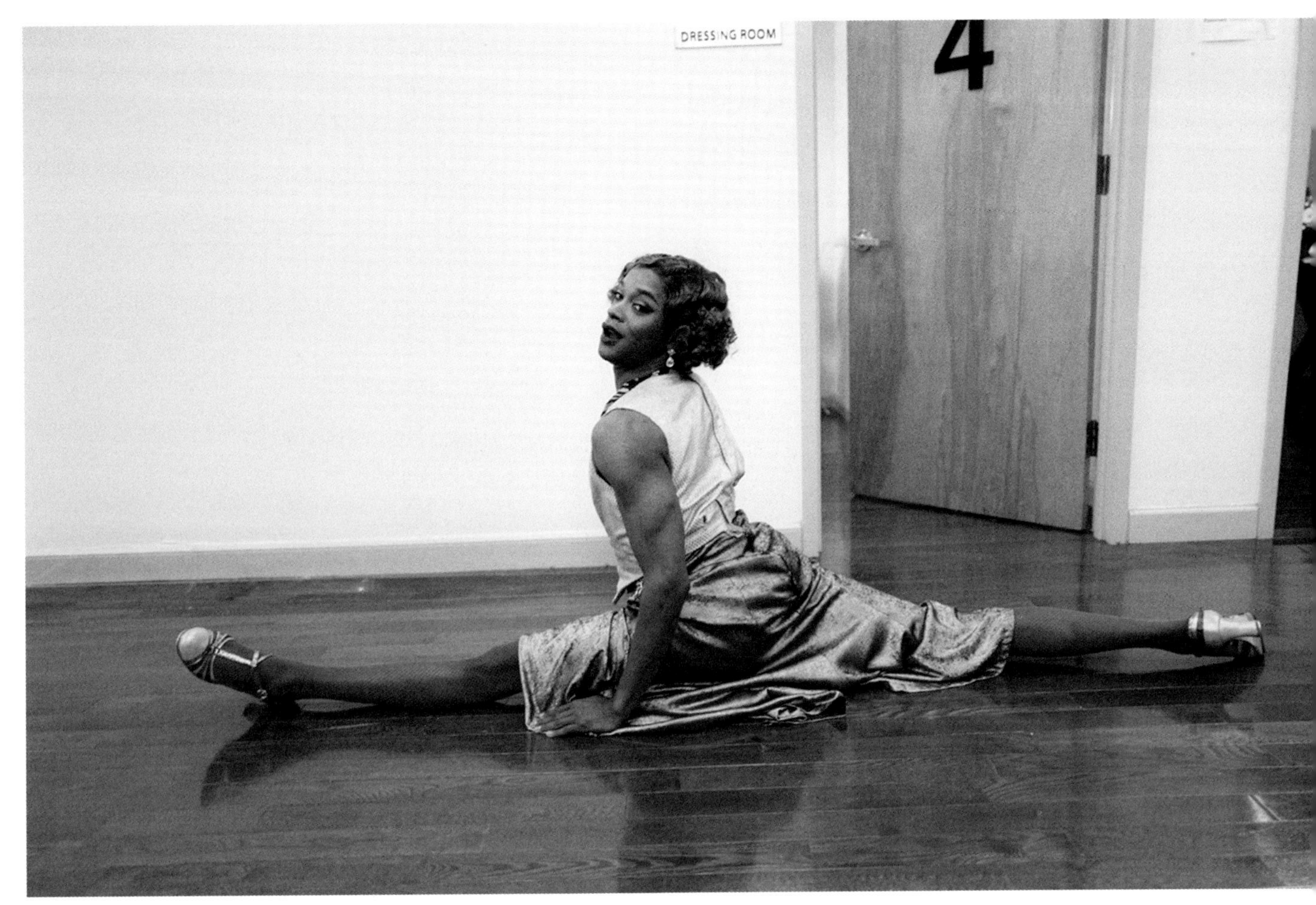

J. Harrison Ghee
Some Like it Hot
The 75th Annual Tony Awards
2023

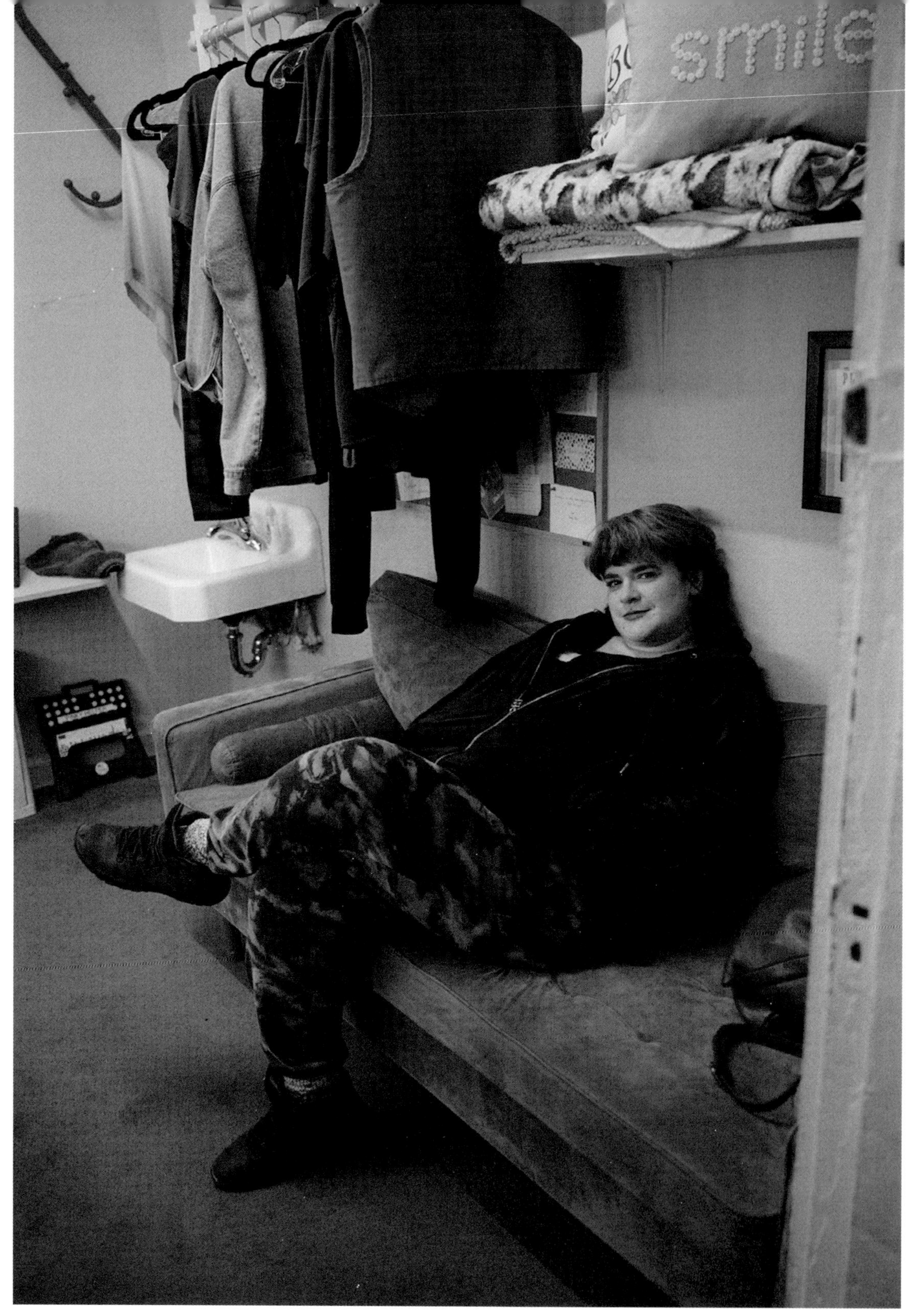

Bonnie Milligan
Kimberly Akimbo
Booth Theatre
2024

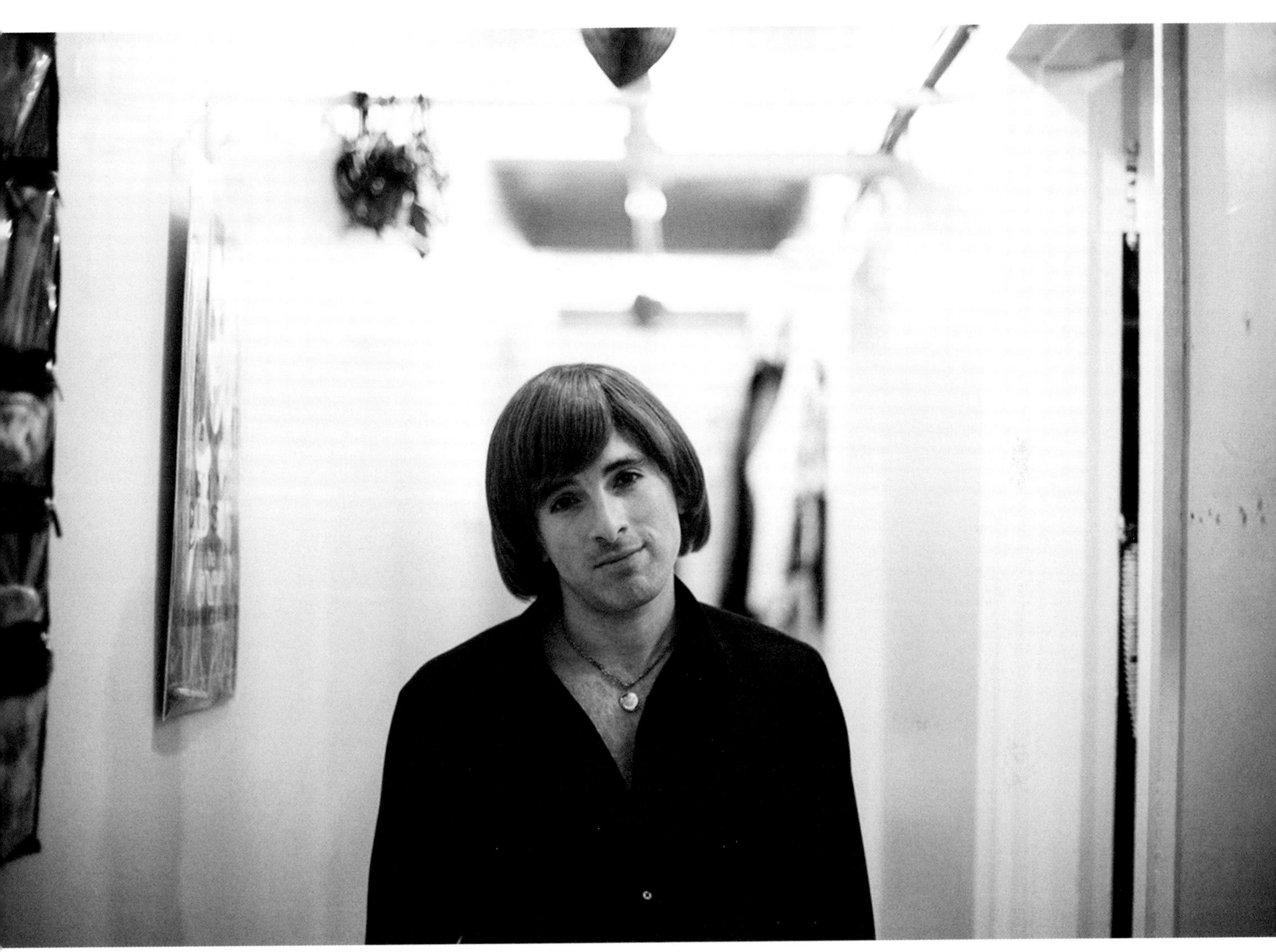

Jarrod Spector
The Cher Show
Neil Simon Theatre
2019

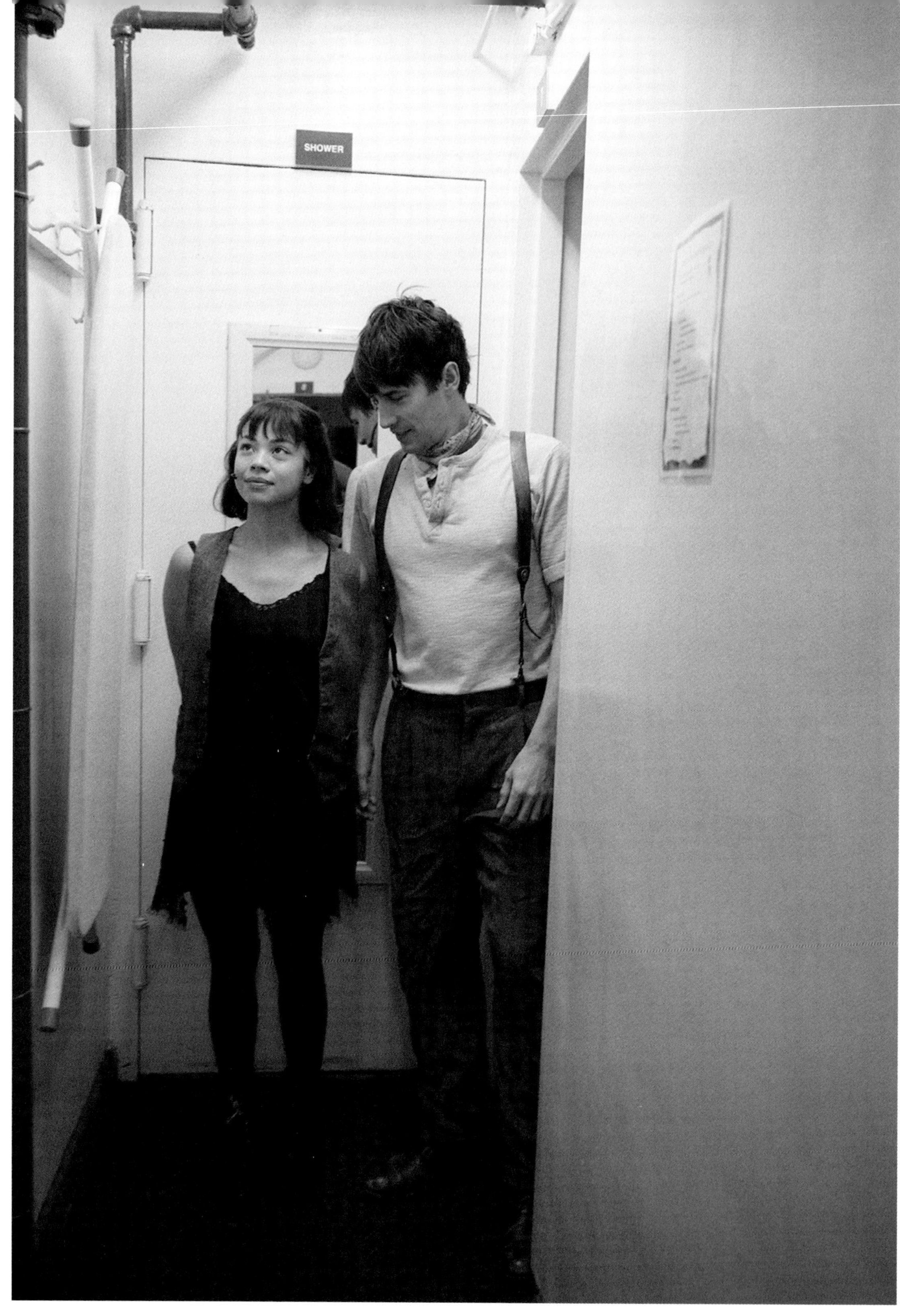

Eva Noblezada and Reeve Carney
Hadestown
Walter Kerr Theatre
2023

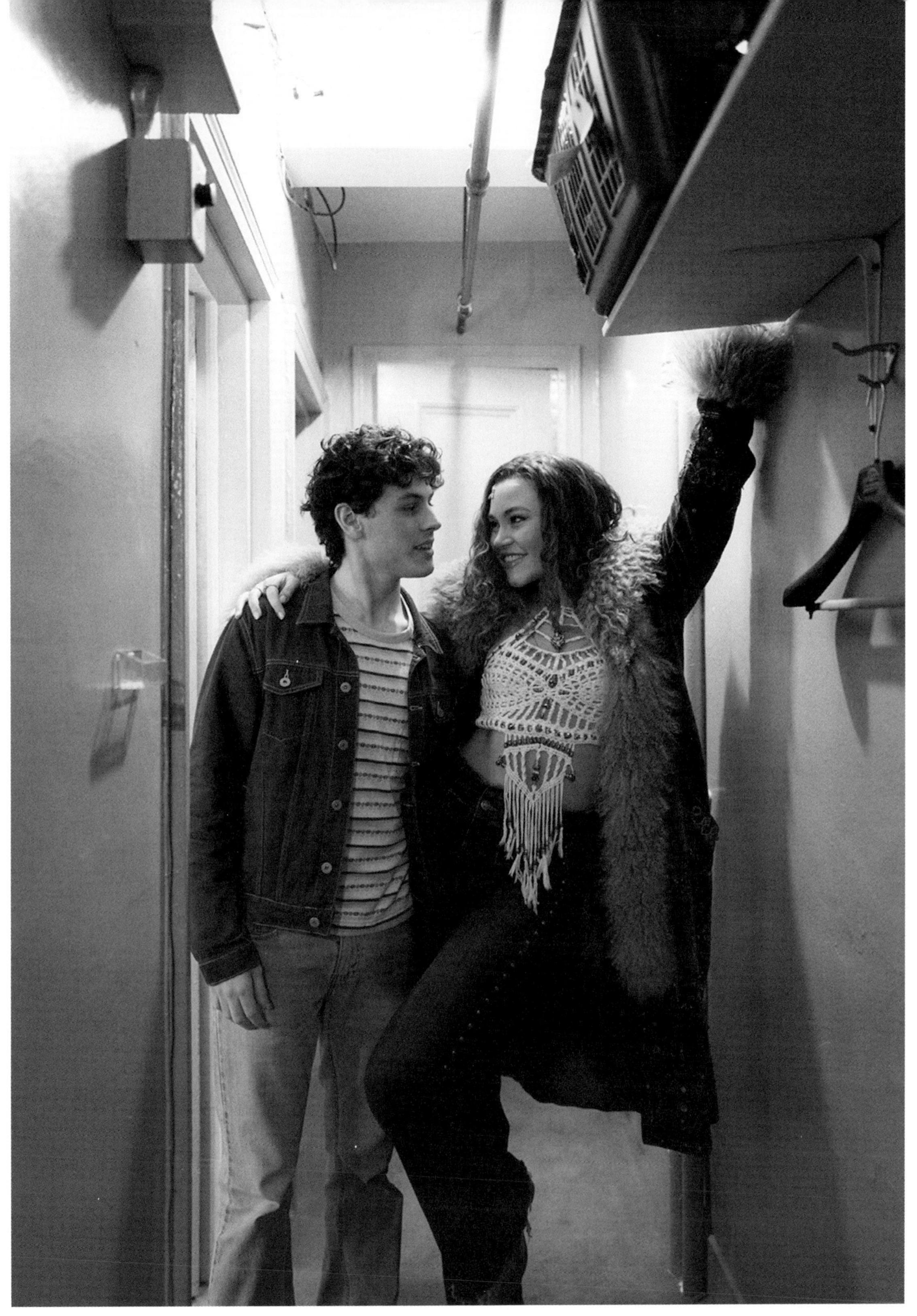

Casey Likes and Solea Pfeiffer
Almost Famous
Bernard B. Jacobs Theatre
2022

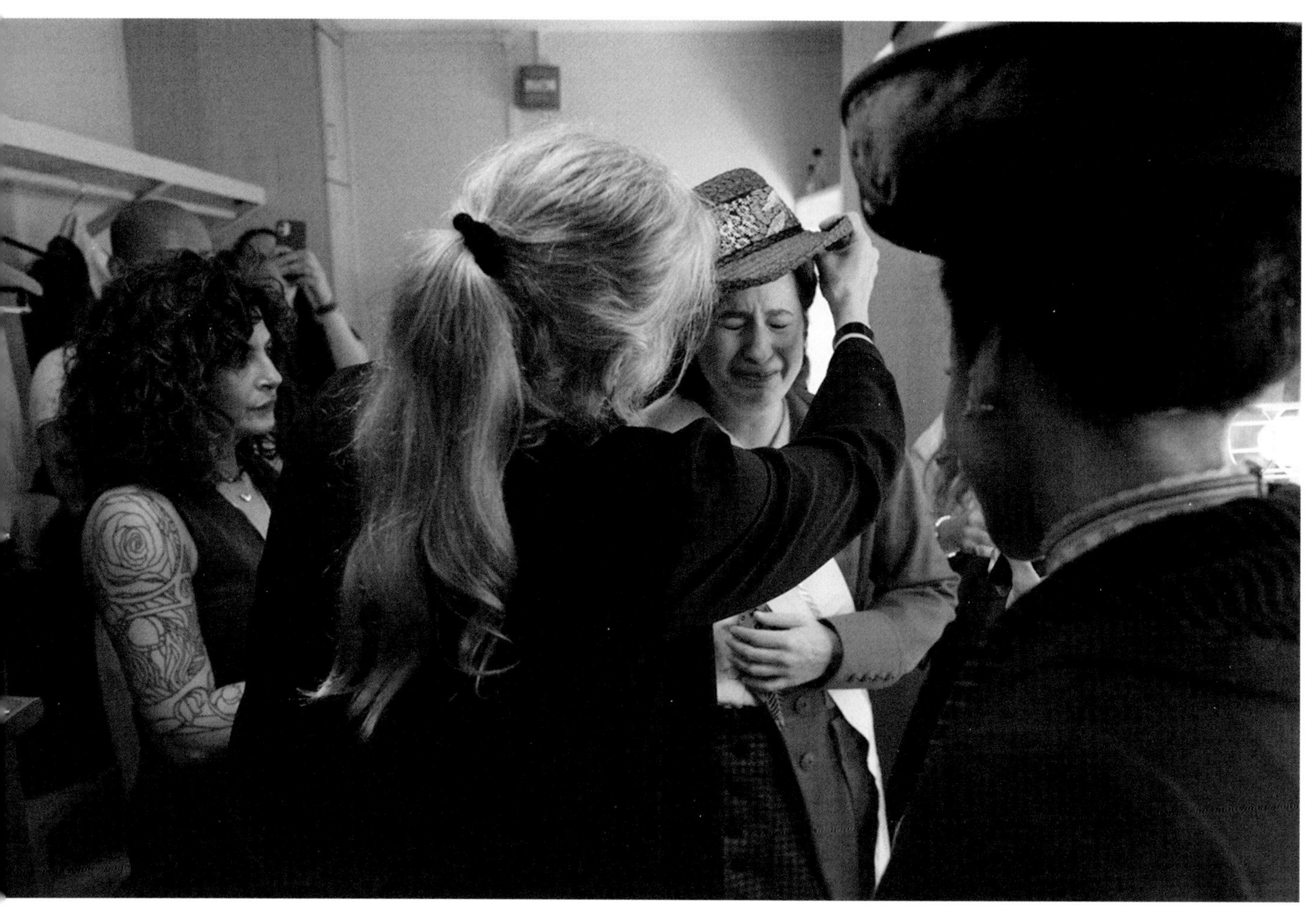

Shaina Taub
SUFFS
The 77th Annual Tony Awards
2024

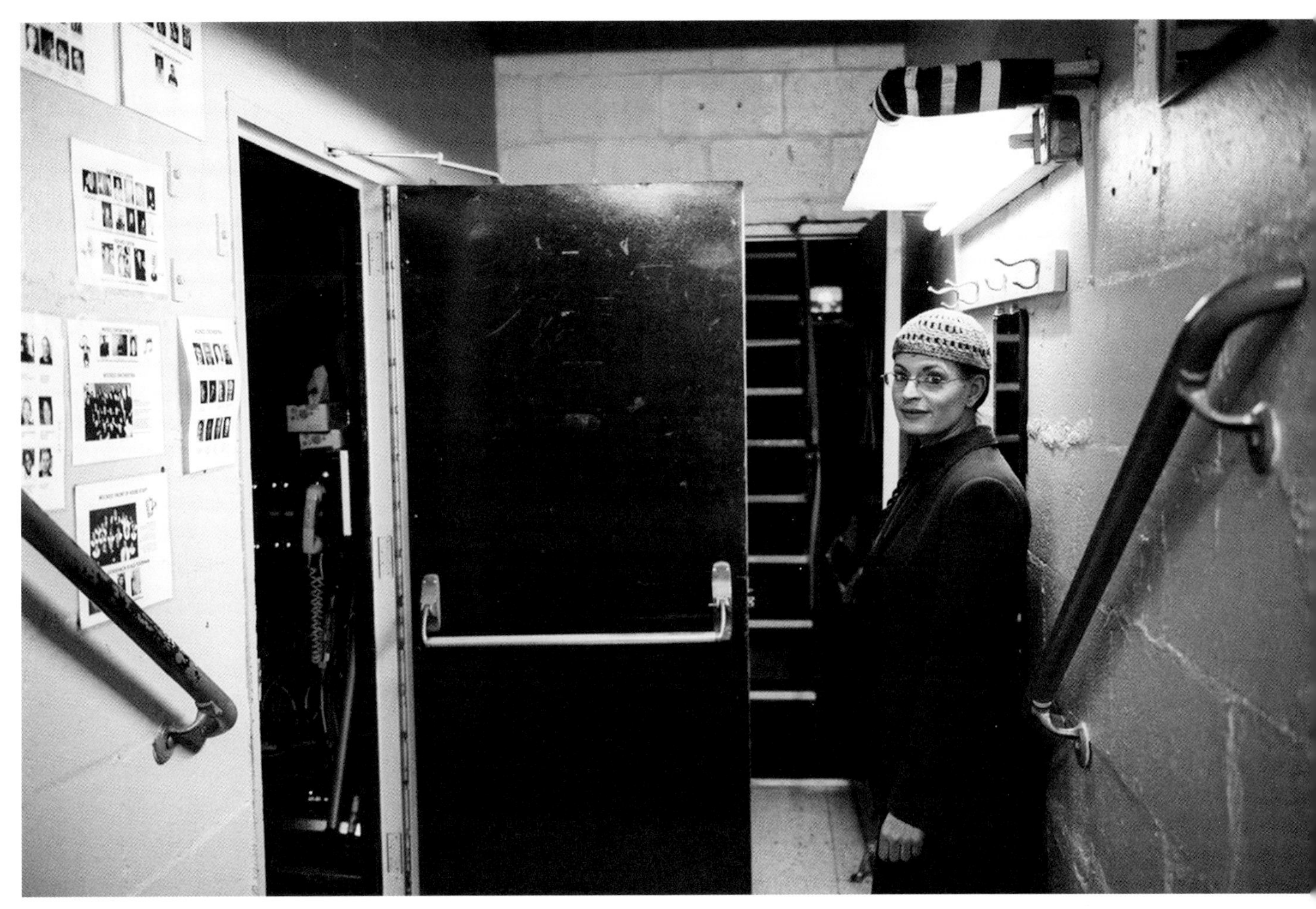

Jackie Burns
Wicked
Gershwin Theatre
2017

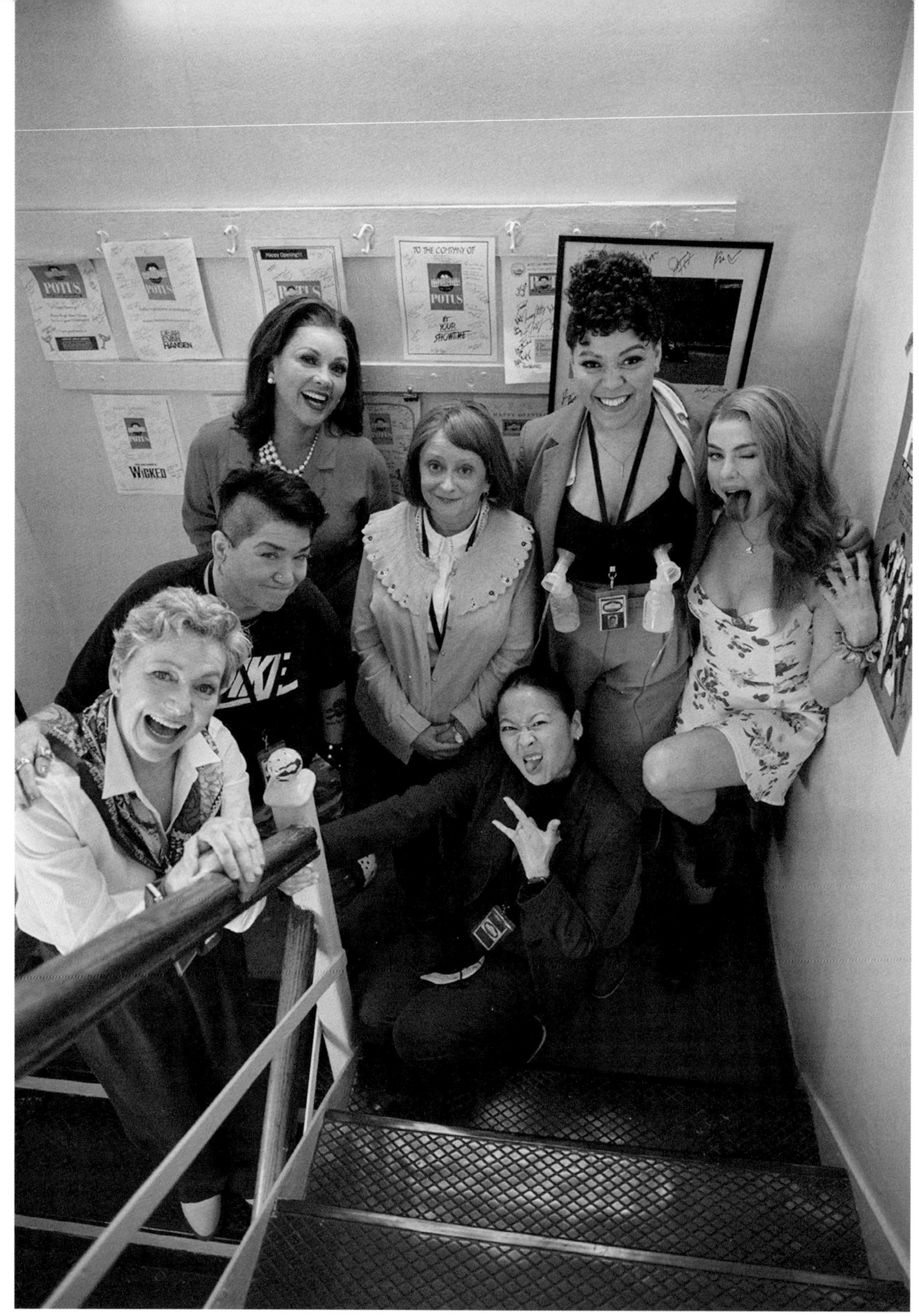

Julie White, Lea DeLaria, Vanessa Williams, Rachel Dratch, Suzy Nakamura, Lilli Cooper, and Julianne Hough
POTUS: Or, Behind Every Great Dumbass Are Seven Women Trying to Keep Him Alive
Shubert Theatre
2022

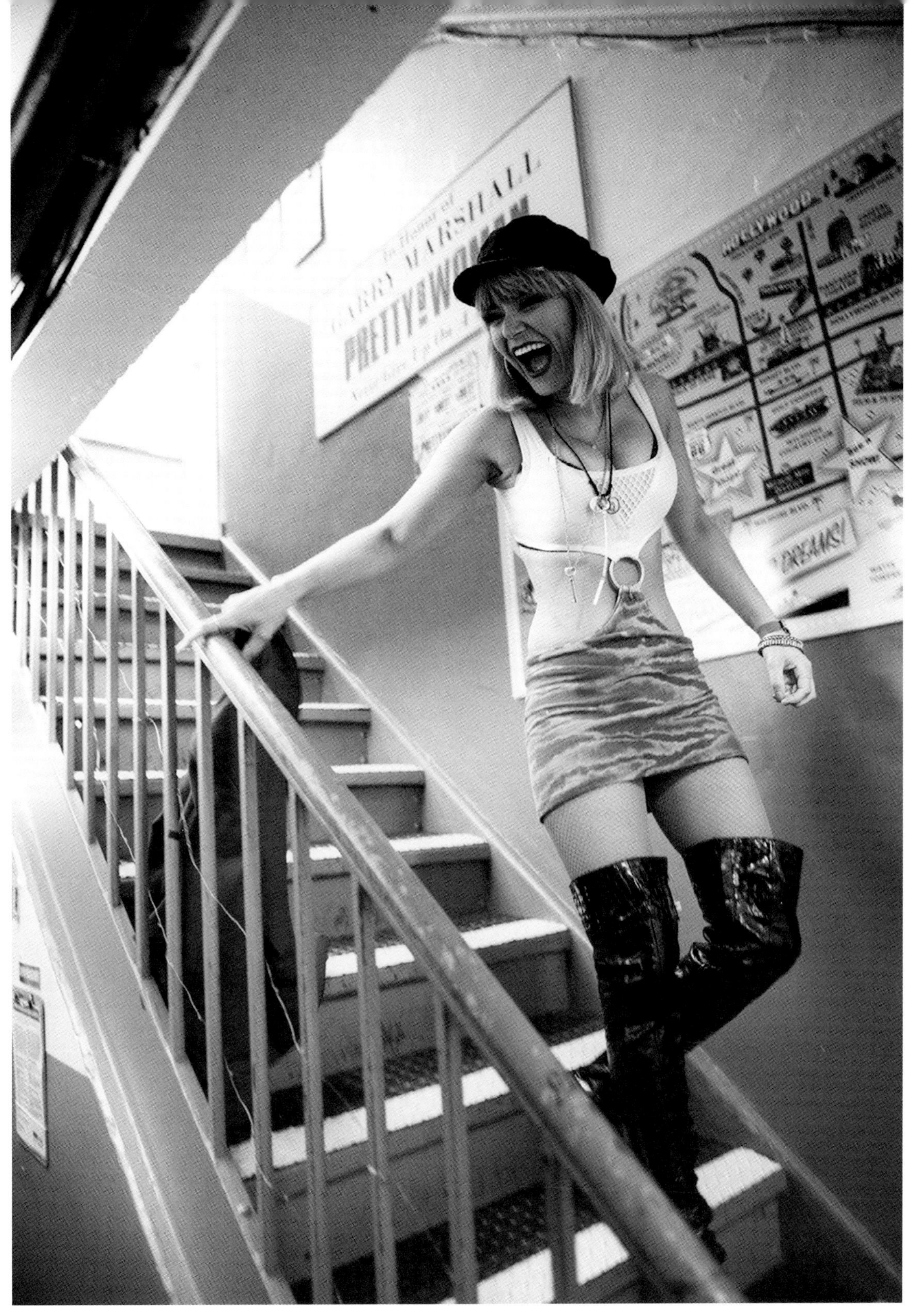

Samantha Barks
Pretty Woman
Nederlander Theatre
2018

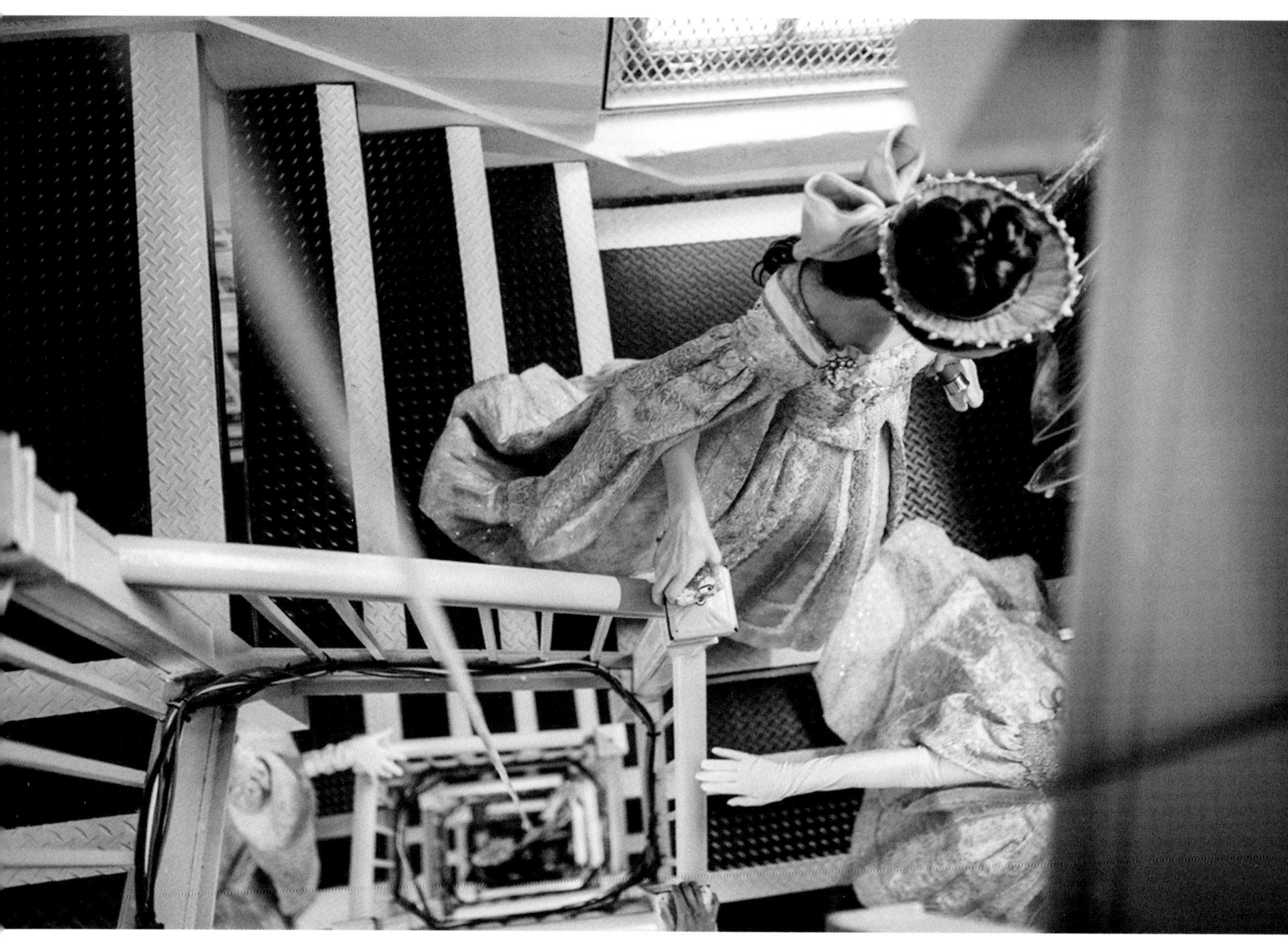

Anastasia
Broadhurst Theatre
2018

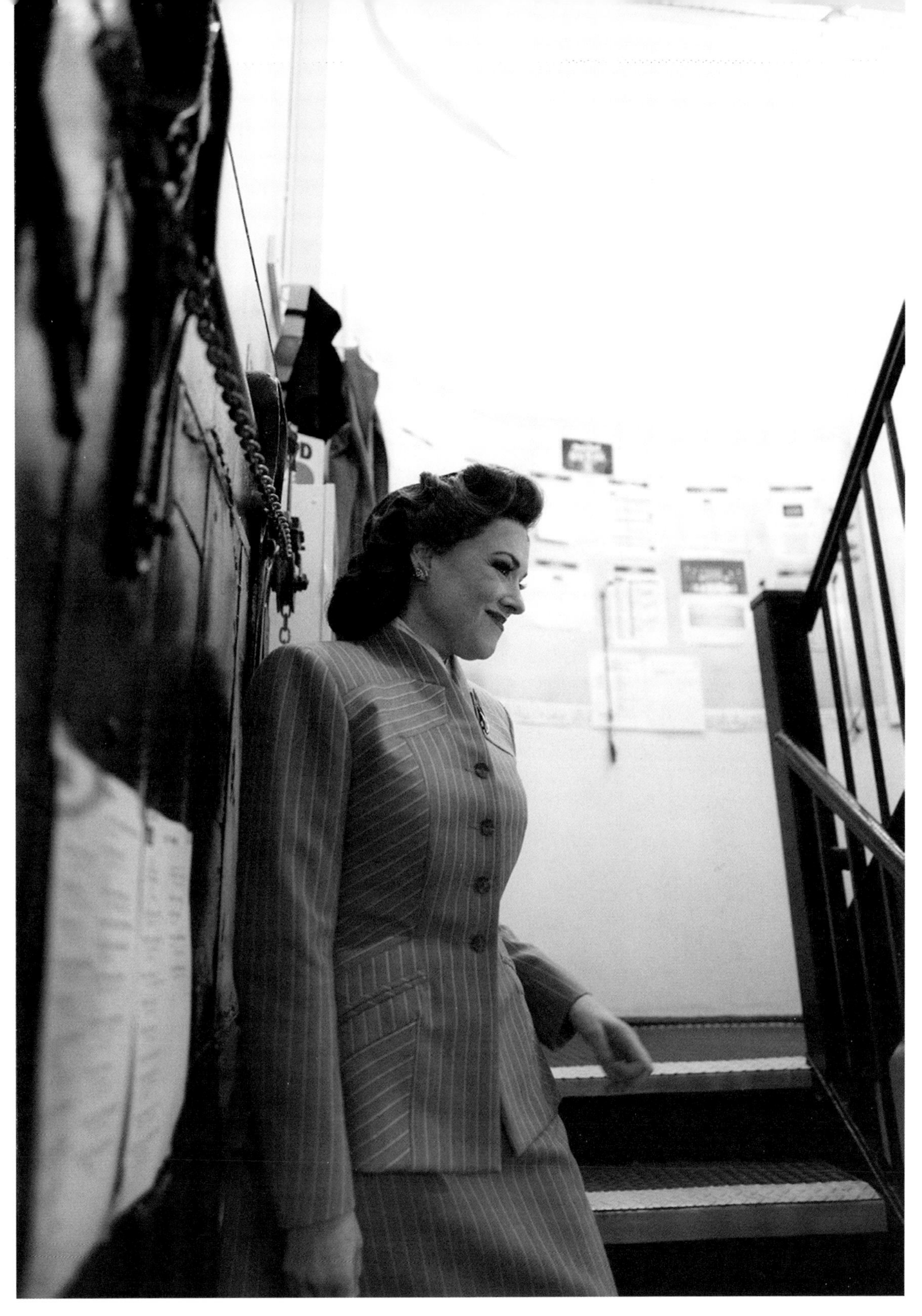

Emily Skinner
New York, New York
St. James Theatre
2023

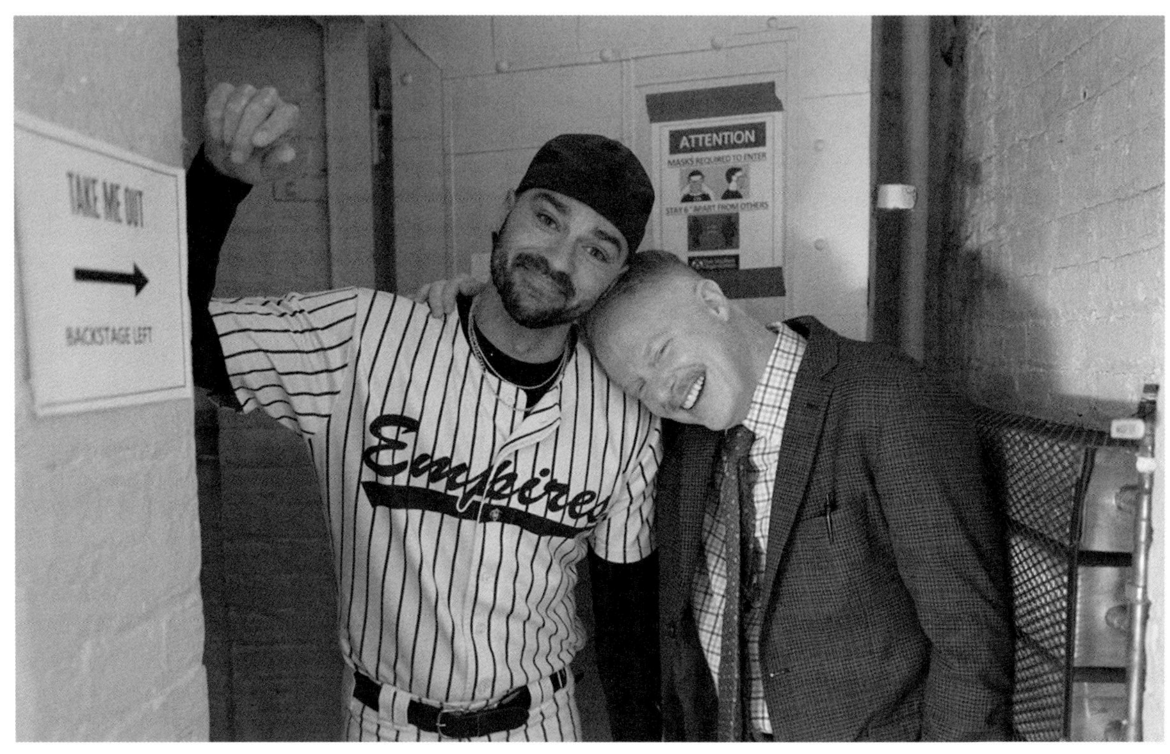

Jesse Williams and Jesse Tyler Ferguson
Take Me Out
The Hayes Theater
2022

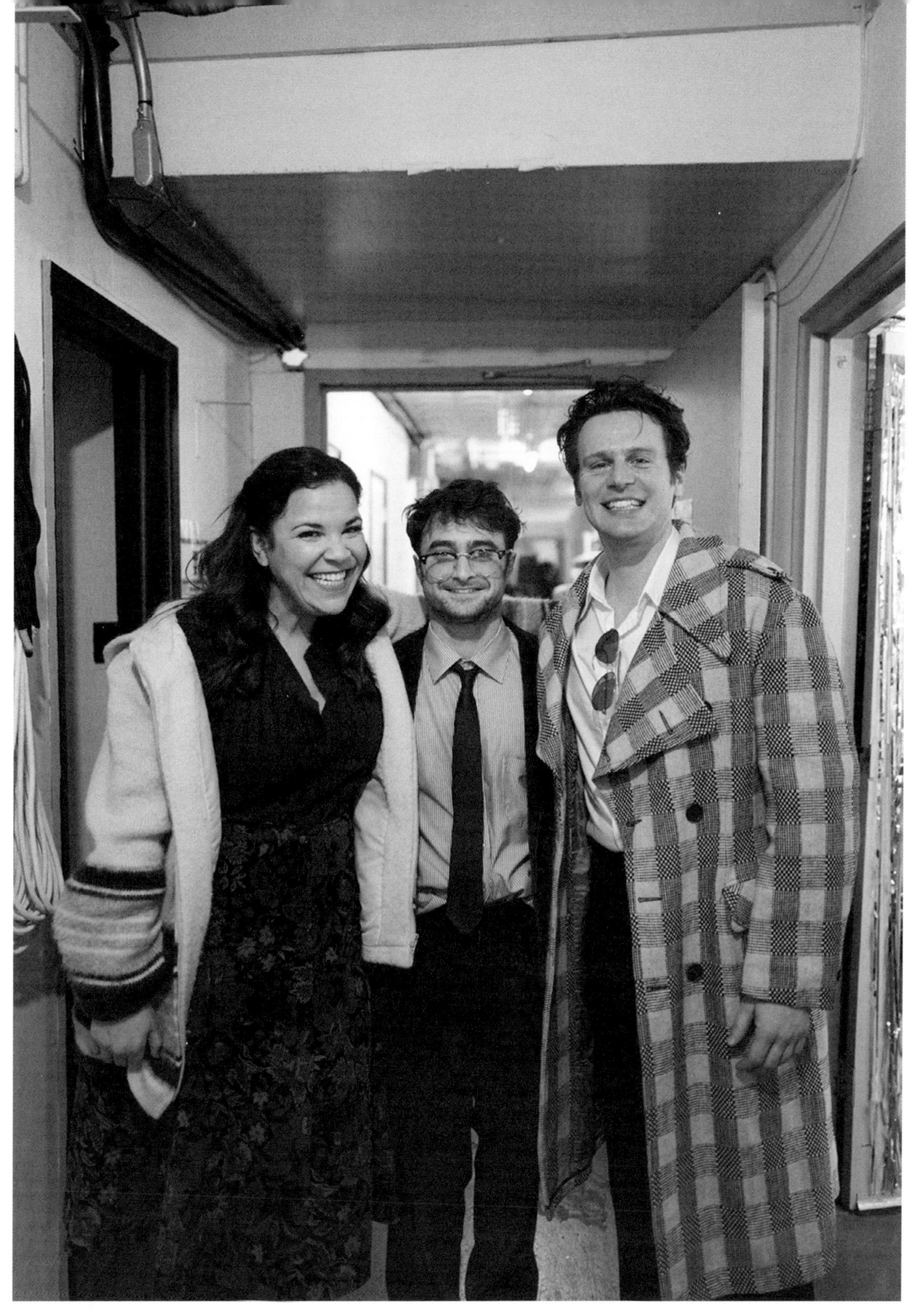

Lindsay Mendez, Daniel Radcliffe, and Jonathan Groff
Merrily We Roll Along
New York Theatre Workshop
2023

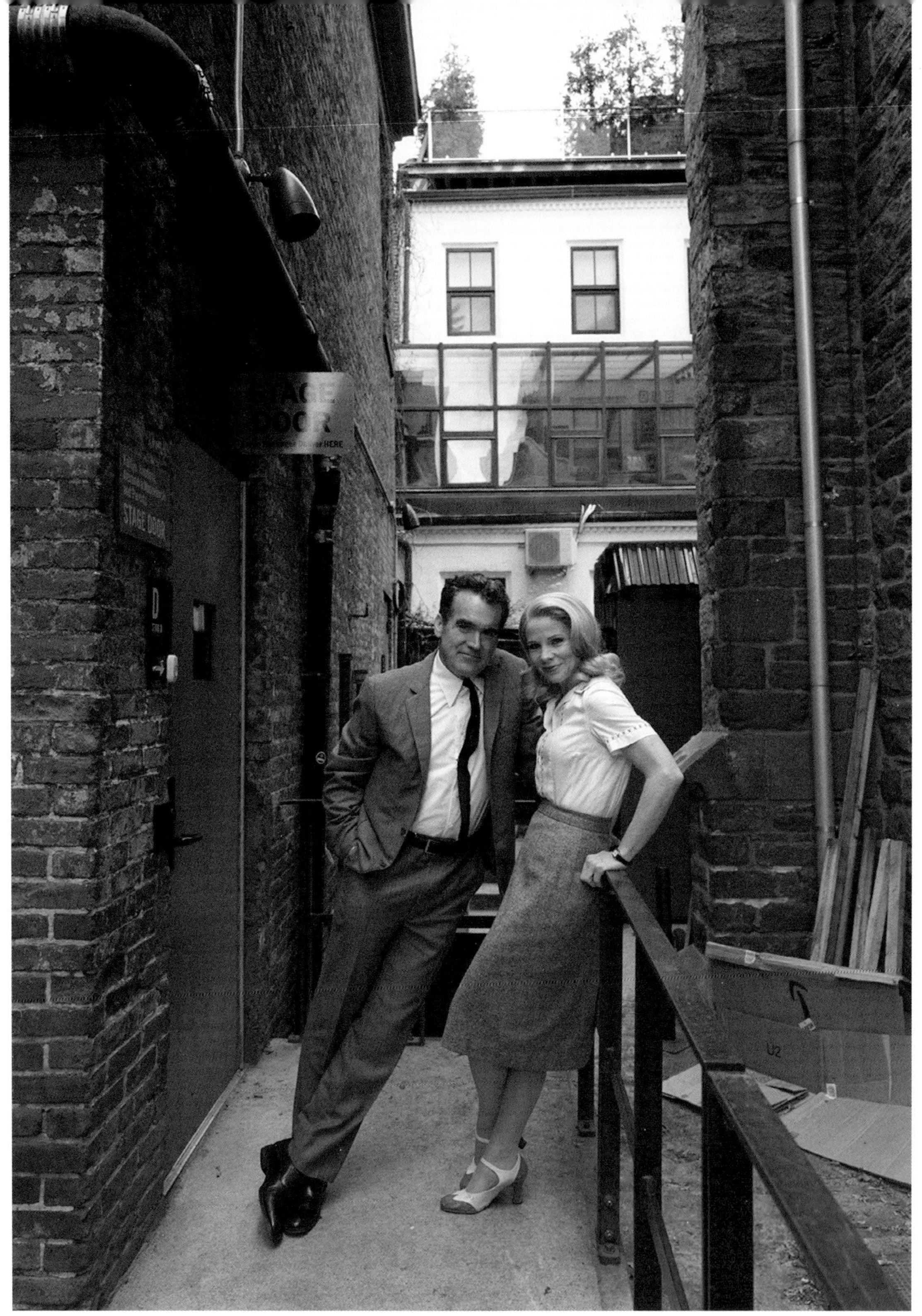

Brian d'Arcy James and Kelli O'Hara
Days of Wine and Roses
Atlantic Theater Company
2023

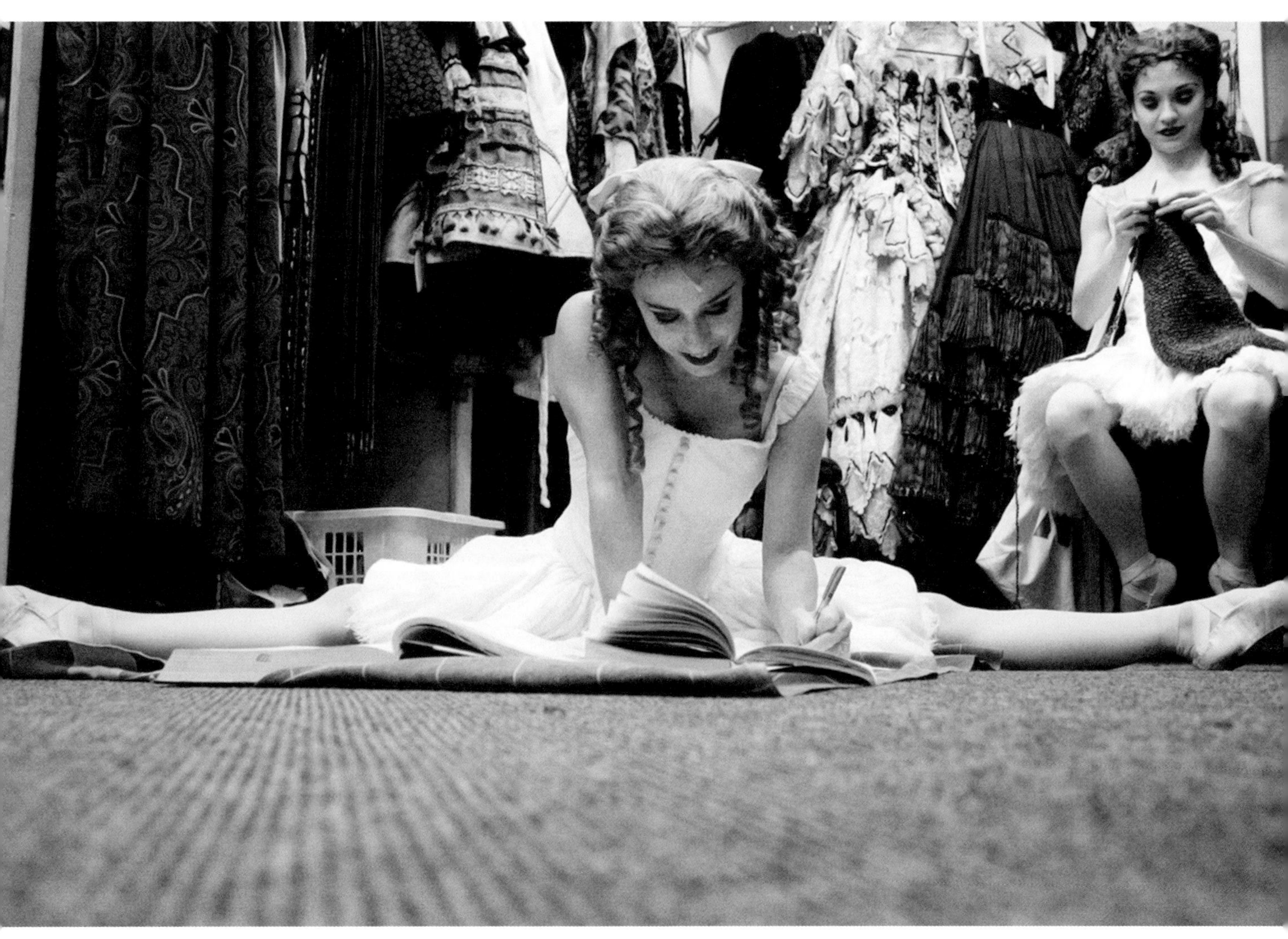

Heather McFadden and Kara Klein
The Phantom of the Opera
Majestic Theatre
2010

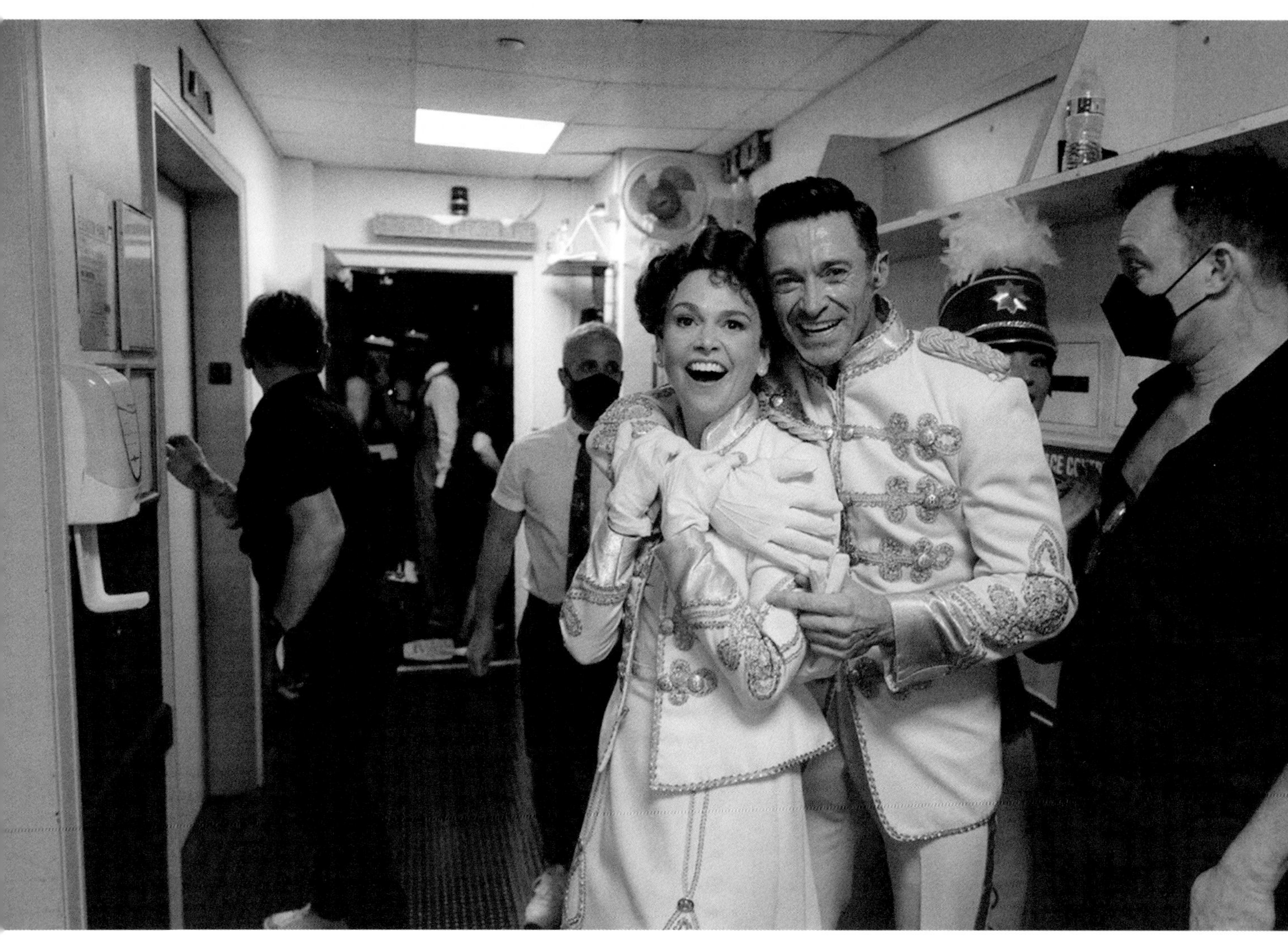

Sutton Foster and Hugh Jackman
The Music Man
The 75th Annual Tony Awards
2022

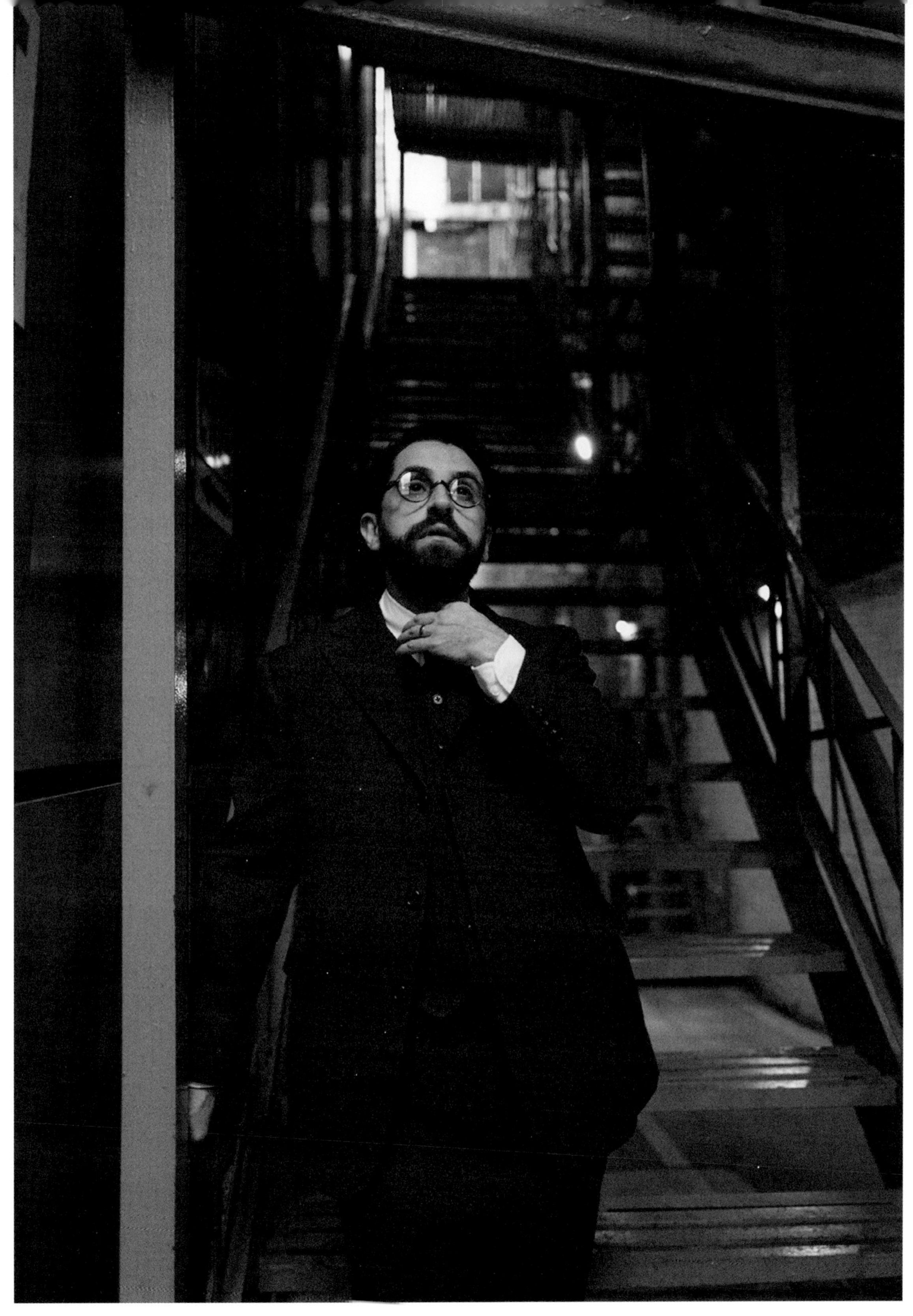

Brandon Uranowitz
Leopoldstadt
Longacre Theatre
2022

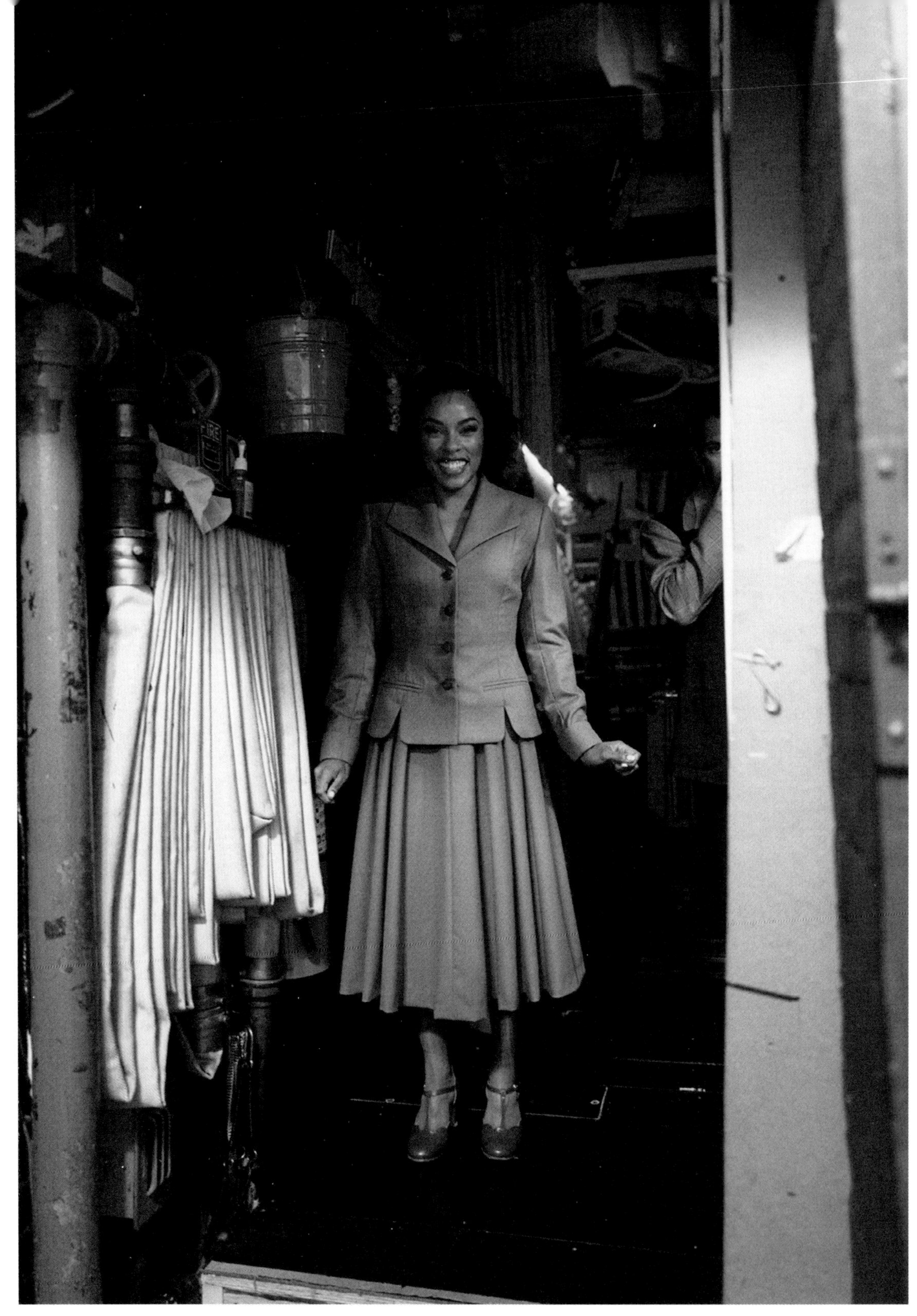

Anna Uzele
New York, New York
St. James Theatre
2023

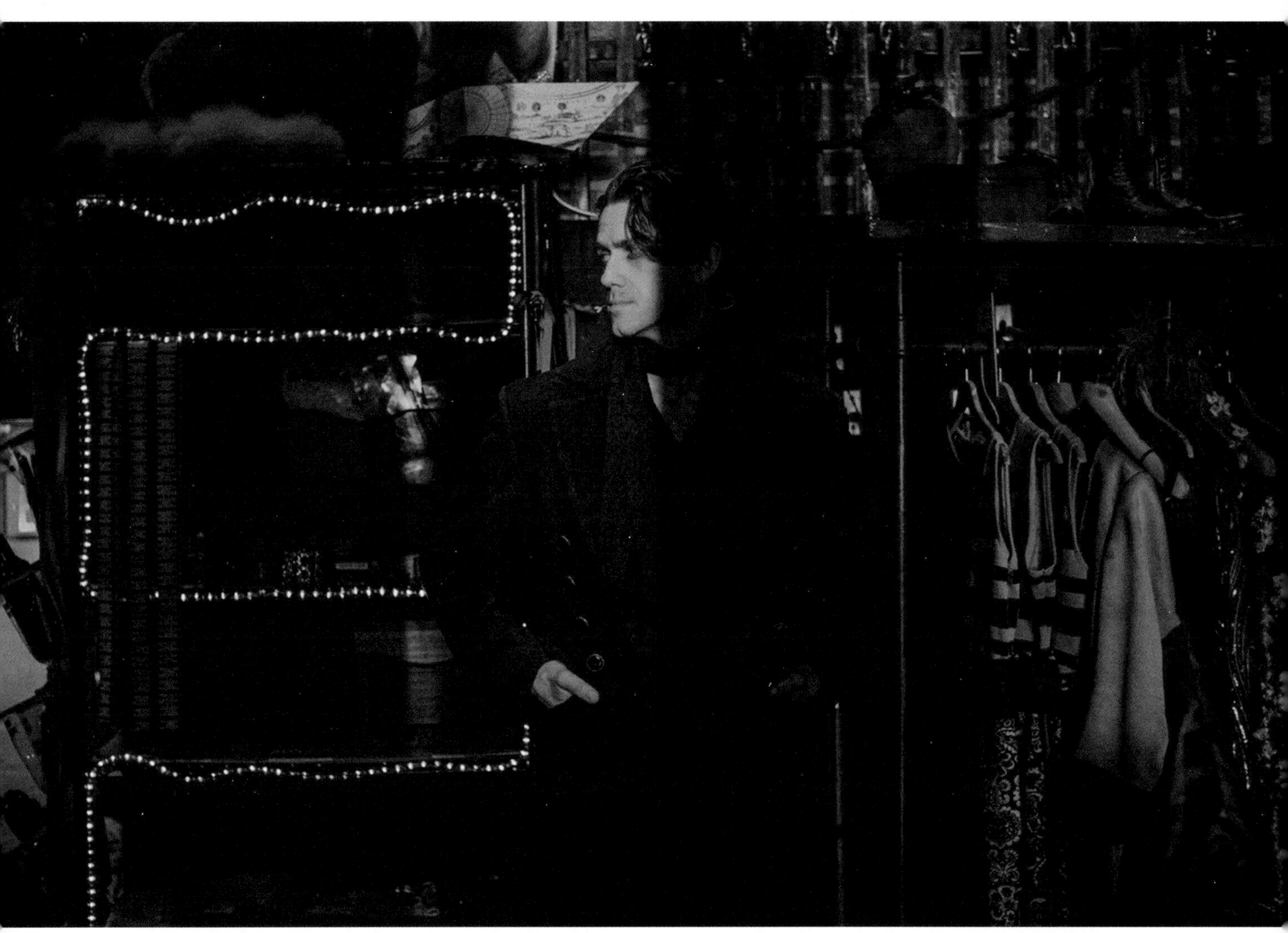

Aaron Tveit
Moulin Rouge!
Al Hirschfeld Theatre
2020

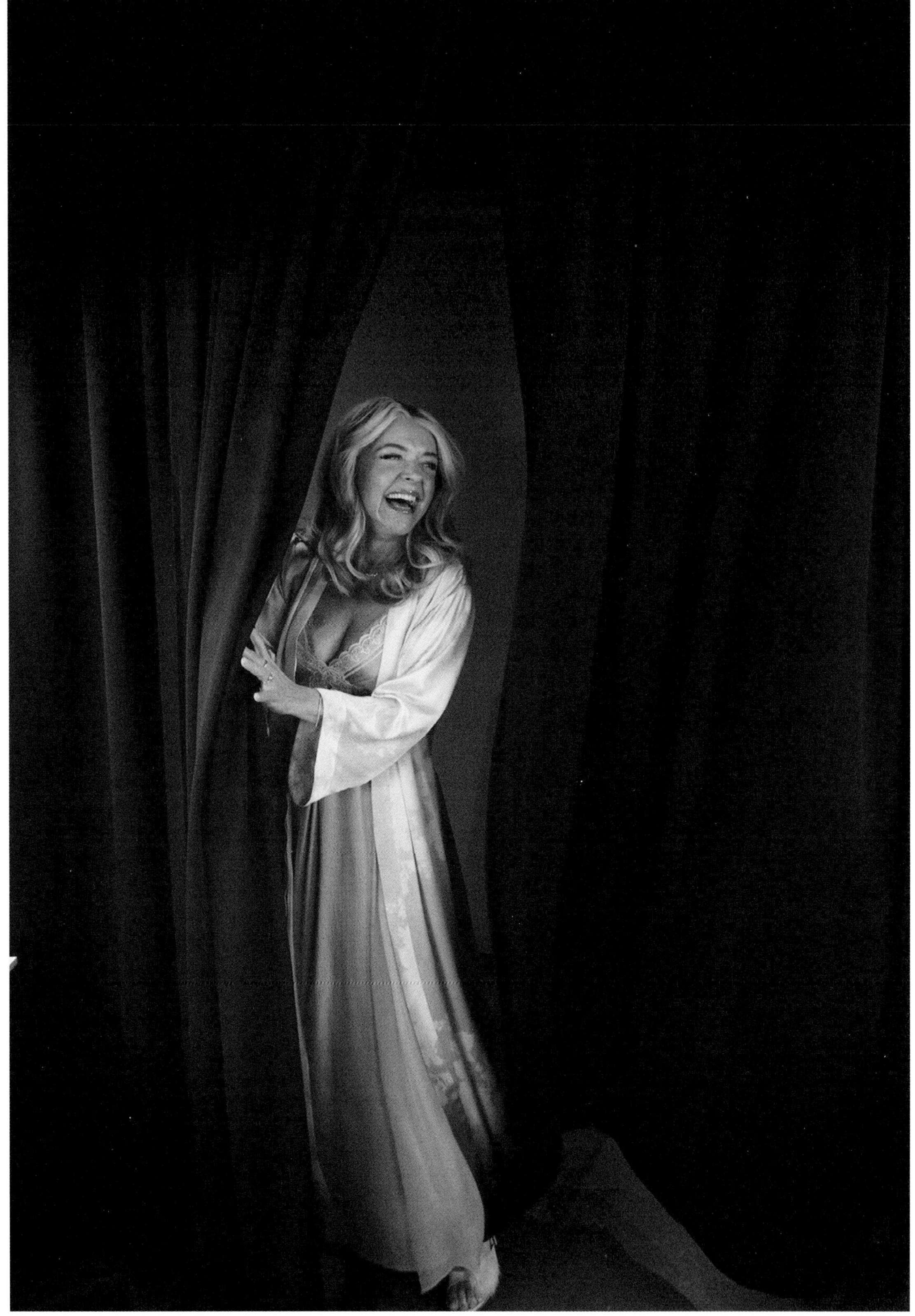

Rachel Bay Jones
Here We Are
The Shed
2023

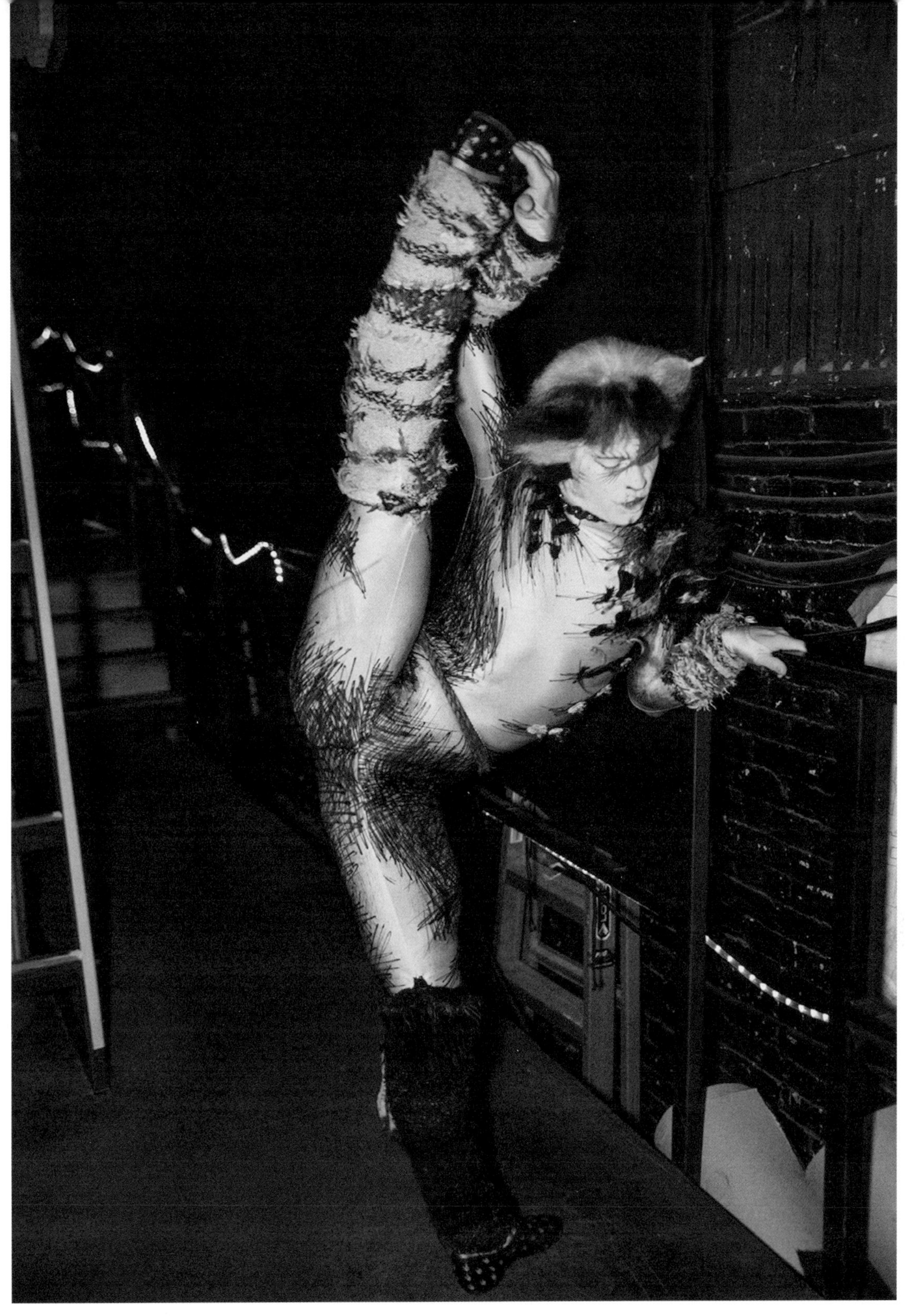

Jakob Karr
Cats
Neil Simon Theatre
2016

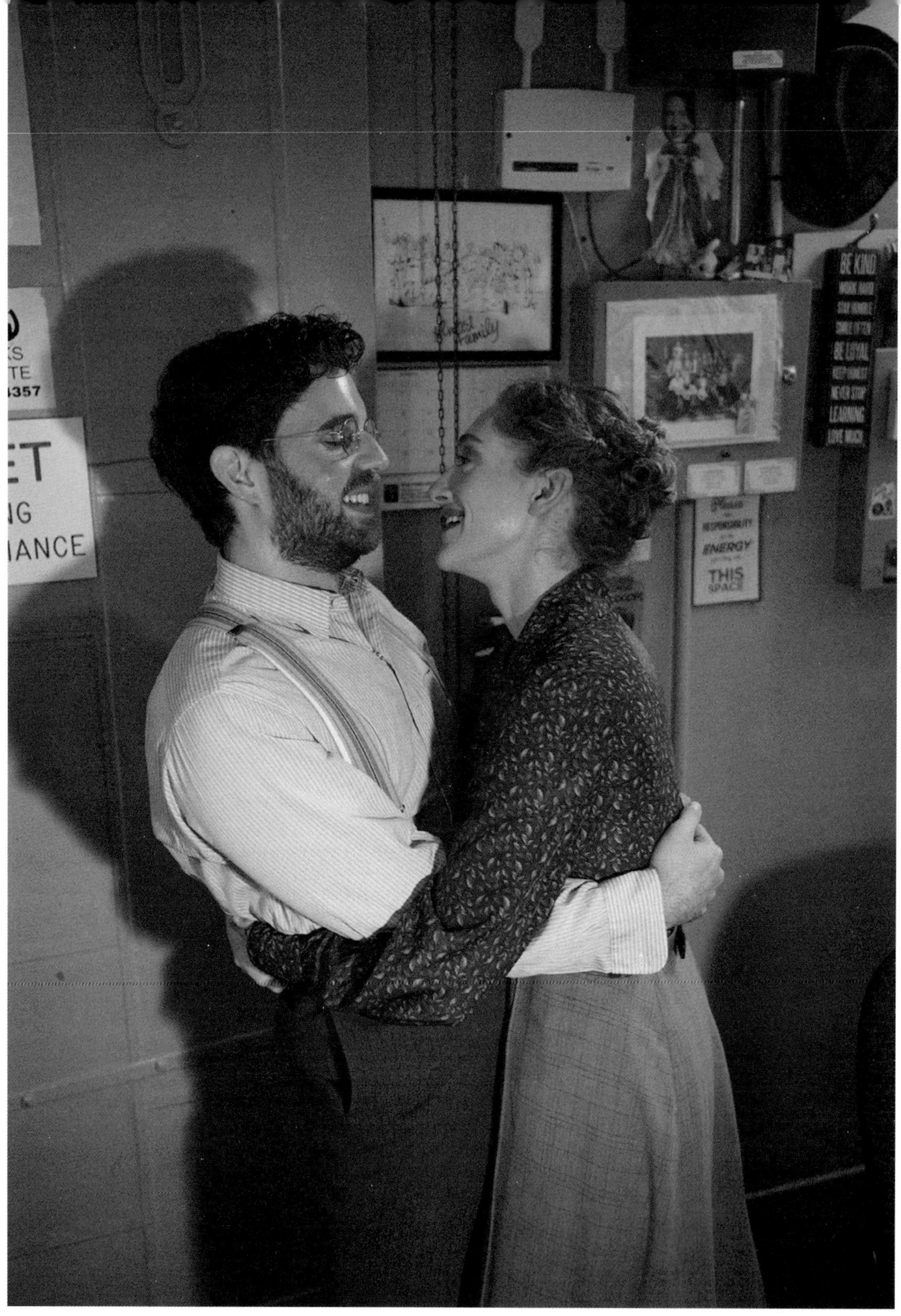

Ben Platt and Micaela Diamond
Parade
Bernard B. Jacobs Theatre
2023

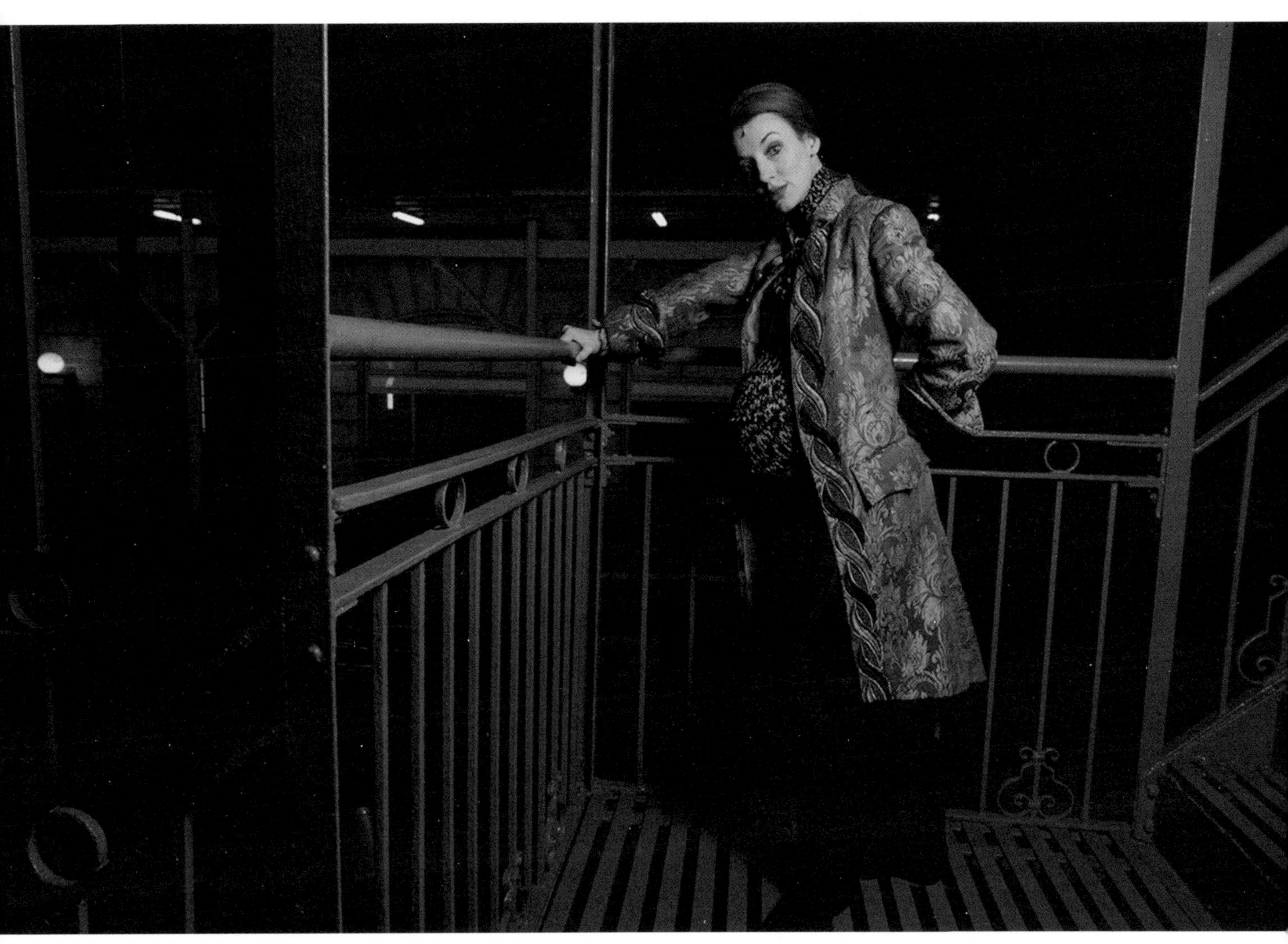

Elizabeth Davis
1776
American Airlines Theatre (now Todd Haimes Theatre)
2022

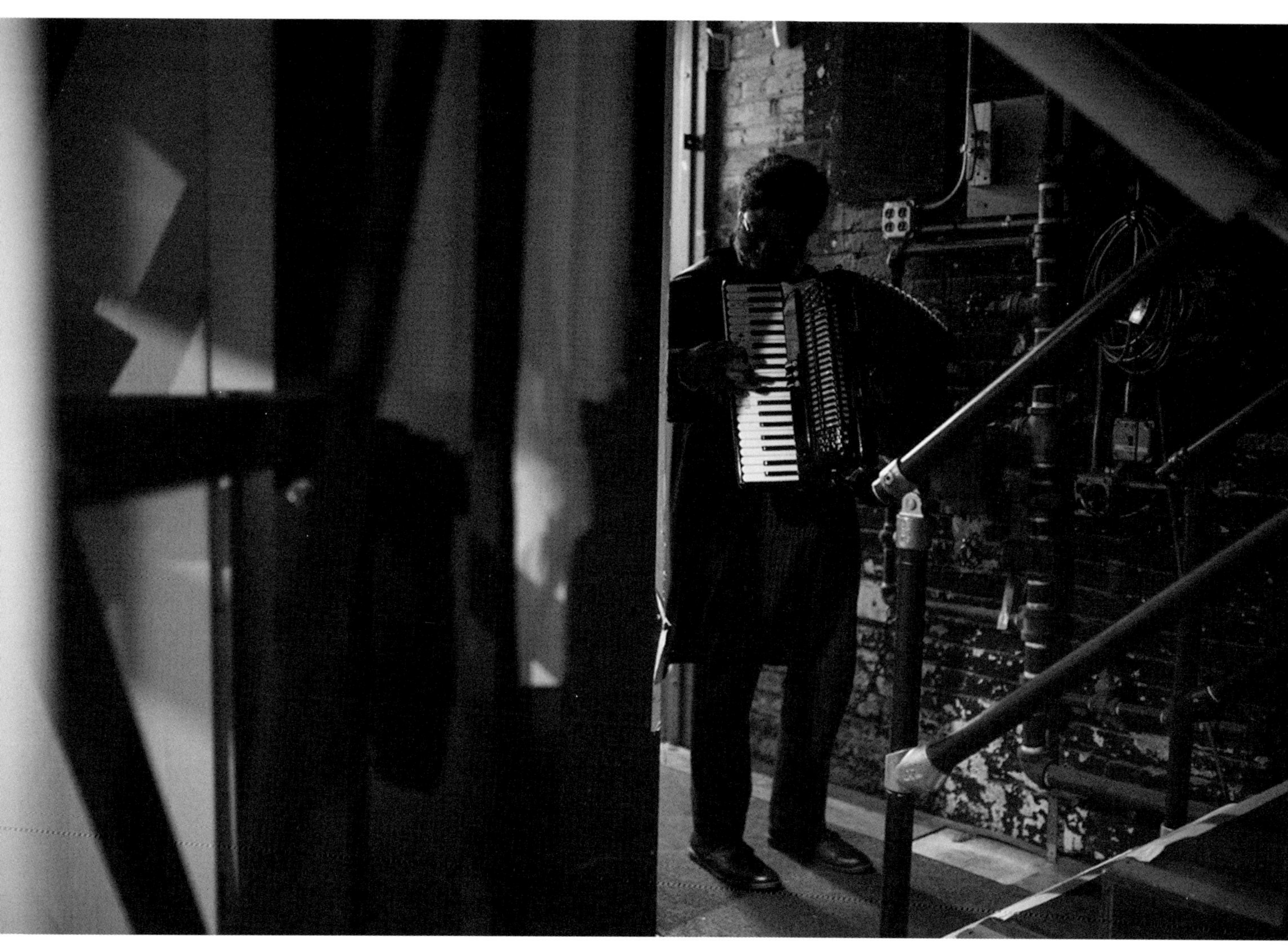

Okieriete Onaodowan
Natasha, Pierre & The Great Comet of 1812
Imperial Theatre
2017

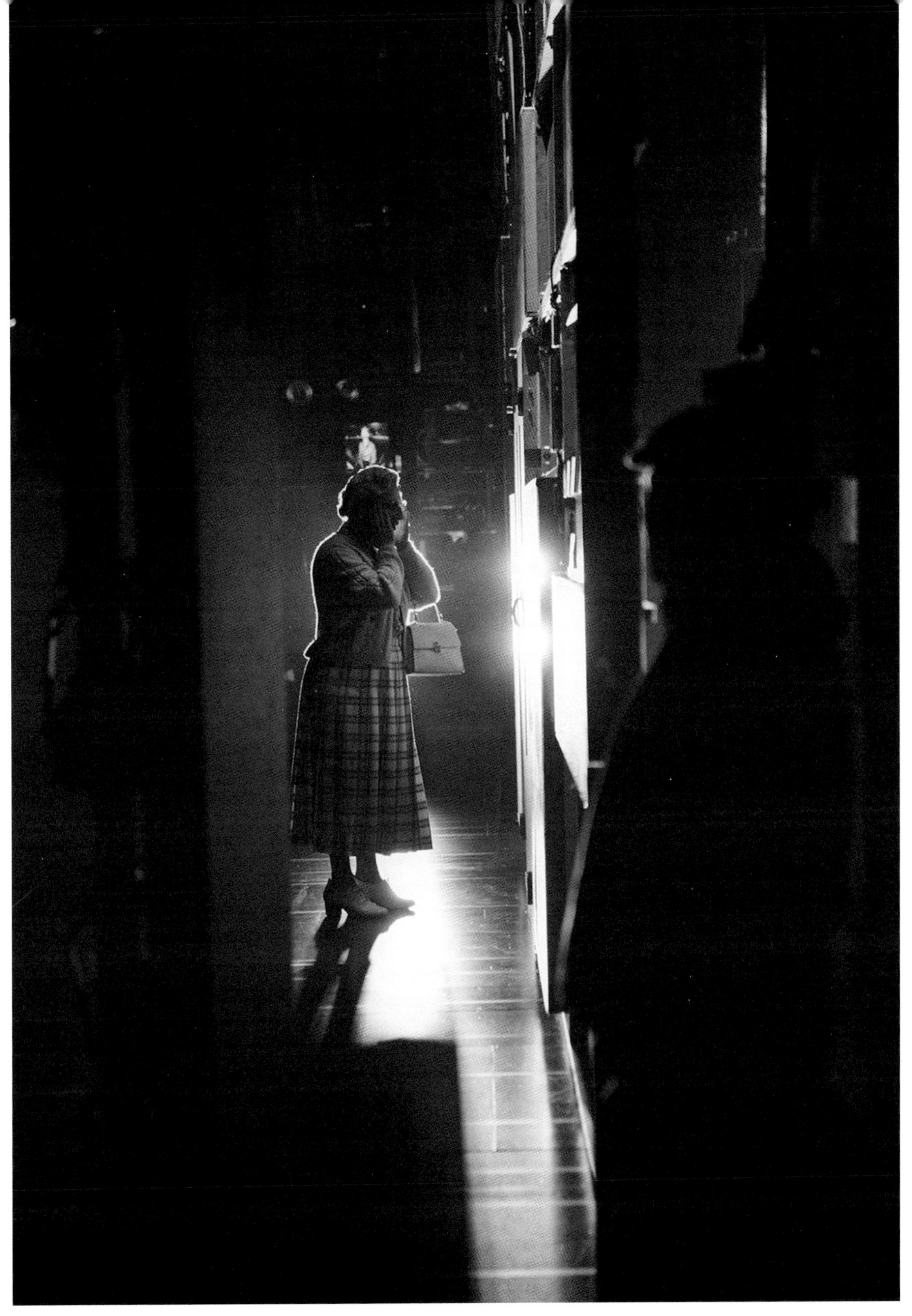

Rob McClure
Mrs. Doubtfire
Stephen Sondheim Theatre
2022

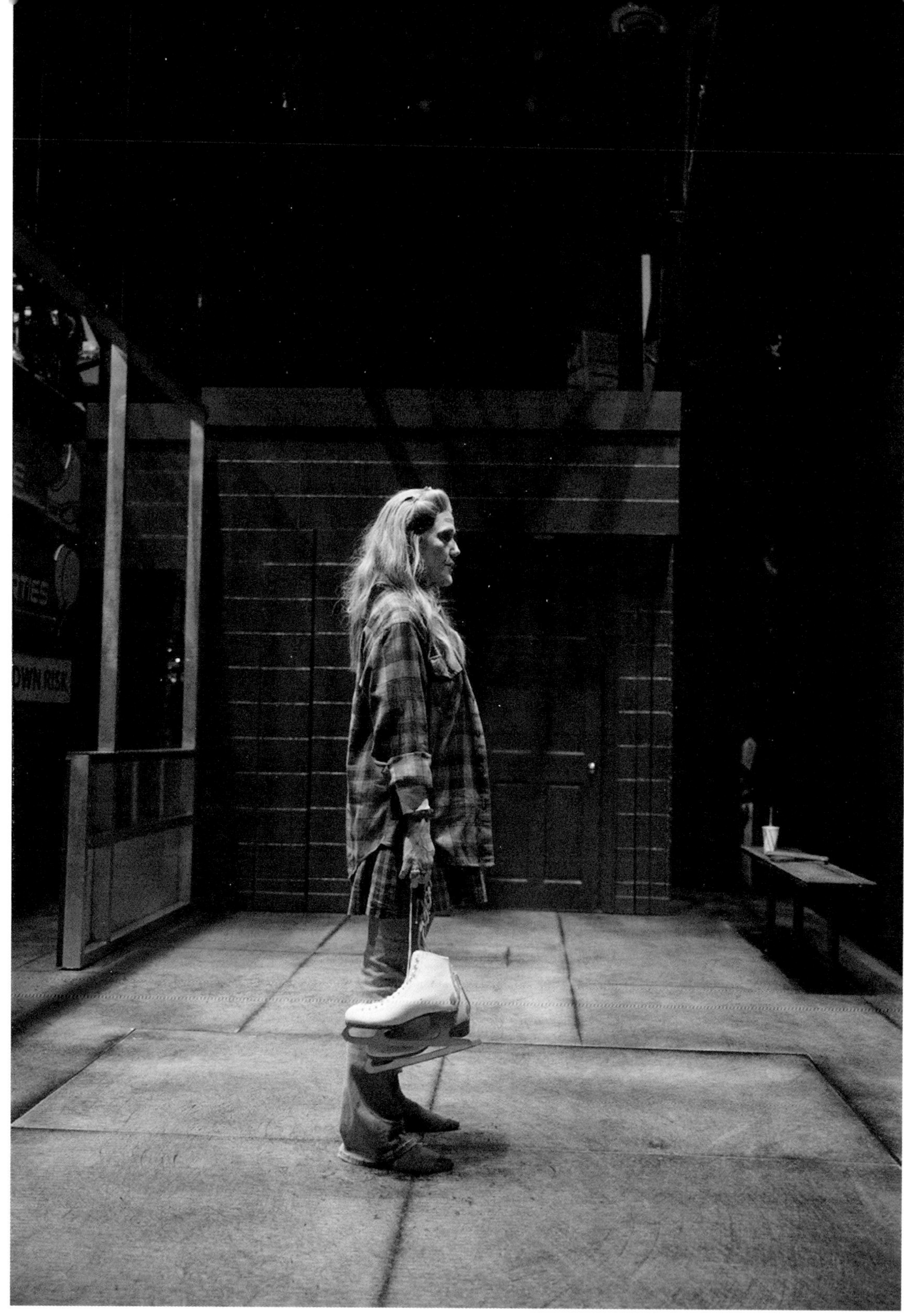

Victoria Clark
Kimberly Akimbo
Booth Theatre
2023

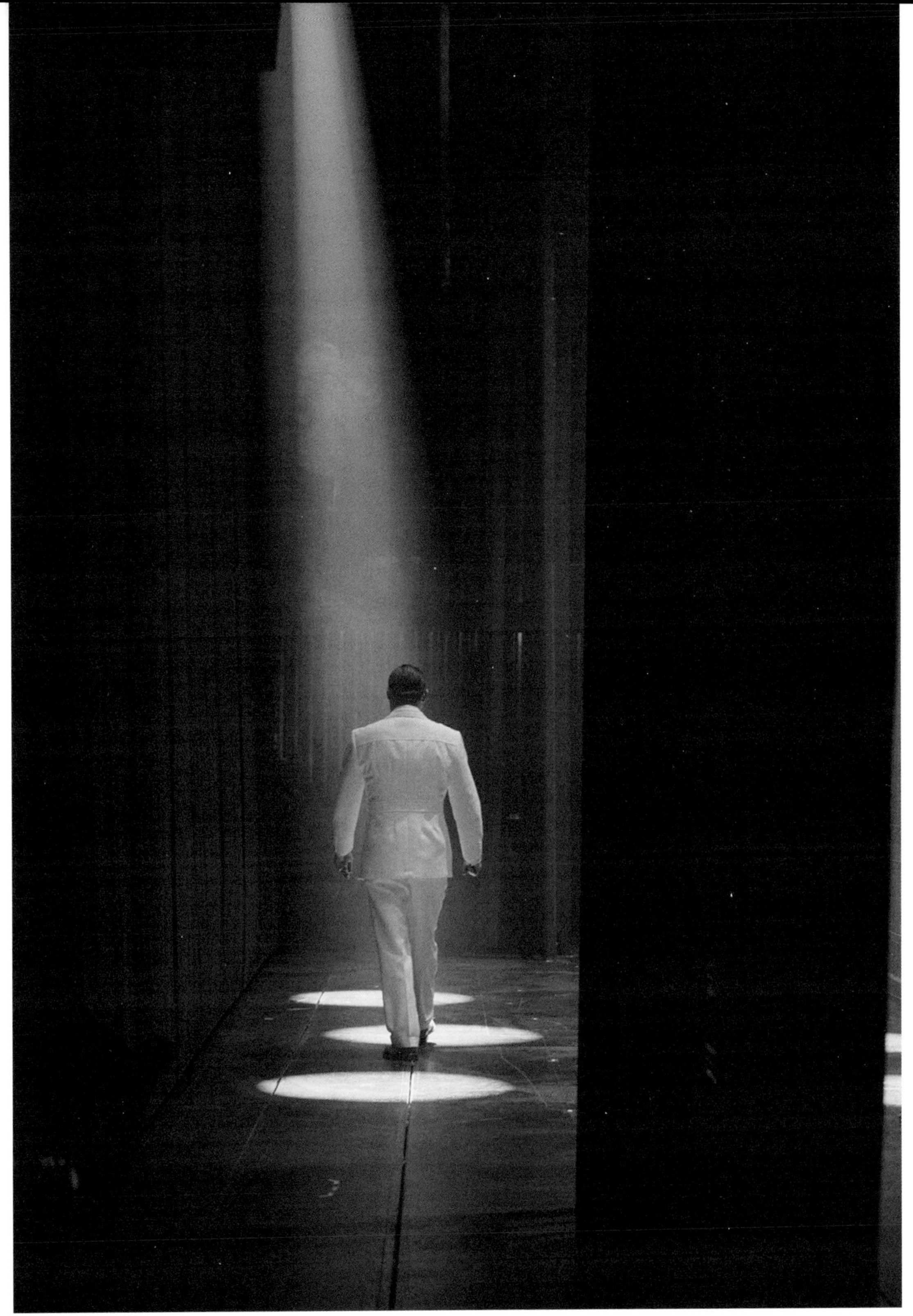

Jeremy Jordan
The Great Gatsby
Paper Mill Playhouse
2023

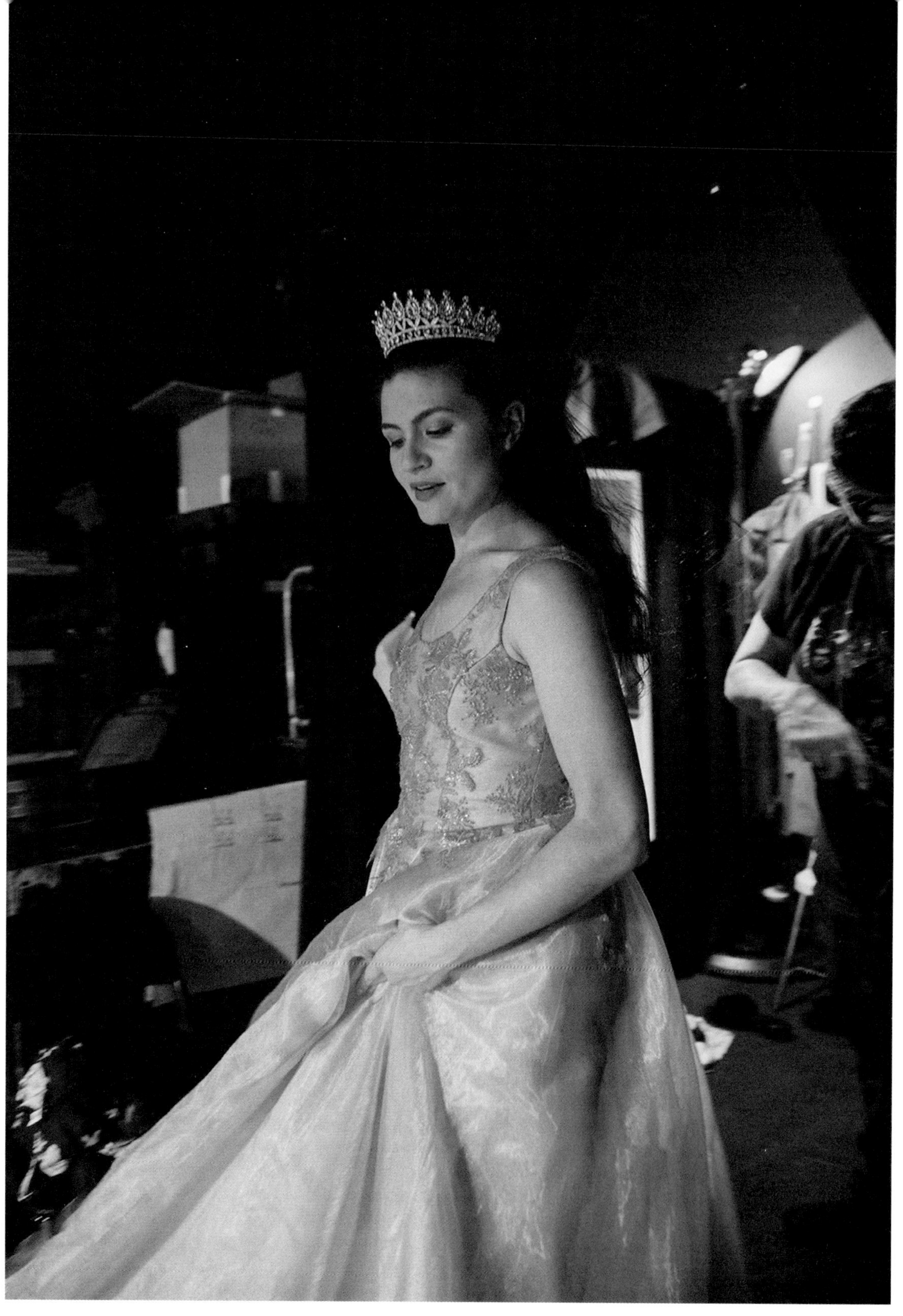

Phillipa Soo
Into the Woods
St. James Theatre
2022

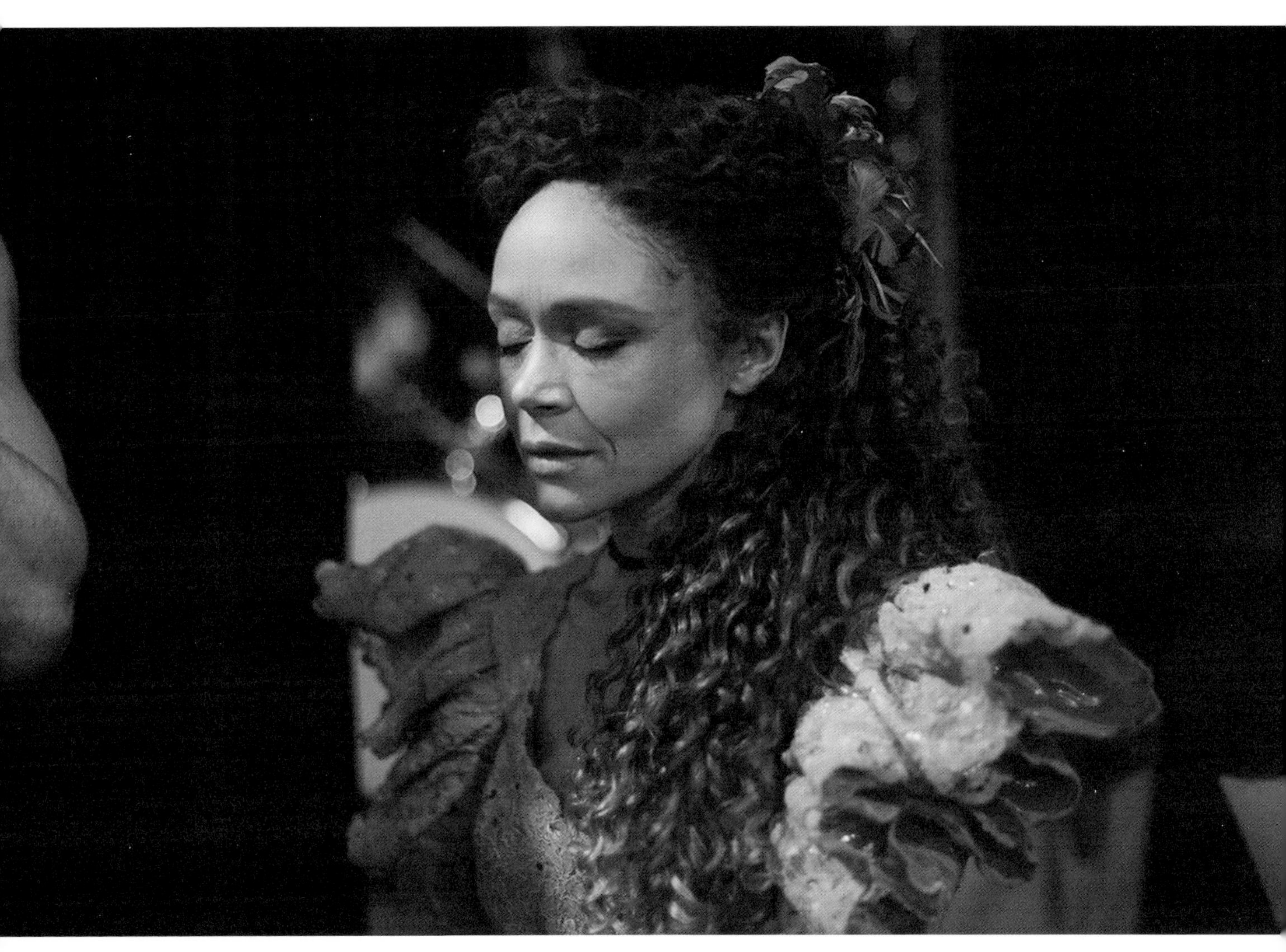

Amber Gray
Hadestown
The 73rd Annual Tony Awards
2019

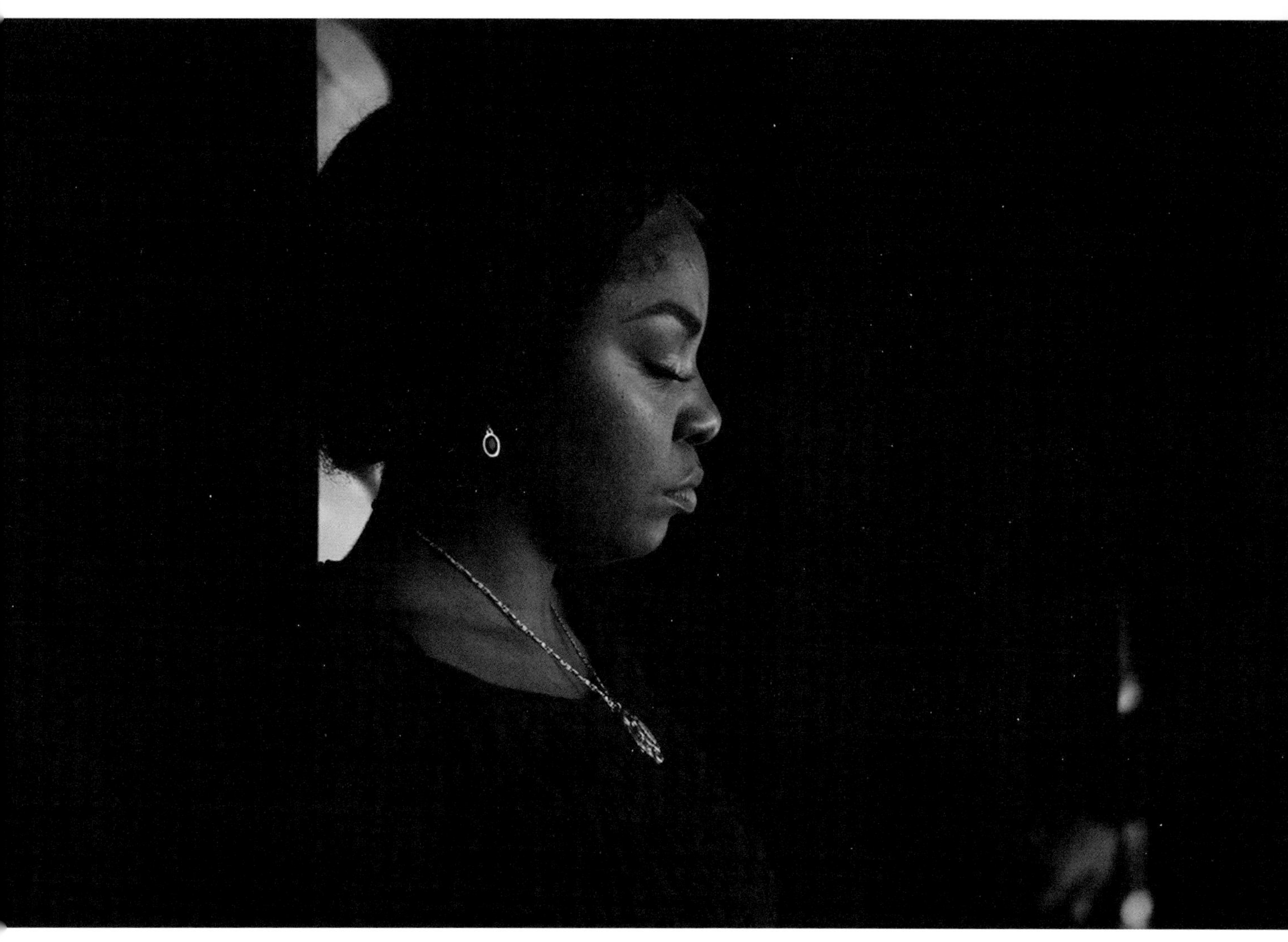

Joaquina Kalukango
Paradise Square
The 75th Annual Tony Awards
2022

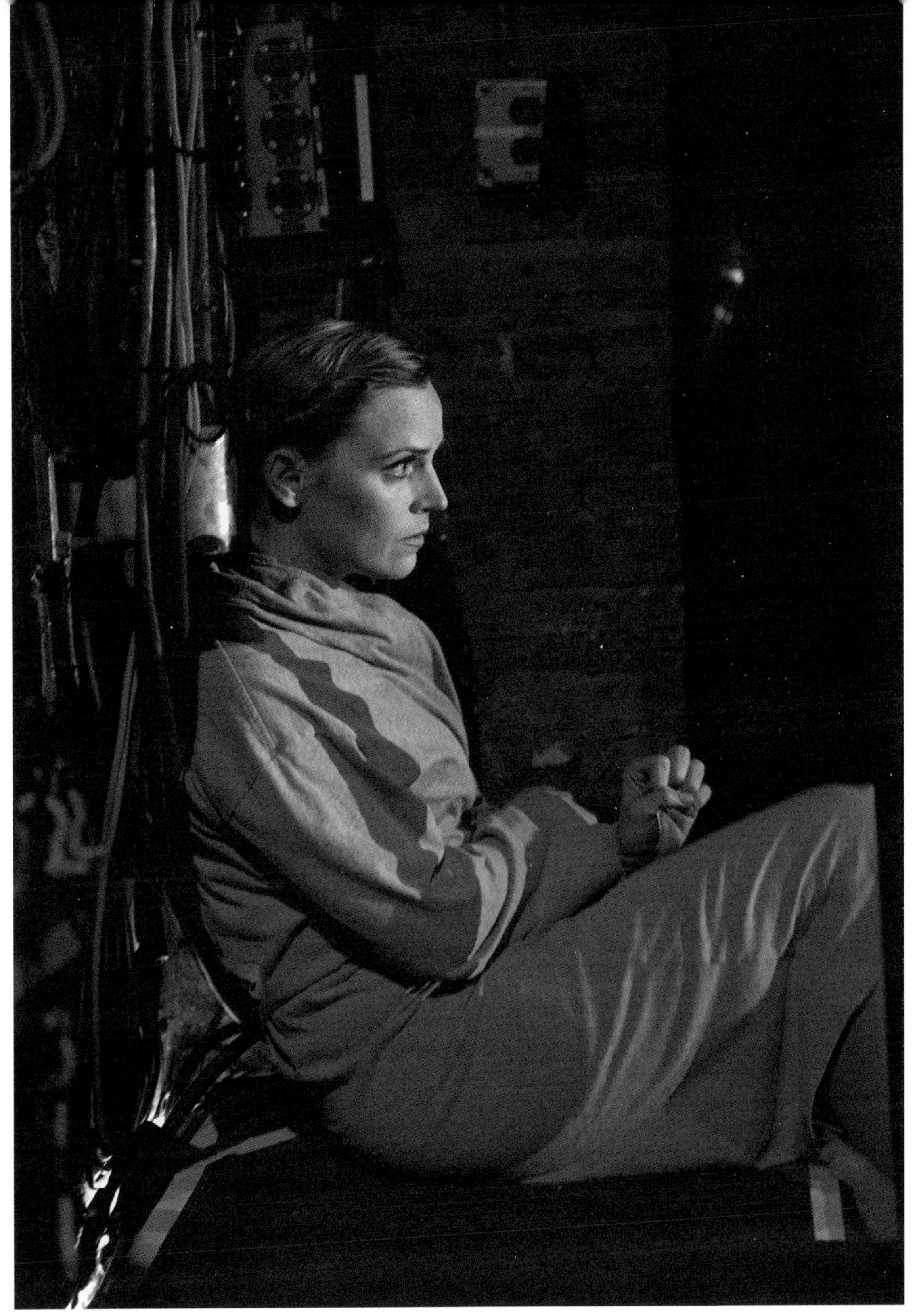

Katie Rose Clarke
Merrily We Roll Along
New York Theatre Workshop
2023

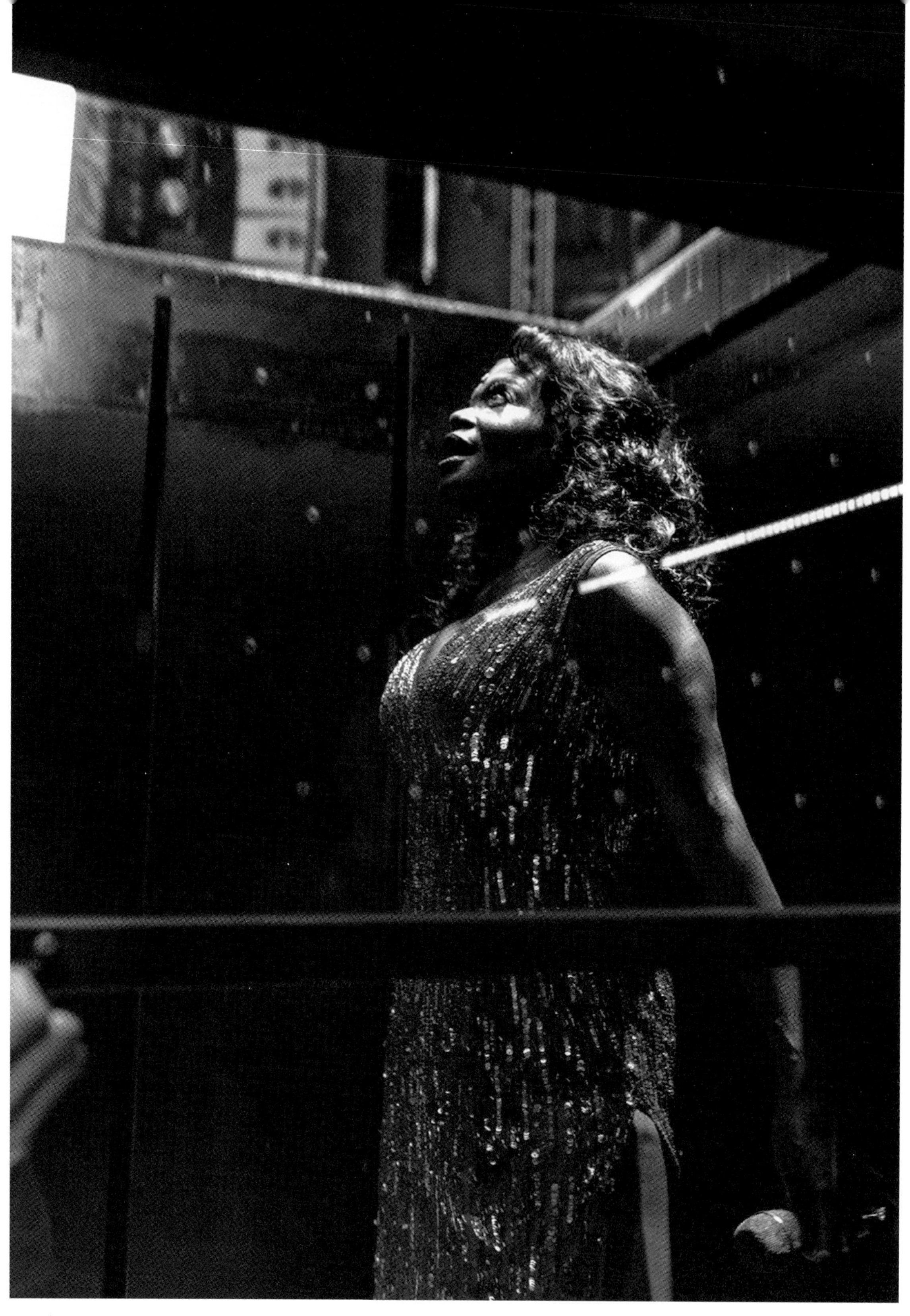

LaChanze
Summer: The Donna Summer Musical
Lunt-Fontanne Theatre
2018

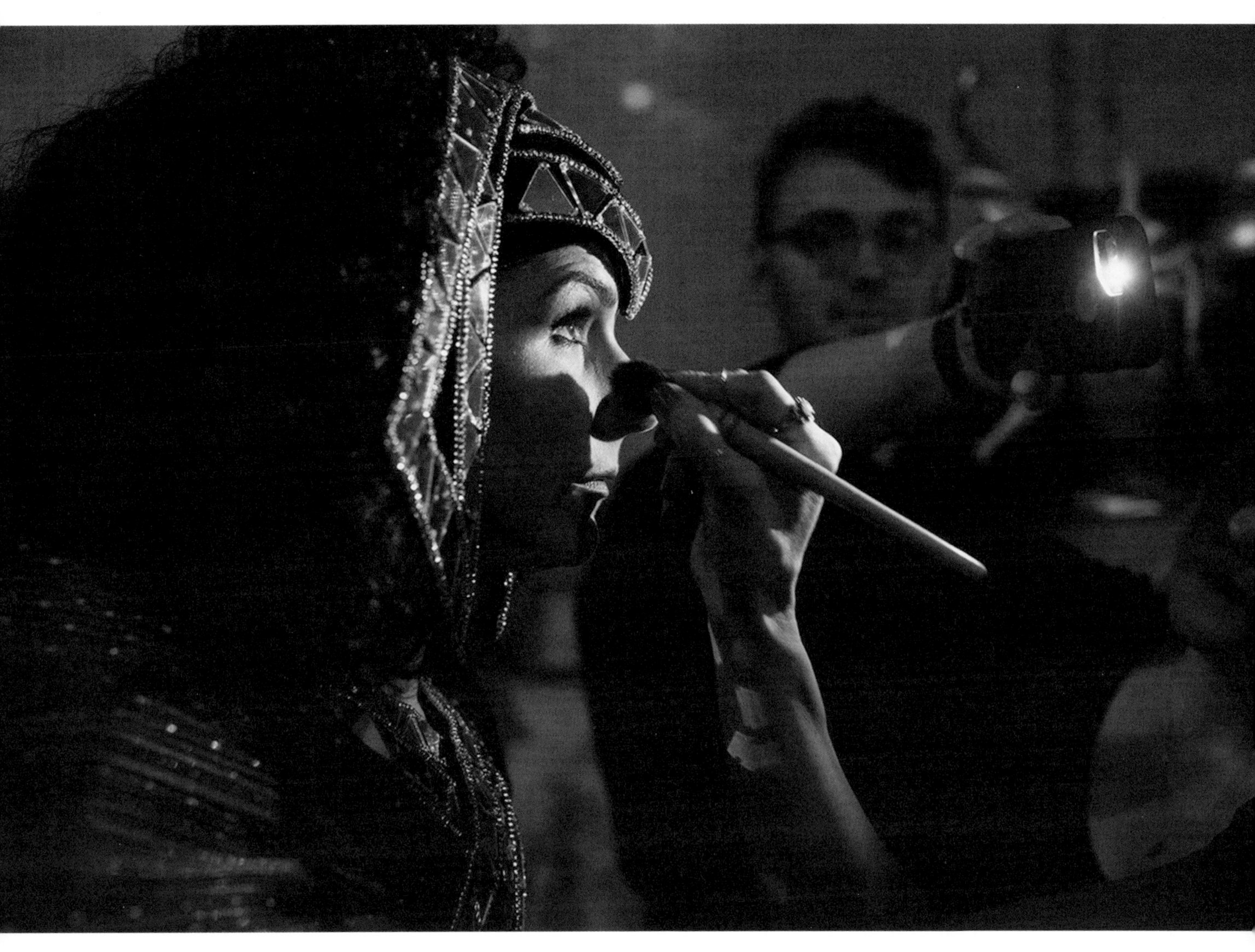

Stephanie J. Block
The Cher Show
The 73rd Annual Tony Awards
2019

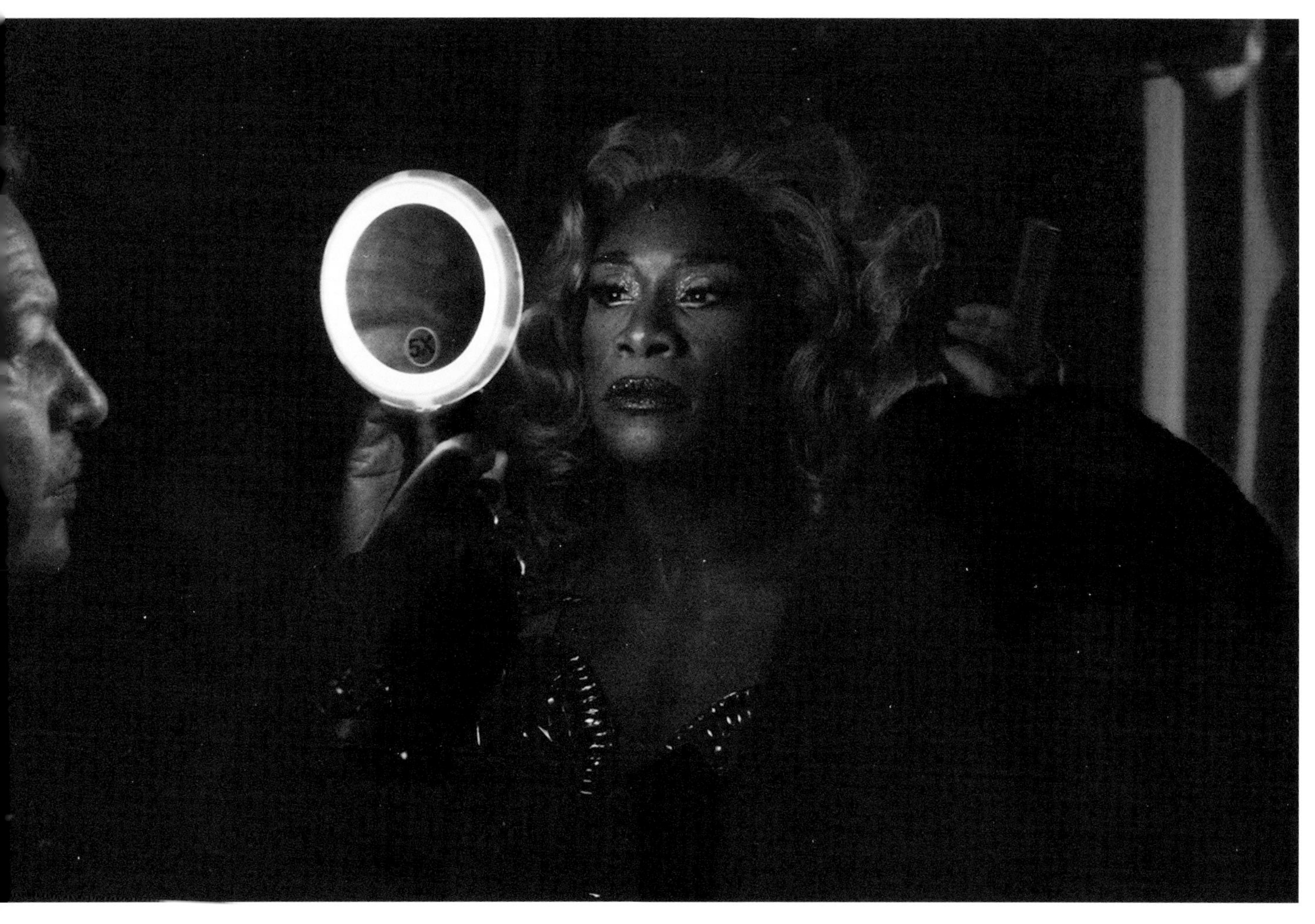

Billy Porter
Kinky Boots
Al Hirschfeld Theatre
2017

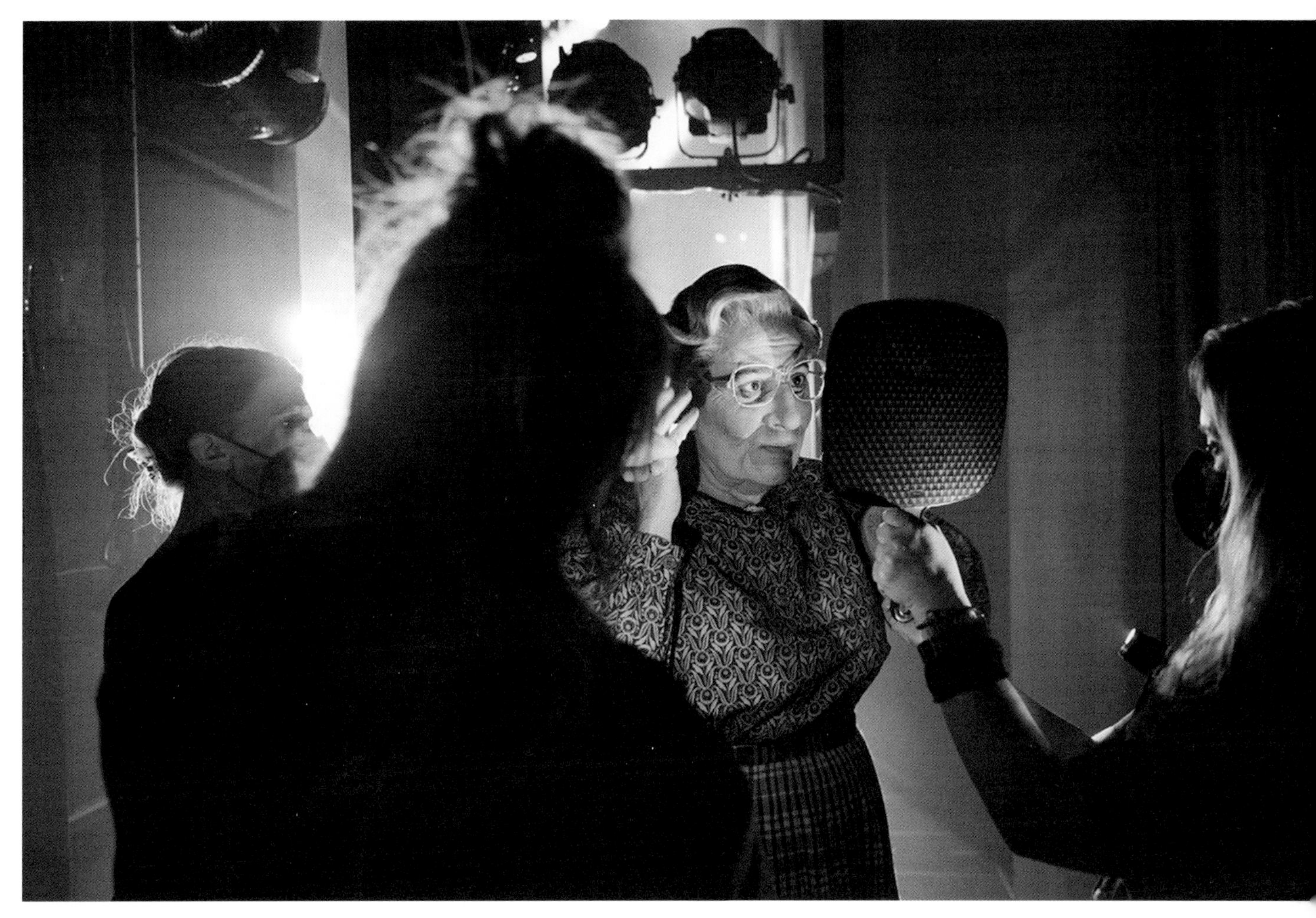

Rob McClure
Mrs. Doubtfire
Stephen Sondheim Theatre
2022

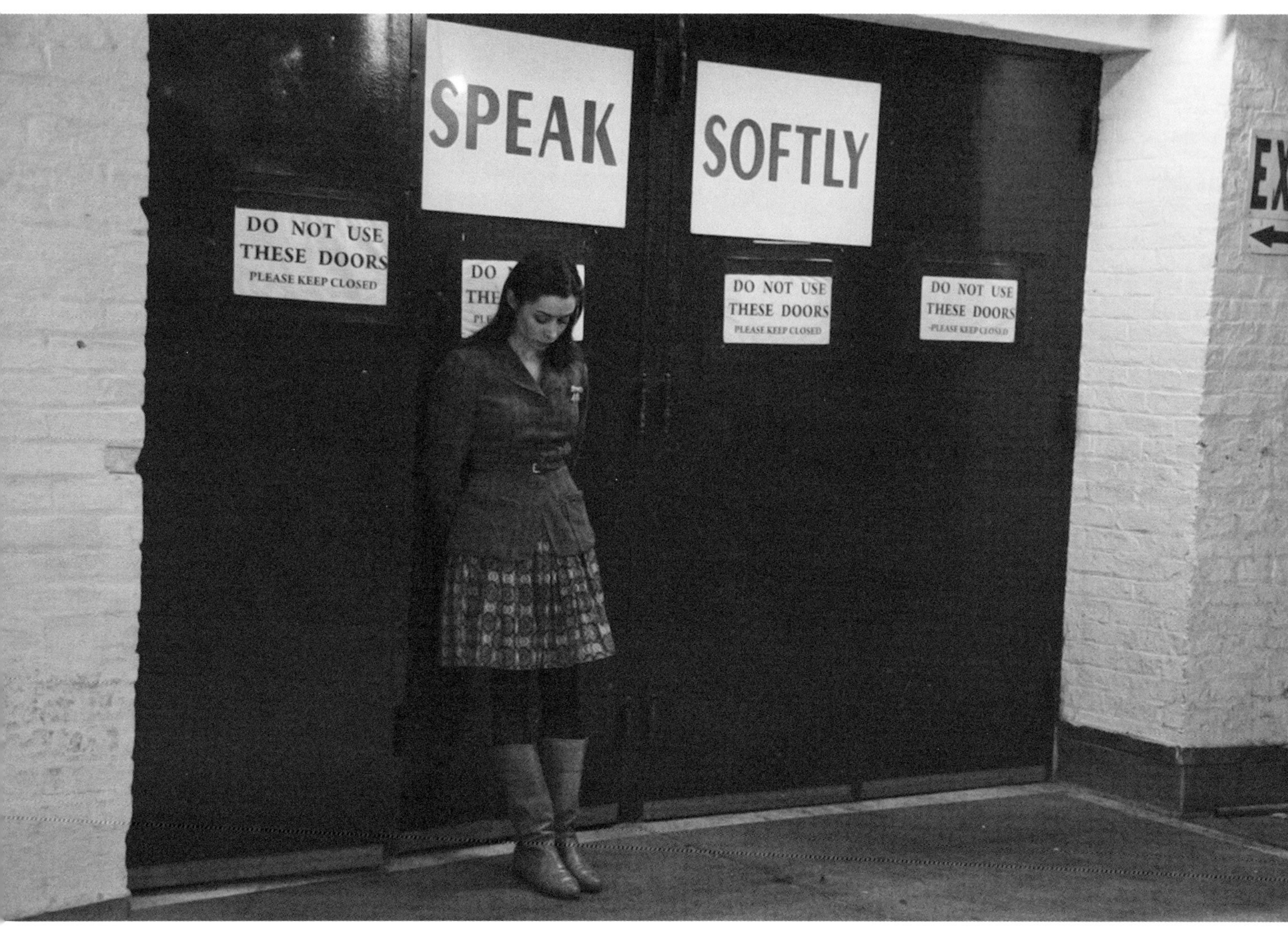

Cristin Milioti
Once
Bernard B. Jacobs Theatre
2012

ACKNOWLEDGMENTS

As a people-pleasing double Cancer this task has kept me up at night. Seriously, I've come back to this section an embarrassing amount. If I could, I would literally thank every human I have ever come into contact with since the minute a camera was put in my hand. Every move I've made during my career and every opportunity I've been given along the way has been paved by friends and family, colleagues and mentors, too many to count. There are so many who have championed me, hired me, held me up, fed me, housed me, and given me encouragement. So below is the list that I have begrudgingly tried to narrow down, but just know if we've ever met or you've ever said one nice thing to me, I thank you, and I honestly mean it.

For taking a chance on me and believing in this book from the beginning: my agents, Mia Vitale and Sarah Passick at Park & Fine; editors John Cerullo and Emily Burr at Applause; and my intrepid lawyer, David Manella at Loeb & Loeb.

Paul Wontorek, Beth Stevens, Kathy Henderson, and everyone at Broadway.com for hiring and mentoring a 22-year-old right out of college and giving me a platform to start my career.

Laura Benanti, Celia Keenan-Bolger, Gavin Creel, Caissie Levy, Lin-Manuel Miranda, Sutton Foster, Megan Hilty, Kelli O'Hara, Leslie Odom Jr., Nicolette Robinson, Danny Burstein, Cherry Jones, Ashley Park, Erika Henningsen, Stephanie J. Block, Annaleigh Ashford, Brandon Uranowitz, Ben Platt, Micaela Diamond, Alex Newell, Shoshana Bean, and Ariana DeBose for opening their doors and allowing me into their dressing rooms and lives in the early days and continually to capture their careers over the last decade and a half.

Publicity firms and publicists who have always allowed me into their shows to photograph and have continued to hire me for the last 12 years: Polk & Co, O&M, Boneau Bryan Brown, Vivacity, Imprint, Rubenstein, and Grapevine PR.

Special thank you to the life-blood of the theatre; the dressers, stage managers and crews that let me invade their space and occasionally capture them in the background while they work so tirelessly.

Glass House Tavern and Chris for letting me sit at their bar for hours on end editing between jobs and shows. And for the corn couscous!

Fellow photographers, colleagues, and collaborators who have taught me, elevated me, hired me, become friends, and said my name in hundreds of important rooms: Joan Marcus, Matthew Murphy, Sara Krulwich, Kevin Thomas Garcia, Tony Marion, Kevin Lin, Eleni Gianulis, John Vermeer, Liviya Kramer, Chelsea Hayes, Shawn Purdy, Butch Vincencio, Molly Barnett, Jordan Roth, John Johnson, Sue Wagner, Rachel Sussman, Rick Miramontez, and Frank DiLella.

Natalie Powers and Brooke Bell for assisting me and keeping me sane daily.

First responders, Chelsea Nachman and Alyson Ahrns, for being by my side continually through this career and this life.

My college mentors Ellen Meachum, Robin Street, and Joe Turner Cantu.

My brothers, Jesse and Duncan, for keeping me humble, loving me unconditionally, and being my first photo subjects.

My guidepost and fellow "20-nothing" Jessie Rosen for championing my career since the moment we met and this book since before it was a book, and for writing/re-writing anything and everything I've ever needed over the last 18 years. And her husband and my number one fan, Robby Luchow.

My New York/theatre soulmates-turned-family: Jessica Keenan-Wynn, Jarrod Spector, Kelli Barrett, Lora Lee Gayer, Julia Murney, Jenn Colella, Jessica Phillips, Julia Mattison, Drew Gehling, Jessica Vosk, and LJ Behlmann.

My lifers, best friends, and biggest cheerleaders Zac Wilson, Brittany Bell Faulkner, Lindsay Fine Smith, Dana Colagiovanni, Stephanie Gibson, Meggie Duke, Kate Dickson, Harry Ford, Leanne Barrineau, Jocelyn Brunot, Corrie Cockrell Fulweiler, KK Gillespie, and all their beautiful partners, husbands and babies.

Zac, thank you for being there literally from day one as my sounding board, artistic eye, and first collaborator. Brit and Linds, thank you for constantly showing up for me no matter when or where. I love you, Broads! Dana, thank you for your unfailing loyalty.

My grandaddy who bought me my first camera, my meme despite hating having her picture taken for being my favorite muse, my grandma who was my musical theatre guru, and my dear beautiful friend Susan who all aren't here to see this book but who would have been the firsts to want to.

To everyone in the pages of this book who welcomed me into their havens, their sacred spaces: I am forever grateful!

In loving memory of sweet Gavin.

INDEX